A History of Dogs in the Early Americas

Marion Schwartz

A History of Dogs in the Early Americas

with selected drawings
by Susan Hochgraf

Yale University Press

New Haven & London

Published with assistance from the Charles A. Coffin Fund.

Designed by Nancy Ovedovitz and set in Simoncini Garamond type by The Composing Room of Michigan, Inc. Printed in the United States of America by Edwards Brothers, Inc., Ann Arbor, Michigan.

Library of Congress Cataloging-in-Publication Data

Schwartz, Marion.

A history of dogs in early Americas/Marion Schwartz.

p.   cm.

Includes bibliographical references and index.

ISBN 0-300-06964-2 (cl. : alk. paper)

    0-300-07519-7 (pbk. : alk. paper)

1. Indians–Domestic animals. 2. Dogs–America–History.

3. Indians–Social life and customs.   I. Title.

E59.D69S38 1997   96–46927

636.7´0089´97—dc21   CIP

A catalogue record for this book is available from the British Library.

The paper in this book meets the guidelines for permanence and durability of the Committee on Production Guidelines for Book Longevity of the Council on Library Resources.

10   9   8   7   6   5   4   3   2

For Alison and Bob

In the very earliest time when both people and animals lived on earth a person could become an animal if he wanted to and an animal could become a human being. Sometimes they were people and sometimes animals and there was no difference. All spoke the same language.—*Eskimo hunting song*

Contents

Plates follow page 76

Preface   ix

Acknowledgments   xi

Chronology of Sites, Cultures, and People   xii

Maps   xiv

1 The Creation of the American Dog   1

2 Hunting, Hauling, and Herding Dogs   29

3 The Edible Dog   60

4 Dogs in the Land of the Dead   93

5 Molded, Carved, and Painted Dogs   125

Epilogue: After the Conquest   161

Appendixes   169

Notes   179

References   197

Index   221

Preface

Right at the start, I should state that I do not own a dog. I am not a dog person. For fourteen years I have been a lab technician in the physical anthropology lab at Yale University, and I have also spent time working with Alison Richard to learn about the life histories of a lemur species in Madagascar. One year, for a change of pace, I sat in on a course in North American prehistory. That was the beginning. I soon became captivated by the so-called New World and what it must have been like before the Europeans and their diseases arrived. The phrase "a world apart" was always in my mind. Then, a couple of years ago, I was taking a course on the Amazon with archaeologist Warren De-Boer and looking for a research topic. I do not remember how the decision came about to write on dogs. As dogs were not present in the Amazon before Contact it now seems an odd choice. I only know that, once I started, I was carried along from one place to another with ever more excitement and enthusiasm in a great search for the truly American Dog.

One of the first books that captured my imagination was the Varners' book *Dogs of the Conquest*. Two things intrigued me. One, I had never heard before that the Spanish had brought huge dogs trained on human flesh with them to the Americas to control native populations. In reading the sixteenth-century accounts of these "hero" dogs it became clear to me that the conquistadors regarded their dogs as more noble and intelligent than any of the people they were conquering. The Spanish talked about their dogs as if they were more human than the American "savages." That struck me as a strange attitude, but, as I said before, I am not a dog owner. The second question that the book raised for me was this: If these dogs were so startling and frightening to the Native Americans, what were their own dogs like? Was it true that, along with superior weapons, the invading Europeans also had "better" dogs? It was at this point that I began to understand that the word *dog* had many meanings. Dogs were as different as the people they served. What I wanted to understand was *how* different, and how one species—one nonhuman species at that—could be so many things to so many people.

Now I was on my way, unable to stop until I had some sense of how the Inca, the Aztec, and the Maya regarded dogs. And what about the Iroquois and the Tlingit and the Hopi? What about people whose names we do not know, the residents of urban Cahokia or the isolated hunting and fishing groups that lived 7,000 years ago and buried their dogs with such care? I found myself unwilling to limit the scope of my enquiry. I wanted to explore the entire American past and all of America's first people and use any type of evidence I could discover. I knew that this approach had many pitfalls and that my work might be sketchy and scattered. But still I proceeded, through the genetics and behavioral literature, onto the archaeological record and faunal reports, next to the chronicles, the ethnohistorical accounts, and the ethnographies, and then to myths, the codices, and hieroglyphics, followed by works of pre-Columbian art and of Western artists choosing Native American subjects and on and on. Then I started on linguistics, and a whole new avenue opened. I did all this because each time I looked I found another little part of the puzzle. Now I had to struggle mightily to place all this data into a meaningful context and into some kind of a story. This proved far harder than amassing the information. I decided to write primarily about the special cases in which dogs played a prominent or at least retrievable role. I tried to cover a representative spectrum of societies that existed in America, but I am not confident that I have always succeeded in presenting a general overview with adequate detail. I have, however, succeeded in writing about what I found most compelling. I have also provided lists of references to supplement my account. There is much more to this story than I have had space and time to explore.

Now, of course, I am becoming a dog person. One day I think the right dog for me is an Alaskan malamute. The next day I think that I should have a Mexican hairless, or maybe a Carolina dog. It is hard to find dogs these days that can trace their ancestry to American origins, so perhaps a Siberian husky might serve my needs. Not for me the mastiffs, greyhounds, and wolfhounds that proved so successful at "dogging" Indians. I am a thoroughly non-Western dog person, and I hope, in the pages of this book, to persuade the reader to take a dog's-eye look at the American past.

Acknowledgments

I have received massive amounts of help and encouragement from many good-hearted and patient people during the time I worked on this book. My special thanks goes to those who read and commented on the manuscript, to my reviewers, and to those who put up with my endless talk about dogs. Thanks to Susan Hochgraf for her wonderful drawings. The following people contributed to this endeavor and made its successful completion possible. You all have my deeply felt gratitude: Andrew Balter, Richard Burger, Juliet Clutton-Brock, Michael Coe, Harold Conklin, Warren DeBoer, Amos Deinard, Robert Dewar, Megan Doyon, Jill Leslie McKeever Furst, Rosemary Gianno, Thomas Gundling, Martha Hill, Frank Hole, David Kelley, John Kingston, Floyd Lounsbury, Patricia Mathews, Gisela Mattsson, Jerald Milanich, Mary Miller, Barbara Narendra, Danny Povinelli, Patricia Princehouse, Alison Richard, Peter Roe, Irving Rouse, William Sacco, Peter Schwartz, Michael Seaman, Meg Soulsby, and Elizabeth Wing.

Chronology of Sites, Cultures, and People

Date	North America	Mesoamerica	S. America/Caribbean
A.D. 1800–1900	*Catlin, Kane, Morgan, Bodmer, Murrey, Berlandier, Bourke*		*Von Tschudi, Darwin, Fitz-Roy*
A.D. 1600–1800	*DuPratz, Sagard, Lescarbot, Verendryes, Hearne, Henry MacKenzie, VanCouver,* Barcal Buffalo Pasture, Burr's Hill	*Wafer*	*Garcilaso de la Vega*
A.D. 1500–1600	*The Great Sun, DeSoto, Coronado, Zaldivar*	*Motecuhzoma, Cortés, Bernal Diaz, Camargo, Sahagún, Duran, Landa*	*Atahualpa, Pizarro, de Cieza de Leon, Acosta, Guaman Poma, Pané*
A.D. 1300–1500	MISSISSIPPIAN, Spiro, Grasshopper, Belcher	AZTEC, *Ahuitzotl,* MIXTEC	INCA, *Pachacuti,* Cuzco, HUANCA, Machu Picchu
A.D. 1100–1300	MISSISSIPPIAN, Mimbres, Arroyo Hondo, deChelly	TOLTEC, MIXTEC	HUANCA Chancay, Lambayeque, CHIMU
A.D. 900–1100	Mimbres, Flushing, Lambert Farm	TOLTEC, Cozumel, Cacaxtla, Marimas	
A.D. 700–900		CLASSIC MAYA, Seibal, Tikal, Altar	
A.D. 500–700		CLASSIC MAYA, Veracruz, Sitio Conté	NAZCA, MOCHE, Pampa Grande

Date	North America	Mesoamerica	S. America/Caribbean
A.D. 300–500	McKeithern, Weeden Is.	FM. MAYA, Cuello, Cerros, Kamnaljuyu, Teotihuacán	NAZCA, MOCHE, Cahuachi, Sipán
A.D. 100–300	White Dog Cave, Adena, Copena	FM. MAYA, ZAPOTEC, Teotihuacán, Colima	NAZCA, MOCHE, Hacienda Grande, Sorcé
100 A.D.– 500 B.C.	Ipiutak, Dinwoody, Coso	FM. MAYA, ZAPOTEC, Teotihuacán, Colima, Monte Alban, Tehuácan	GALLINAZO, SALINAR, PARACAS, Lighthouse, Tomaval
1000–500 B.C.		OLMEC, Tehuácan	Tembladera, Chavin
2000–1000 B.C.	Ventana Cave, South Indian Field	OLMEC, San Lorenzo, Tlatilco Tehuácan	CHORRERA, Pacopampa, Kotosh
3000–2000 B.C.	Port au Choix, Indian Knoll, Read, Carton Annis, Perry	Tehuácan: Santa Maria Phase	VALDIVIA, Real Alto, Loma Alto
4000–3000 B.C.	Lamoka		Paloma, Guitarrero Cave
5000–4000 B.C.	Rogers Cave, Eva		Los Vegas, La Moderna
6000–5000 B.C.	Koster		Los Toldos, Telar-machay
7000–6000 B.C.			Fells Cave
8000–7000 B.C.	Danger Cave, Agate Basin, Olsen-Chubbock		Elbert Cave

Note: italic type = Individuals; Roman type = Archaeological Sites; CAPITALS = Cultures

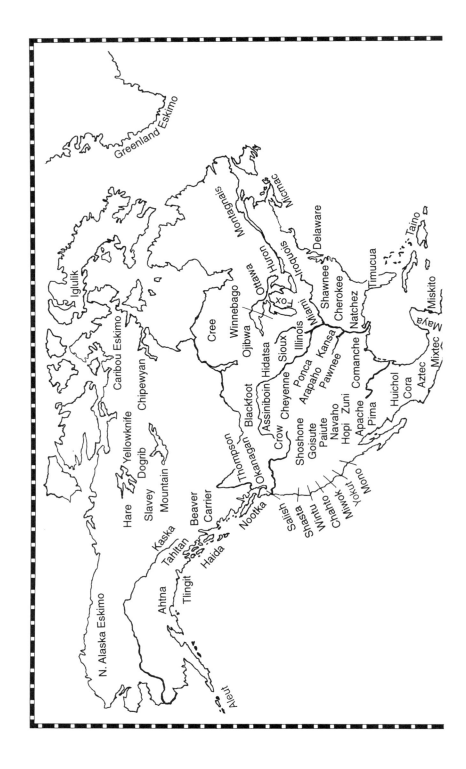

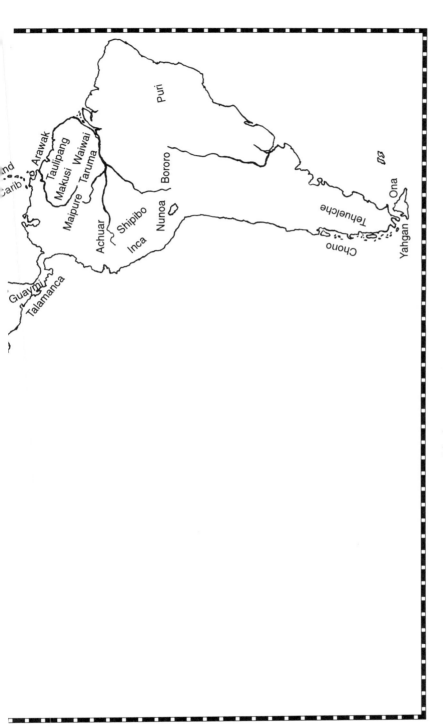

Ethnohistoric groups discussed in the text.

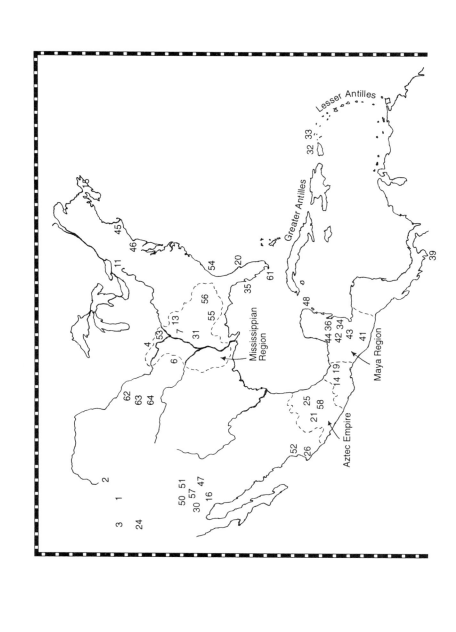

Lesser Antilles

32 33

Greater Antilles

45

46

11

54

20

61

35

56

13

55

53

7

31

4

6

Mississippian
Region

48

44 36

42 34

43

41

Maya Region

14 19

25

58

21

52

26

Aztec Empire

39

62

63

64

2

50 51

30 57 47

16

3

1

24

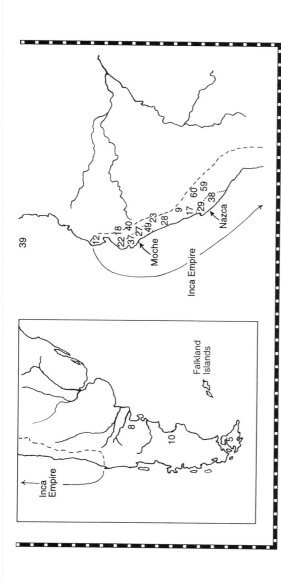

Archaeological sites discussed in text, numbered according to their relative age from oldest to youngest.

1. Olsen-Chubbock, 2. Agate Basin, 3. Danger Cave, 4. Koster, 5. Fell's Cave, Elbert Cave, 6. Rogers Cave, 7. Eva, 8. La Moderna, 9. Telarmachay, 10. Los Toldos, 11. Lamoka Sites, 12. Real Alto, Loma Alta, 13. Indian Knoll, Read, and Carlson Annis, 14. Tehuacán Valley, 15. Port au Choix, 16. Ventana Cave, 17. Paloma, 18. Pacopampa, 19. San Lorenzo, 20. S. Indian Field, 21. Tlatilco, 22. Tembladera, 23. Chavin, 24. Coso, 25. Teotihuacán, 26. Colima, 27. Tomaval, 28. Lighthouse Point, 29. Paracas, 30. White Dog Cave, 31. Copena Mound, 32. Hacienda Grande, 33. Sorcé, 34. Cuello, 35. Weeden Island, 36. Cerros, 37. Sipán, 38. Cahauchi, 39. Sitio Conté, 40. Pampa Grande, 41. Kaminaljuyu, 42. Seibal, 43. Altar de Sacrificios, 44. Tikal, 45. Lambert Farm, 46. Flushing, 47. Mimbres, 48. Cozumel, 49. Chimú, 50. Arroyo Hondo, 51. C. de Chelly, 52. Marimas, 53. Cahokia, 54. Ossabaw Island, 55. Moundville, 56. Etowah, 57. Grasshopper, 58. Tenochtitlan, 59. Cuzco, 60. Machu Picchu, 61. Marco Island, 62. Buffalo Pasture, 63. Barcal, 64. Big Village.

A History of Dogs in the Early Americas

1 *The Creation of the American Dog*

Our domestic dogs are descended from wolves and jackals and though they may not have gained in cunning, and may have lost in wariness and suspicion, yet they have progressed in certain moral qualities, such as affection, trust-worthiness, temper, and probably in general intelligence.—Charles Darwin, *The Descent of Man and Selection in Relation to Sex* (1871)

Then the Woman picked up a roasted mutton-bone and threw it to Wild Dog, and said, "Wild Thing out of Wild Woods, taste and try." Wild Dog gnawed the bone, and it was more delicious than anything he had ever tasted, and he said, "O my Enemy and Wife of my Enemy, give me another."

The Woman said, "Wild Thing out of the Wild Woods, help my Man to hunt through the day and guard this Cave at night, and I will give you as many roast bones as you need. . . ."

Wild Dog crawled into the Cave and laid his head on the Woman's lap, and said, "O my Friend and Wife of my Friend, I will help your Man to hunt through the day, and at night I will guard your Cave."—Rudyard Kipling, *Just So Stories* (1912)

At a remote time in the past, the earth was inhabited by people other than those created by the sun-god. They were very bad and fought among themselves all the time.

When the sun-god saw this he decided to annihilate these people and to create another population in their stead. To destroy the bad people, the sun-god sent torrential and continuous rain, the springs opened, and the ocean overflowed. In the deluge all mankind was swept away. . . .

Then the sun god decided to create new people. First he made a man, then a woman, and finally a dog to keep them company. Later he created the guanaco and the rhea as food for the couple he had brought forth.—*Folk Literature of the Tehuelche Indians*

Dogs are remarkable animals because they are uniquely sensitive to the cultural attributes of the people with whom they live. Not only are dogs a product of culture, but they also participate in the cultures of humans. In fact, dogs were the first animals to take up residence with people and the only animals found in human societies all over the world. Because of their ubiquity across cultural boundaries, dogs have been so commonplace that their history seemed to warrant little consideration. And yet for the past twelve thousand years dogs have played an integral part in human lives. What is most remarkable about dogs is their ability to adapt to the needs of the people with whom they live. Dogs have proved themselves amazingly flexible beings, and this was as true in the Americas as it was elsewhere in the world.

The Western Hemisphere was first populated with people, accompanied by dogs, who migrated from Northeast Asia. People spread and settled in every region of the Americas, in the varying latitudes, climates, altitudes, and topographies. They established their own cultural identities, their own languages, their own traditions and beliefs. Although their common origins united them, they remained isolated from events in Europe, the Near East, China, and India. Before the fateful voyage of Christopher Columbus in 1492, societies in the Americas were largely untouched by outside influences, and unlike the early societies on which Western culture is based, did not possess domesticated goats, sheep, cattle, pigs, or horses.[1] Dogs were the only domestic animals present in the majority of Native American groups, the only animal allied with humans.

What we know about dogs in Native American societies is limited. But we do know that the dogs brought by the Spanish were much different in character and breeding from those already present. How these non-European animals meshed with humans in everyday life, how they functioned in the symbolic realm, and how their roles varied across cultural boundaries are questions basic to our understanding of American dogs.

A few themes emerge from the details of the dog's lot in America. First and foremost, the dog was an ambiguous animal. Native Americans understood that even though dogs resided in the human camp they had a close kinship with coyotes and wolves. Because of these relationships, dogs occupied and operated on several levels: they connected the wild and the tame, and they joined nature and culture. Even though dogs were seen as almost human, they were also known to be carnivores and, as such, were linked not only to wolves, coyotes, and foxes but also to bears and jaguars. On the one hand, dogs were esteemed as companions, hunters, and guards. On the other hand, they were associated with promiscuity and filth. Among some groups, eating dogs was strictly taboo, whereas other groups ate them with great relish. Some cultures relied on dogs for transportation and hauling. Others found them to be of no use at all. Dogs played key roles in the myths of some people; in other myths, dogs were scarcely mentioned. In addition, the numbers of dogs and their physical appearance varied widely from locality to locality and through time.

Thus, a multitude of stories about dogs exist. And they are by no means simple tales. Our own concept of the pet dog must be discarded as we examine these dog stories in the context in which they occurred. If that human context is not kept in mind we will lose sight of the complexity and richness of the lives of those who inhabited a world far different from our own. One of the most eloquent if unintentional expressions of this sentiment is in Alexander Pope's *Essay on Man,* written in the early eighteenth century. Although Pope's tone is patronizing and his view of American peoples uninformed, he recognizes that differences in perspective did exist and that each had validity.

> Lo, the poor Indian! whose untutor'd mind
> Sees God in clouds, or hears him in the wind;
> His soul proud Science never taught to stray
> Far as the Solar Walk, or Milky Way;
> Yet simple Nature to his hope has giv'n,
> Behind the cloud-topp'd hill, an humbler heav'n;
> Some safer world in depth of woods embrac'd,
> Some happier island in the wat'ry-waste,
> Where slaves once more their native land behold,
> No fiends torment, no Christian thirst for gold.
> To be, contents his natural desire,—
> He asks no angel's wing, no seraph's fire;
> But thinks, admitted to that equal sky,
> His faithful dog shall bear him company.[2]

The last line seems to refer to the dog's connection to the Land of the Dead. Dogs were thought to be essential guides for tricky afterlife journeys. They were part of human existence and the cycle of life, death, and rebirth that was at the core of all Native American belief systems. In addition, dogs were utilitarian animals exploited for human survival.

The Family Canidae in the Americas

The family Canidae—the wolves, dogs, jackals, and foxes—has wild members on all continents except Australia, which has only the dingo. The thirty-eight species of wild canids live in habitats ranging from tropical rainforest to arctic tundra. The North American wolf (*Canis lupus*) is social and eats mainly meat from large mammals. The South American maned wolf (*Chrysocyon brachyurus*) spends most of its life alone, and fruit forms the bulk of its diet.

Although their members are diverse, the Canidae as a group possess some distinctive characteristics. They seem to be unique among mammals in that the larger canids produce, on average, more infants per litter than do the smaller canid species. Generally, litter size among mammals is inversely related to body size; the large cats, for instance, have fewer offspring than do the small ones. Canids usually live in complex social groups, are highly adaptable, form pair bonds, and hunt cooperatively. Food is shared among family members, and fathers and siblings help to raise the pups.[3]

When humans first arrived in North America the dire wolf (*Canis dirus*) was still sharing the landscape with the smaller gray wolf (*Canis lupus*). The dire wolf's range at 10,000 B.C. extended from southern Alberta to Peru.[4] At least 1,646 dire wolves died at the Rancho La Brea tar pits in southern California. These pits, centers of asphalt accumulation for 25,000 years, have trapped thousands of animals, the most common of which are dire wolves. This suggests that dire wolf populations were substantial at 10,000 B.C., but within a few thousand years the dire wolf had disappeared. The most recent occurrences of the extinct canid are from the western United States in 7500 B.C., well after humans crossed the Bering Strait.[5]

The extant wild canids of North America are the gray wolf, the coyote (*Canis latrans*), the hybrid red wolf (*Canis rufus*), the arctic fox (*Alopex lagopus*), the gray fox (*Urocyon cinereoargenteus*), the red fox (*Vulpes vulpes*), the swift fox (*Vulpes velox*), and the kit fox (*Vulpes macrotis*). In addition to the dire wolf, other members of the genus *Canis* may have inhabited South America, but all these "wolflike" canids were extinct by the end of the Pleistocene. The gray wolf and the coyote never moved farther south than the table land of Mexico. The gray fox has extended its range into northern Venezuela and Colombia, but all the other South American canids are unique to that continent.

The canid with the widest distribution in South America is the culpeo (*Dusicyon culpaeus*), which ranges all along the western coastal region of the continent from southern Colombia to Tierra del Fuego. *D. griseus,* the chilla, is now scarce, but its home is the southern tip of South America, below 25 degrees south latitude. The pampas fox (*D. gymnocercus*) is found in east-central South America, whereas the sechura fox (*D. sechurae*) occurs only in a small region on the northwest coast. The final member of this group of foxes is the hoary fox *(D. vetulus)* which lives in the open grassland of Brazil.[6]

The short-legged and stockily built bush dogs (*Speothos venaticus*) are found in tropical rainforest, particularly along forest borders and wet savannas. These animals are highly social and, when tamed, act much like domestic dogs. They are good swimmers. Bush dogs hunt in packs and, though small, can bring down peccaries and even small tapirs.[7] The small-eared dog (*Atelocynus microtis*) is found only in lowland tropical forest. Like the bush dog, its body is

*The pampas fox, or zorro (*Dusicyon gymnoceras*), is one of five extant species of closely related foxlike canids living in South America. These canids hunt singly or in pairs, are predominately gray, and are of intermediate size, weighing 4.5 to 6.5 kilograms. Photograph by Russ Mittermeier/Bruce Coleman, Inc.*

The bush dog (Speothos venaticus), *found only in tropical South America, lives in packs, has a heavily carnivorous diet, and commonly shares its food with group members. Males play an important part in the care of infants. Weight ranges from 5 to 7 kilograms. Photograph by Tom Brakefield/Bruce Coleman, Inc.*

stocky and its legs short, but the small-eared dog is larger and has a bushy tail. Nothing is known about its behavior in the wild. The fourth and largest genus of South American canid, the maned wolf (*Chrysocyon brachyurus*), has been referred to as the "fox on stilts" because of its long legs. Maned wolves, which live in the grasslands of eastern central South America, are the least social members of the canid family and are not closely related to any other taxa. They may be the sole survivors of the large canid species that existed in South America before the arrival of people.[8] The crab-eating fox (*Cerdoyon thous*), more vulpine in appearance than the bush dog, short-eared dog, or maned wolf, lives in woodlands and savannas in Brazil, Uruguay, and Argentina. As its name suggests, crustaceans are part of its diet. Like the bush dog, the short-eared dog, and the maned wolf, it is the sole member of its genus.

The gray wolf (*Canis lupus*), the red wolf (*Canis rufus*), the coyote (*Canis latrans*), and the dog (*Canis familiaris*) are the American members of the genus *Canis*. In the Eastern Hemisphere the genus is represented by four species of jackals, all living on the African continent, and by the gray wolf, which has lived throughout the northern latitudes until being exterminated in well-populated areas by people and dogs. *Canis familiaris,* of course, has as wide a distribution as *Homo sapiens.* Members of the genus *Canis* are interfertile. These two canid characteristics—global ranges and interfertility—make the history of the domestic dog exceedingly difficult to tease apart from the history of its relatives.

Coyotes are among the most adaptable of carnivores. Consider, for example, the behavioral range of this versatile North American mammal, now extending its range eastward. The coyote has been around for at least 500,000 years. It joined the dire wolf and the gray wolf at the La Brea tar pits, but as a much smaller cousin it had to content itself with scavenged leftovers. Today, five types of social organization have been observed among coyotes. They have been seen in packs, in resident pairs, as solitary residents, as transient nomads, and in temporary aggregations.[9] Such social flexibility, as well as their opportunism as predators, scavengers, and omnivores, has allowed coyotes to move into areas where wolves cannot survive.

Coyotes are believed to have hybridized with gray wolves to form the red wolf population in the southeastern United States.[10] Moreover, roughly 40 percent of the offspring between coyotes and dogs are fertile, but the coyotes that started invading the northeast United States forty years ago seem not to have interbred with dogs regularly.[11] In spite of their ability to produce fertile offspring, wolves, dogs, and coyotes have maintained their distinctiveness through time because each species has a preferred way of life. To understand the relationships of these family members it may be useful to think of the wolf and coyote as siblings, the wolf as parent to the dog, and all three as second cousins to the foxes and other canid species. Although the coyote may have contributed to the gene pool of the native North American dog, genetic, behavioral, and geographic evidence overwhelmingly points to only one direct ancestor: the wolf.[12]

The Making of a Species

Before we can understand the domestication of parts of the wolf population and the creation of a new species we have to grapple with what a species is, something still debated long and hard by evolutionary biologists. When does a wolf stop being a wolf and become a dog? What makes a species domesticated as opposed to tamed? And, once a dog, why not become a wolf again or a wolf-coy-dog?

Let us use the following definition of *species*: a population with morphological, ecological, and genetic traits that distinguish its members from other species. These biological units have mechanisms that hold them together and keep outsiders away. One such mechanism is the female's ability to recognize appropriate mates by their behavior and odor. In addition, species members occupy the same ecological niche, develop at similar rates, and are ready to breed at the same time. Mating opportunities cannot be too restricted if genetic cohesiveness is to be maintained. When something disrupts these mechanisms—geographic isolation, developmental or ecological shifts—cohesion breaks downs and the unit splits apart. Although canids can and do form fertile hybrids, such matings occur only under unusual circumstances, such as when a member of the same species is unavailable. Females will continue to show definite preference for males meeting their criteria of suitability, and hybrids tend not to breed with other hybrids.[13]

During speciation (the creation of a new species), a stable, cohesive population gives way to transitory groups of animals in a state of flux.[14] Among wolves living in and around human settlements 12,000 years ago, a developmental and ecological schism was occurring that tended to separate species members: some wolves were becoming domesticated.

A standard definition of domestication contains two parts: a cultural component, in which humans control the breeding of the animal over which they claim ownership, and a biological component, in which an animal becomes different in form as well as behaviorally distinct from its wild ancestor.[15] Often stated as part of this definition is that humans saw the utility in controlling certain animals and set about domesticating them. A less anthropocentric approach, and one with more explanatory power, considers domestication a more dynamic process and a coevolutionary relationship between species. By associating with humans, members of these species greatly increased their reproductive success, and a subset of these "weedlike" animals, which thrived in environments disturbed by people, became fully domesticated. The earliest and perhaps the best example of an animal whose nature was "preadapted" for domestication is the gray wolf.

Two criteria considered important to understanding which animals are "preadapted" for domestication are the existence of well-defined dominance hierarchies and a high degree of sociality. If animals roam singly much of the year, if they do not look toward a leader for guidance, and if they spread out when threatened instead of banding together, domestication is unlikely. The white-tailed deer is a good example of an animal whose solitary behavior precludes its domestication even though it prefers to live in areas that people have opened up. Deer have been tamed and herded but not truly domesticated.

Gray wolves (Canis lupus) engaging in dominant/submissive behavior. The wolf lying on its back and underneath the other animal is acknowledging its lower status. Such submission keeps group conflicts to a minimum and packs stable. Wolves, the largest canid species, range in weight from 18 to 80 kilograms. Coat colors include white, brown, gray, yellow, and black. Photograph by Joe McDonald/Bruce Coleman, Inc.

With the wolf-dog interface, the dominance relationships tell the tale. Wolves, to keep group conflicts to a minimum, are programmed to be submissive toward the dominant member, usually a male. This inherited tendency to accept a submissive stance toward other wolves must be continually reinforced by adults as wolf pups become socialized to the group. Otherwise the social order would be in continual flux. If a person consistently works to maintain a leadership role over a young wolf pup, control over the adult animal is possible. Other humans, however, will not be accorded the same status. Submissive behavior is also pronounced in dogs, but dogs more readily transfer their docility to other humans.[16]

The wolf is among the most social of all canids. Wolf society functions because of highly developed social responses, which include strict hierarchies, cooperative systems, and sophisticated communication skills. Howling serves a number of functions, but it primarily allows the pack to reconvene after a separation.[17] Wolves live almost exclusively on the meat of large mammals, traveling long distances and relying on teamwork to secure their prey. Their enormous geographic distribution, at least until recently, proves how successfully they have filled their niche. But wolves in the northern latitudes have often found themselves in direct competition with human hunters. A competitor—and a successful one, at that—is a strange choice for domestication. Why would humans encourage close association with another predator? The answer, in part, lies in the human's ability to interject himself into the wolf's social system. The results of this ability have had far-reaching consequences.

Recent work on the genetics of canids proves that the ancestor of the dog is the gray wolf. In fact, the geneticist Robert Wayne states, "dogs *are* grey wolves, despite their diversity in size and proportion; the wide variety in their adult morphology probably results from simple changes in developmental rate and timing."[18] The results of Wayne's analysis show that gray wolves and dogs vary by just 0.2 percent in their mitochondrial DNA; the distance between wolves and coyotes is twenty times this amount. In other words, as far as their mitochondrial DNA is concerned, dogs are virtually identical to wolves.[19]

If a dog is, genetically speaking, a wolf, what are the differences between the two species? The differences in the morphology and in behavior of dogs are the result of their retention of juvenile characteristics into adulthood. The biological term for this arrested development is *neoteny*. Many of the physical variations among dog breeds result from the same process, the neotenization of wolf morphology. In his 1986 paper on the cranial morphology of canids, Robert Wayne states that "all dog breeds are exact allometric dwarfs with respect to measures of skull."[20] Though their skull size is comparable to that of foxes, the shape is different. Dogs have the skull proportions of juvenile wolves, and the smaller the dog, the more puppylike the appearance of the adult animal. The dog's skull is much wider relative to its length than that of any of the wild canids.

General reduction in size and retention of juvenile features in the adult have been noted in other animals altered by domestication. Smaller snout size was not what people were selecting for when they interfered with breeding populations. They were interested in behavioral traits, not morphological ones. With the wolf/dog, it was puppylike behavior that humans wanted in their adult animals.[21] Wolf pups, not yet incorporated into the adult hierarchy, exhibit a freedom of behavior usually described as play. In wolf society, subadults and adults follow very different sets of behavior.[22] A playful adult will be expelled from a wolf pack, but in human society a playful wolf is the only kind likely to be tolerated. Perhaps it is the wolf's great need to be part of a group that leads it to human habitation. Might the wolf recognize a kindred spirit in the human camp?

Some scholars have suggested that the maternal instinct of women coupled with the universally appealing canid pup orphan was the path by which animals entered human camps.[23] Indeed, there are many ethnographic accounts of women suckling dog pups.[24] Without question, humans, and perhaps women in particular, feel a strong connection with those cuddlesome creatures that have the ability to look humans straight in the eye. But an immature animal's appeal to humans does not explain the dog's place in all manner of societies. Pet keeping, the bringing of wild animals into camp to be raised and even pampered, has always gone on. Among the Guianas of northern South America, it was reported in 1924 that "women will often suckle young mammals just as they would their own children; e.g. dog, monkey, opossum-rat, labba, acouri, deer and few, indeed, are the vertebrate animals which the Indians have not succeeded in taming. It is the women who especially cultivate the art of bird taming, some of them holding quite a reputation in this respect."[25] Taming an animal does not make it domesticated, and most wild animals raised as pets either do not reproduce in captivity, become unmanageable as adults, or run away.

Dog and wolf pups have a set of behaviors that other animals do not possess. Dog owners frequently will state that their dogs love them, but love is impossible to test. The behaviors that make the human feel loved are easier to deal with. In particular, the welcoming behavior and attentiveness that the animal confers on the human can be observed, and the tail wagging and the eye contact on the part of the dog are interpreted as affection. This expressiveness, also seen among wolves who have elaborate greeting behaviors, cements the bond between owner and pet. As James Serpell states, "In short, the dog is almost human, but, owing to its subordinate status, it displays few of the signals which people perceive as competitive or threatening in their interactions with each other."[26]

Were Dingoes America's First Dogs?

The dingo (*Canis familiaris dingo*) is a primitive dog that evolved in Asia from either the Indian wolf (*Canis lupus pallipes*) or the Arabian wolf (*Canis lupus arabs*). Asian fossils with dingolike morphology date to 3000 B.C. Dingoes, most closely associated with Australia, were transported to that continent by seafaring Asians in about 2000 B.C. Less well-known primitive dogs still live on mainland Asia and in New Guinea, as well as in isolated populations in subpolar regions throughout the world. These dogs can be linked to each other by features of their skull and separated from other domestic dogs that have been subjected to intensive selective pressure by people.[27] Because the Australian dingo lives on its own far more than other primitive dogs, it provides the best analog to the first American dogs and how they may have existed in relation to the first American people.

In undisturbed areas, Australian dingoes live in stable packs of three to twelve, hunt cooperatively, and howl or moan rather than bark. They breed seasonally, and females are monestrous, unlike domestic dogs, which have two estrous cycles and breed throughout the year. Most dingoes have ginger-colored coats, but black and tan, all black, and all white coats also occur. More than 70 percent of their diet is from medium and small mammals, but dingoes also hunt large kangaroos. The average-sized dingo weighs 15 kilograms.[28]

An Aborigine woman from Western Australia carries her dog around her waist in the same manner as she would carry her child. Although Aborigine women commonly suckle pups, no one feeds the adult animals. Here the woman covers the dog's eyes so that it will not see the candy she is about to receive for having her picture taken. Photograph courtesy of Richard Gould.

The relationship between Aborigines and dingoes is often one of commensalism, "in which two organisms 'eat from the same plate' without affecting each other's well-being, either for good or ill."[29] For some Aborigines, their association with adult dogs, which are barely tolerated and never fed, is a by-product of the tremendous appeal the animals possessed when they were young. The woman-puppy bond is so strong among some aboriginal Australians that barren and post-reproductive women are required to nurse a dog pup.[30] Women frequently hold pups around the back of their waist in the same way they hold their children.

Aborigines bring other animals into camp as playthings for children, but these are eaten when the children grow tired of them. The same fate does not await dogs. But even though men show as much fondness for the pups as the women do, the Aborigines have little use for adult dogs and must continually guard their food from them. Many of the adopted dingoes return to the wild at maturity, leaving the Aborigines free to adopt more pups without affecting the dog population in the camp. In contrast, introduced European dogs, no matter how ill-treated, will stick around the campsite, valiantly defending it against all intruders.[31]

In other areas of the world, as in Australia, dogs with primitive morphology associated with people and moved into new territories with them. It is easy to imagine a dingolike dog traveling into North America, and in fact one American scientist claims to have identified a population that closely resembles the earliest dogs. I. Lehr Brisbin discovered and named Carolina dogs, which he says have been living in a remote area of South Carolina for centuries. Carolina dogs are almost identical to dingoes in appearance and bone structure. They have erect ears, a pointed muzzle, and a fishhook-shaped tail that is sometimes bushy. Bitches dig elaborate nursery dens and carefully bury their excrement with their muzzles when they are in estrus or lactating.[32] Dingoes and Carolina dogs still retain much of the primal body design from which most other dog forms are derived.

Another possible candidate for an American dingo is an extinct canid with uncertain taxonomic status, the Falkland Islands "wolf" (*Dusicyon australis*). When early European explorers arrived on the Falkland Islands, situated 400 kilometers from the coast of southern Argentina, large "wolf-like foxes" were the only mammals on the island. These animals did not resemble mainland South American foxes, which typically are gray with black tips on their tails. Instead, their coats were gray and tan with white on the tail and feet. Falkland wolves were very tame and waded out to meet landing parties.[33] They were still tame and abundant when Charles Darwin and the HMS *Beagle* visited the Falklands in 1833. Darwin reports:

> The only quadruped native to the islands, is a large wolf-like fox, which is common to both East and West Falklands. I have no doubt it is a peculiar species, and confined to this archipelago; because many sealers, Gauchos, and Indians, who have visited these islands, all maintain that no such animal is found in any part of South America. These wolves are well known, from Byron's account of their tameness and curiosity; which the sailors, who ran into the water to avoid them, mistook for fierceness. To this day their manners remain the same. They have been observed to enter a tent, and actually pull some meat from beneath the head of a sleeping man. The Gauchos, also, have frequently killed them in the evening, by holding out a piece of meat in one hand, and in the other a knife ready to stick them. As far as I am aware, there is no other instance in any part of the world, of so small a mass of broken land, distant from a continent, possessing so large a

quadruped peculiar to itself. Their numbers have rapidly decreased. . . .
Within a few years after these islands shall have been regularly settled, in all
probability this fox will be classed with the dodo, as an animal which has
perished from the face of the earth.[34]

Darwin was right. In 1876 the last Falklands wolf was killed by ranchers who
considered it a pest.

The puzzle, of course, is how these animals got to the islands and where they
should be placed on the canid family tree. Either they arrived at some much
earlier time, when a land connection may have existed, or early people brought
domesticated dogs to the islands. The latter scenario, with the people moving
on and the dogs becoming feral, is supported by some of the anatomical features of the Falklands wolf. Juliet Clutton-Brock argues that the wolf shows
affinity to *Canis familiaris dingo* in its large skull, inflated frontal sinus, and
somewhat compacted teeth in the premolar region.[35] Another view is that this
animal was a close relative of the extinct *Dusicyon avus,* known from Eberbert
Cave (8000 to 10,000 B.C.) in southern Chile. This argument proposes that the
wolves became isolated on the Falklands and, like maned wolves, were the only
survivors of an ancient lineage.[36]

*Falkland Islands "wolves," now extinct, were described by the HMS Beagle's
captain, Robert Fitz-Roy, as being as big as midsized mastiffs and having thick
wooly coats, sharp canines, and broad faces. Like dingoes and foxes, they
burrowed in dens to have their young. Their favorite prey species were birds.
After Hamilton Smith, 1843.*

The correct answer to this puzzle is crucial to our understanding of early domestic dogs in South America. So far, a definitive resolution has not been possible with only eleven specimens of the Falklands wolf in existence, and most of these in Europe, and the relevant fossil material in South America. However, some recent genetics tests using skin from one of the specimens indicate that Falklands wolves were more closely related to coyotes than to any South American canid.[37] The questions remain: Did any wild species of *Canis* ever live in South America, and was the Falklands wolf related to other members of the genus *Dusicyon,* or was it an American dingo?

Early Dogs in the Americas: The Fossil Record

The problems of identifying a newly domesticated species, whether animal or plant, is that the initial differences between wild and controlled organisms are very slight. And invariably, it seems, the sample is small. In the case of early dogs, fragments of mandibles (the jaw bone) make up the bulk of the fossil material. With what reliability can one recognize a mandible fragment as that of a dog and not a small wolf? Luckily for investigators, teeth are evolutionarily conservative and slow to change. Thus, reduction in tooth size lagged behind the decrease in mandible size, so that the first dogs had large teeth crowded in small jaws. When more of the skull is preserved, several features help to distinguish dog from wolf. One of the most important of these is the facial foreshortening that the wolf undergoes in becoming a dog.[38]

A statistical approach, known as discriminant function analysis, has been used effectively with fragmentary archaeological specimens to distinguish between dogs and wolves and dog-wolf hybrids. A series of measurements from the fossils is plotted against animals of known taxonomic status to reveal which extant animal most closely resembles the fossil material. Thus, even though the behavioral changes that are driving the morphological shifts are not visible, the neoteny of the skull has been preserved and left for us to discover. Beginning sometime before 10,000 B.C., populations of canids worldwide were changing their ecological niches, and some left the evidence behind.

Wolf skulls have been collected near Fairbanks, Alaska, from deposits dated to 8000 B.C. Stone tools were found near the canids but not in association with them. Several of the crania were very short-faced for wolves. Stanley Olsen believes that the Alaskan animals were forerunners of Eskimo dogs. Walker and Frison mention the Agate Basin Site in Wyoming, dated at about 8000 B.C., as having a very early dog-wolf hybrid.[39] A specimen with a more secure date, be-

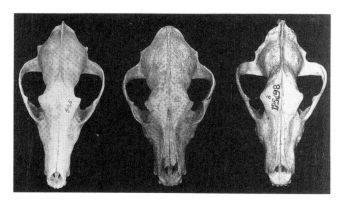

The skull in the center is that of a dog from Indian Knoll, an Archaic site in Kentucky, and is about 4,000 years old. The skull at left is from a modern coyote, and the one at right is from a modern wolf. All have been reproduced to the same size. Note the relatively shorter, wider face and less projecting crest at the back of the cranium of the dog. Also note that the eye orbits are more rounded in the dog. Large eyes are a neotenous feature. Photograph courtesy of the William S. Webb Museum of Anthropology, University of Kentucky.

tween 8000 and 7000 B.C., and a clearer taxonomic position as a true dog, is the mandible fragment from Danger Cave in Utah.[40] In the Illinois River Valley, at the early Archaic site of Koster, three complete dog skeletons were recovered from shallow pits, giving clear evidence that they were deliberately buried in 6500 B.C.[41] By 2000 B.C., dog burials in the Eastern Woodlands of North America had become commonplace.

At Jaguar Cave, Idaho, skull fragments from several dogs were discovered at a human hunting camp that was dated to 9,500 to 8,000 B.C. Not only were the dog mandibles very modern in appearance, they belonged to animals of two different sizes. Until recently, the Jaguar Cave dogs were judged the oldest in the Americas and among the most ancient worldwide. They lost that distinction when the site was redated by radiocarbon in 1987 to about 3,500 years old.[42]

The Paleoindian period constitutes the earliest time of human adventures in the Americas. Human occupation of the Western Hemisphere was well established by 10,000 B.C., and the end of the Paleoindian period is generally considered to be about 8000 B.C., when the Archaic period began. Although fossil evidence is lacking, it is reasonable to believe that when people trekked from Asia into North America they were accompanied by dogs, either by dingoes or more northern Siberian dogs. Mammoths, mastodons, dire wolves, saber-toothed cats, equids, and other soon-to-be extinct mammals filled the land-scape. A major wave of extinction of the largest animals followed the intro-duction of humans and dogs. Whether the new arrivals were good enough hunters to precipitate these extinctions is under debate.[43] Indeed, the evidence that Paleoindians were skilled hunters is mostly circumstantial, and the use of dogs in hunting or for transportation is entirely speculative.

Mammoth kill sites, where elephant bones are associated with stone tools, have been documented from the Basin of Mexico throughout a corridor stretching from western Texas into eastern Arizona and northward through Colorado, Wyoming, and Montana.[44] On close inspection, it appears that the animals met their death by human hand only after becoming mired in a bog or marsh rather than being felled in the open field. Such indicators and the lim-ited number of such kill sites point to opportunistic but isolated events rather than to a hunting strategy specializing in mammoth procurement. No evidence linking dogs to these hunting activities has been found in the Americas, al-though doglike wolves were associated with mammoth hunting camps in the Ukraine.[45] At this point, we simply have no idea whether dogs helped bring down the biggest animal the Paleoindians ever tackled.

It is more likely that dogs were involved in the most familiar Paleoindian ac-tivity: the communal bison drive. The largest bison kill sites are in the north-western plains and include the Agate Basin, Horner, and Casper sites in Wyoming and the Jones-Miller and Olsen-Chubbock sites in Colorado. Both Agate Basin and Casper have the remains of roughly 75 bison, and Olsen-Chubbock, Horner, and Jones-Miller each have more than 200 bison skele-tons.[46] With such large-scale single-event hunts, dogs could have provided as-sistance in two ways: stampeding the buffalo and transporting surplus meat from the kill site.

The bison at the Olsen-Chubbock site, identified as the extinct species *Bi-son occidentalis,* were stampeded into a shallow arroyo and killed in about 8000 B.C. Joe Ben Wheat has calculated the processing time and meat weight for the roughly 200 bison killed at the site. First, he estimated how much meat would have been consumed in the initial feasting and then how the remaining pre-served joints of meat could have been transported to base camp areas. He thinks that only certain parts of the killed animals were transported from the site because many skeletal elements are missing. It is reasonable to assume that 30 to 50 percent of the kill was removed, and, if ethnographic analogy is ap-plied, dogs and women would have carried the load. If no dogs were available, hundreds of people would have been needed. If 33 percent of the preserved kill was removed from the site, 104 dogs would have been required for the task.[47] Whether Paleoindian hunting groups could have supported such large numbers of dogs when mass kills were not available is an open question.

In Wyoming, evidence has been found for the occasional interbreeding between dogs and wolves starting at 8000 B.C. An upper jaw from a dog-wolf was recovered from the Paleoindian Horner site. Such hybrids are also found in archaeological contexts as late as the seventeenth century.[48] Further reinforcement for the existence of dog-wolf hybrids comes from several early visitors, including the following report: "The Indian dogs which I saw here so very closely resemble wild wolves, that I feel assured that if I was to meet with one of them in the wood, I should most assuredly kill it as such. . . . I saw an abundance of semi-wolf dogs. . . . I looked at the Indian Dogs again with much attention, and was assured that there is much cross breeding between these dogs and wolves, and that all the varieties come from the same root."[49] Unfortunately, only the single large dog-wolf mandible has been found in association with a bison kill site, and the animal's status as a domesticate is unclear.

Although never abundantly represented in the faunal remains of early South American sites, there are scattered bits of dog bone at several Andean sites. The caves at Jaywamachay, Panaulauca, Uchumachay, Telarmachay, and Lauricocha, all in the highlands of Peru, contain deposits with dates ranging from 9,000 to 2,500 B.C. The initial occurrence of dog in these caves coincides with the first indications that the South American camels—which were to become the llama and alpaca—were coming under human control on the high, treeless plains of Peru and Bolivia.[50] Although we have no direct evidence that dogs were used to help herd these animals, their presence at the same sites is suggestive.

Dog remains have been claimed for three early sites in southern Argentina: Fell's Cave (8700–4000 B.C.), Los Toldos (5200–2800 B.C.), and La Moderna (4500 B.C.).[51] If there was a domestic dog at Fell's Cave in Tierra del Fuego in 8000 B.C., and if it has been correctly identified at Los Toldos, then the dog had trekked a long way from Asia and must have been present from the earliest human occupation. However, several recent researchers have identified the fossils from Argentina as belonging to the extinct canid *Dusicyon avus*.[52] Others have placed this material in the genus *Canis* but not *Canis familiaris*.[53] Considering the conflicting opinions, the timing of the arrival of the domestic dog at the southernmost tip of South America remains a mystery. Indeed, knowledge about the early history of all American dogs is hampered by a lack of well-dated fossils that can be indisputably assigned to *Canis familiaris*.

The Origin of Dogs and Their Human Relatives:
Other Stories

Because the dog is as much a cultural construct as a biological species, the story of its creation has a second part. The first part concerns the processes of natural selection transforming a wild animal into a domesticated one, from living apart from humans to joining them. Rudyard Kipling, in his *Just-So* story "The Cat That Walked by Himself" (see epigraph), has written a story with this first point of view at its core. In addition, Kipling credits Woman with throwing the bone that tempts Wild Dog into the cave. A bargain is struck between them. Woman will feed Dog and Dog will hunt for Man and guard his cave. What the Wild Dog loses is its freedom and most of the fruits of its own labor. The Cree of Central Canada tell a similar story: At first, Dog was bigger than Wolf. He was called Narrowtail. He and Wolf decided to have a race. The winner would get to live with people. Because he was bigger, Narrowtail won and Wolf was angry. "You will eat too much," he said. But Narrowtail said, "No, I'll be much smaller than you when I live with people." Today, when wolves howl at night they are crying because a dog is in camp and not working for himself, not having to hunt.[54] Dog won, and Wolf lost the right to live with people.

The Cheyenne of Wyoming explain the acquisition of dogs in the following way: First their creator, Great Medicine, "showed them a field of corn and a herd of Buffalo. But the Cheyenne had no way to carry their equipment or to follow the buffalo, and other tribes disputed their hunting rights and attacked them at night. To prevent this, the Cheyenne captured young wolves or wild dogs and raised them as pets and they would guard their camps at night and now since they were killing buffalo they could provide plenty of meat for these dogs and they soon had a large number of them in camp. They began to pack their camp equipage on these dogs when they followed the buffalo on their way south in the fall."[55] In this story, the Cheyenne needed help, both in guarding their camp and carrying their goods, so they captured and raised young canids knowing that the animals would be useful. This next story, about the origin of the Sun-Dance, illustrates how helpful dogs have been to the Cheyenne: Early in their history, the Cheyenne endured a great famine. People had only dried vegetation and their dogs to eat. A young medicine man went off in search of food. He chose a beautiful woman to accompany him. Her five dogs carried their camping equipment. They finally arrived at the Sacred Mountain, which they entered through a concealed passage. Great Medicine told them to follow his instructions regarding the Sun-Dance ceremony and that the buffalo would follow them off the mountain. The next day the medicine man put on a cap of buffalo horns and departed from the Sacred Mountain with his woman and their dogs. They led the buffalo to the place where the hungry Cheyenne were camped.[56]

The tradition of the Hidatsa concerning the origin of dogs is as follows: Yellow-Dog, a Hidatsa with supernatural powers, taught his people about the four varieties of dogs: Forehead-Raised, Lodge-Digger, High-Catcher, and Four-Eyes. The squash that the Hidatsa grow purportedly got its colors from these dogs. Forehead-Raised was bad-tempered, Lodge-Digger dug holes in the earth roof, and High-Catcher stole meat, but Four-Eyes was very gentle. Yellow-Dog told his people to kill the first three dogs but not to kill "gentle dogs like Four-Eyes. Dogs are magic friends. They have mystery power."[57] A "four-eyes" dog, one that has two tan spots above its eyes, was also common among other Plains people, including the Mandan, Ponca, and Sioux, suggesting that it might have been an ancient and widespread "breed."[58]

The Shawnee creator is Kokomhøena (Our Grandmother). During the first period of creation, so the legend goes, she descended from the void and formed the earth on the back of a turtle. Most of the heavenly bodies were created while

After visiting the creator Great Medicine, a medicine man, his woman, and their five dogs lead the buffalo from the Sacred Mountain for the Cheyenne people. Drawing by Richard Davis, Cheyenne. After Dorsey, 1905.

the earth was inhabited only by Our Grandmother, her grandson, and her little dog. The second creation period ended with a flood, and in the third period the grandson made mischief. In the fourth period, the present day, Our Grandmother retired from the earth with her grandson and dog but continued to mete out occasional punishments from above.[59]

The Penobscot of northern Maine have a mythical hero known as Deceiving Man. According to legend, Deceiving Man called all the animals together to ask them what their behavior would be like when men appeared in their midst. The moose said that it would take flight, and the squirrel said that it would gnaw off the humans' heads. The other animals went away angrily, saying that men would be too poor. Only the dog offered to live with people and share their poverty. Deceiving Man then decreed that all those animals who went away in anger would henceforth live in fear, not only of men but of dogs as well.[60] The Penobscot hero gave all the animals a chance to ally with people, but with the exception of the dog, they regarded the approaching humans with hostility. For this attitude, Deceiving Man punished them.

The transformer hero known as Kulóskap was the great teacher and friend of the Micmac of Nova Scotia. When Kulóskap first came into the world, men were as animals and animals were as men, and the land was full of all manner of fiends. During this early period Kulóskap used his two great dogs and his considerable powers to defeat ghosts, goblins, cannibals, and devils. One day on his way to confront a hideous creature, Kulóskap met two monstrous dogs, "but he set his own [dogs] at them, and they, growing to tremendous size, killed the others. His dogs were so trained that when called to come off they went on, and the more they were bid to be quiet the more they bit."[61] Later in his journey he encountered two witches disguised as flirtatious young maidens bringing gifts. Knowing their evil intent, Kulóskap signaled to his dogs with contrary instructions, and they chased the witches away.

In the Guianas, the Waiwai's great culture hero Mawari was father to all people. Mawari, so the story goes, summoned an Anaconda Woman from the river to be his wife. As she rose from the water she carried in her arms the first two dogs. These dogs became Mawari's pets. Previously, Mawari had kept bush dogs as pets, but these he sent back to the forest. When he went to heaven he left the new dogs as pets for his children. In Waiwai legend then, dogs come from the underwater world of the Anaconda people.[62]

When Nagaicho, the creator of the Chahto people of northern California, decided to create the world, "he took along a dog." After he had made many creatures, he said to the dog, "All things are good. We have made them good, my dog." Thus satisfied, he went back north with his dog.[63] And, of course, it is from the north that people said they had received their dogs.

American creation stories frequently start with humans and animals, including dogs, possessing nearly identical attributes. In these myths dogs are more like humans—speaking like them, living in villages like them, and procreating with them. For various reasons, dogs lose most of their human characteristics, but they still understand human speech and retain some of their former magic. In Iroquois thought, dogs once lived in the human world but forfeited their human status through indiscreet behavior. One Seneca storyteller explains human-dog relations this way: "It is true that whenever a person loves a dog he derives great power from it. Dogs still know all we say, only they are not at liberty to speak. If you do not love a dog, he has the power to injure you with his orenda [magic]."[64]

Many North American people attributed great powers to the coyote, which they considered to be quite a trickster. A Miwok story credits the coyote with creating humans. As the story is told, Coyote called together all the animals and asked them what people should look like. Each animal wished people to resemble itself, but they all agreed that no other animal could give people the wit and cunning that the coyote could supply. The other animals, having made a clay model of their prototype human, went to bed. Coyote stayed up all night, destroyed the other animals' model, and made his own version.[65]

A Southern Paiute story has Coyote involved in the creation of people but playing quite a different part than in the Miwok myth. At first, there were no men and a mother sent her daughter out to find one. The daughter, unable to find a human mate, came back with Coyote. When Coyote realized that his wife has a toothed vagina (vagina dentata) he hit her over

The Micmac hero Kulóskap sets his two great dogs on witches. "Kus! [be gone]," he shouted to the dogs, which only caused them to lunge more fiercely at the witches, forcing them to flee in disarray. Woodcut by Charles Godfrey Leland, 1898.

the head with a stick. The woman soon gave birth to a myriad of tiny babies, which she dropped into a jug. When the jug was full, Coyote distributed the contents across the land, and these babies became the founders of the Great Plains groups. The Gosiute version of this story states that the last man to come out of the jug was covered with dust and tougher than all the others. He was the Gosiute.[66]

The Mixtec people who live in the Oaxaca valley of Mexico have a legend about the first time the sun appeared over the earth. Before this, people had lived in darkness, but with the light and heat generated by the sun some of the people became very frightened. They dug deep holes and covered themselves to hide from the sun and perished. Their dogs, unable to find anything to eat, were changed into coyotes so that they could fend for themselves. This is why, according to the Mixtec, there are coyotes today.[67]

The widespread creation myths that attribute people's origins to a mating between a human and a dog has deep roots in Asia. There are a great number of Turko-Mongol people with a dog ancestry myth. Further east, an ethnic group that lived on the western edge of ancient China, the Dog Jung, traced its ancestry to the mating of a pair of white dogs sometime in the first millennium B.C. A heroic dog named P'an Hu was ancestor to the Man and the Mao people who lived to the south and east of China. The Ch'i-tan, who had both dog totems and dog ancestry myths, lived to China's north. It is no wonder that the early Chinese felt themselves surrounded by Dog People.[68]

This Asian tradition is also found in northern North America. The Dogribs, as their name suggests, are among the northern Athapaskan peoples who believe that they are descended from the mating of a woman and a dog. In the Dogrib version, a woman's brothers, realizing that their sister has taken a dog lover, kill the dog and drive the woman into the woods, where she has six pups. A male and female pup marry and become ancestral to all Dogribs.[69] John Mackenzie, an early northern explorer, reported the Chipewyan belief that at first the earth was covered by water and inhabited solely by a giant bird who dived into the water creating land and calling forth all the animals. The Chipewyan themselves, however, "were produced from a dog; and this circumstance occasions their aversion to the flesh of that animal, as well as the people who eat it."[70] Samuel Hearne visited the Chipewyan in 1772 and was given a more detailed account of their origins. According to that legend, the first person on earth was a woman. She found a dog who turned into a handsome man at night and resumed canine shape by day. The woman became pregnant by this dog-man and, soon thereafter, a man so tall that his head touched the clouds appeared and tore the dog to pieces. The guts of the dog were thrown into the river, where they became fish. The dog's flesh became different land animals, and its skin became birds. The tall stranger told the woman and her offspring that they could kill and eat the fish, animals, and birds without worry because he had commanded that they multiply for her use in abundance.[71] Thus, food was produced for the Chipewyan by the scattered bits of the dog who was also their father.

In 1941 an Ojibwa woman, Angeline Williams, narrated, in her native language, a story of a woman who married her dog. This woman had many children by her dog husband, and all the males had dog characteristics and all the females looked like humans. The woman's brothers came to Little Dog Island, where this woman lived with her family, and killed all the males and retrieved the females. These female *aabita-animosh* (half-dog beings) were allowed to stay with the Ojibwa because they looked human, but after this time people lived with dog-husbands only in secret.[72]

The Tlingit, the Haida, and the Nootka are among the Pacific Northwest people joining subarctic and arctic groups in having a dog husband tradition.[73] The Tlingit and Haida myths tell of siblings born from the union of a dog and a woman; the brother became Thunder and the sister became Mistress of Earthquakes.[74] A Nootka woman had dog children who shed their robes and took on human form. One of her sons, who had supernatural powers because his father was a dog, was able to catch a whale with a tiny hook.[75]

The dog husband myth is found as far south as the Plains, and the Arapaho have developed their own twist. An Arapaho woman mated with a White Dog and had seven puppies. Before the pups and their father became human, they lured all the other dogs from the village to teach the people a lesson for ill-treating their dogs. The people, knowing that they could not get along without their dogs, vowed to treat them better. The man and his seven sons (the White Dog and his seven pups) then restored the dogs to their owners. This myth is used to explain the origin of the Arapaho Dog Soldiers, a military society of the bravest of warriors.[76] The Dog Soldiers are descended from those seven puppies. In fact, most Plains people had dog societies in the nineteenth century. The Cheyenne Dog Soldiers were the most famous of these military groups because of their brave stand against the U.S. Army.[77]

Not all Dog People have resulted from women mating with dogs. The Huichol of northwestern Mexico have an origin myth with several reoccurring panamerican themes: multiple creations, a flood, a "grandmother" creator, and the transformation of a dog into human form. After the flood, the story goes, the old woman Nakawé, "The One Who Came First," re-created all the plants and animals. She saved one man and a little black female dog. The man lived in a hut with this dog. One day he saw the dog take off her animal skin and become a beautiful woman. He stole and burned her animal skin and married her. This couple repopulated the earth, and their descendants call themselves Sons of the Dog.[78] A clan of Arawak Indians living on the upper Pomeroon River, Guiana, are known as *pero-kuru-kuyaha,* the "dog spirit people." This clan has an origin myth identical to that of the Huichol except that the dog's coat was white instead of black. Perhaps the different color is more significant than it seems at first. The Arawak clan uses a Spanish derived word for dog, *perro,* and may have chosen a white female dog only after the arrival of the pale-colored Europeans.[79]

Dogs in the Creation Myths of the Inca, the Aztec, and the Maya

The Huarochirí Manuscript is the only colonial document to record a pre-Hispanic religious tradition in an Andean language—Quechua, the language of the Inca. It tells of the "dawning age," before the present race of people existed. In this remote antiquity people lived forever but were forced to sacrifice half their children to feed the insatiable appetite of the fire-monster Huallallo Caruincho. This cruel world was destroyed by the great Andean mountain deity Paria Caca, who defeated and passed sentence on Huallallo, saying:

> Because he [Huallallo] fed on people, let him now eat dogs; and let the Huanca people worship him.
> When the Huanca worshiped him, they'd propitiate him with dogs. And since he, their god, fed on dogs, they also ate them.
> As a matter of fact, we speak of them as "dog-eating Huanca" to this day.[80]

The Huanca were great enemies of the Inca, and *The Huarochirí Manuscript* provides the mythical origins for the opposing viewpoints of the Huanca and the Inca regarding the consumption of dog.

The Aztec believed that there had been four previous suns in the sky before the creation of the fifth sun, the sun whose light shone on their empire. In the Aztec Legend of the Suns, the first sun ended when people were eaten by jaguars. The second sun was blown away and the people changed into monkeys, and in the third sun, people were destroyed by a rain of fire. A worldwide flood concluded the time of the fourth sun. Only one couple survived the deluge, by hiding in a log. When the man and woman started the first fire with a drill stick, the god Tezcatlpoca said, "'Gods, who's doing the burning? Who's smoking the skies?' . . . Then [Tezcatlpoca] cut off [the couple's] rumps, and that way they were turned into dogs."[81]

One deity in the pantheon of gods from central Mexico was frequently depicted as a dog. This canine deity, known as Xolotl by the Aztec, is credited in several stories as being instrumental in creating people. In one tale, Xolotl and his brother Quetzalcoatl journeyed to the underworld to retrieve the people who had been drowned in the flood at the end of the fourth sun. They tricked the God of Death, Mitlantecuhtli, to obtain the people's bones. The precious bones were ground like maize into meal by the gods and mixed with their

blood to create the present race of people. All the gods then retired to the ancient city of Teotihuacán to create the fifth sun, the present-day sun.[82]

In another story, Xolotl traveled to the underworld by himself to procure the bone of the departed races. In his haste he dropped the bone, which shattered into different sizes, just as people are of varying sizes. The gods sprinkled blood on these bone bits, and a male and a female emerged. Xolotl was charged with their nurturing. This couple then founded the human race.[83]

The sacred book of the Quiché Maya, the *Popol Vuh,* or "council book," is one of the world's great creation stories and the most important text written in a Native American language.[84] The *Popol Vuh* was transcribed in the sixteenth

Xolotl (at right), the canine god of central Mexico, played a role in an Aztec creation myth of the coming of the Fifth Sun, the one that currently gives us light. He also helped create the present race of people. Here Xolotl is paired with the dead sun god, who wears a sun disk which is sinking into the jaws of the Earth Monster. Above the pair is the sky sign, and they are framed by water imagery. Xolotl is also the opener of the road from the sky to the watery underworld. From the Codex Borbonicus, 1890, facsimile edition. Courtesy of the Beinecke Rare Book and Manuscript Library.

century from a more ancient hieroglyphic text. It tells of the creation of the earth, the story of the Hero Twins, and the history of the Quiché dynasties.[85] As we have seen, American origin myths are often stories of multiple creations, and the *Popol Vuh* relates three unsuccessful attempts to get it right. In the third attempt, people were carved out of wood, but they soon forgot the masters who made them. As a result, many terrible plagues descended on them.

> The black rainstorm began, rain all day and rain all night. Into their houses came the animals, small and great. Their faces were crushed by things wooden and stone. Everything spoke: their water jars, their tortilla griddles, their plates, their cooking pots, their dogs, their grinding stones—each and every thing crushed their faces. Their dogs and turkeys told them:
> "You caused us pain, you ate us, but now it is *you* whom *we* shall eat."
> . . .
> And this is what their dogs said, when they spoke in their turn:
> "Why is it you can't seem to give us our food? We just watch and you just keep us down, and you throw us around. You keep a stick ready when you eat, just so you can hit us. We don't talk, so we've received nothing from you. How could you not have known? You *did* know we were wasting away there, behind you.
> "So, this very day you will taste the teeth in our mouths. We shall eat you," their dogs told them, and their faces were crushed.[86]

And that was the end of the stick people, eaten by their dogs.[87]

The middle section of the *Popol Vuh* relates the adventures of the mythical Hero Twins, Hunahpu and Xbalanque, who prepare the way for the human race. First they defeated the False Sun. Then they undertook the difficult journey to Xibalba, the Mayan underworld, by going down the face of a cliff, crossing the bottom of a canyon with rapids, passing through some birds, and finally crossing the Pus and Blood rivers to the crossroads of black, white, red, and green. One after the other, they entered the Dark House, the Razor House, the Cold House, the Jaguar House, the Fire House, and the Bat House. After surviving these obstacles the twins were challenged to a ball game[88] by the Lords of Xibalba (the Lords of Death). Again the boys triumphed. They then entertained the lords by dancing and by sacrificing themselves and then bringing themselves back to life. A lord said, "Sacrifice my dog, then bring him back to life again." "Yes," they said.

> When they sacrificed the dog
> he then came back to life.

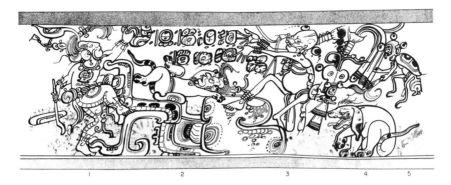

A panting dog with long houndlike ears and jaguar spots, appearing in this scene on a late classic Maya vase, is part of the creation story told in the Popol Vuh. *The dog is happy, having just been brought back to life by the Hero Twins. Hunahpu swings an ax to sacrifice his brother Xbalanque, who has jaguar paws and tail. The ecstatic Death God is tricked by these two into requesting his own sacrifice. In defeating the Lords of Xibalba the Hero Twins prepare the way for the present race of people. Rollout drawing of the "Metropolitan Museum Vase." Courtesy of Michael D. Coe.*

> And that dog was really happy
> when he came back to life.
> Back and forth he wagged his tail
> when he came back to life.[89]

The ecstatic Lords of Xibalba asked to have themselves sacrificed and brought back to life. The twins obliged the first part of their request but of course did not bring them back to life. By such trickery Hunahpu and Xbalanque defeated the lords and prepared the way for humans to live on earth.

Endnote

Whether we consider their mythical beginnings or their wild ancestry, dogs may have gained in their association with people. But through domestication an animal becomes less intelligent and forfeits its freedom.[90] Or, in legend, it loses its ability to speak and become human. Indeed, everyday life for dogs is something quite different from life in myth and story. The reality-based dog serves an owner as a slave must obey a master. The Oneida Iroquois have two words for dog, one of which, *é:lhal,* is a specific noun that cannot be "possessed." To say "my dog" the Oneida must add another word, *kitshene,* which has several meanings including "pet," "domestic animal," "slave," and "prisoner of war." *Akishene é:lhal* means "my dog," "my pet," and "my slave."[91]

2 *Hunting, Hauling, and Herding Dogs*

They [the Micmac] have dogs much like foxes in form and size, and with hair of all colours, which follow them; and although these do not give tongue, yet they know very well how to find the haunt of the beast which they are seeking, on finding which they pursue it courageously, and never give over until they have it down.—Father Marc Lescarbot, *The History of New France* (1618)

And every cur of them [Sioux dogs], who is large enough, and not too cunning to be enslaved, is encumbered with a car or sled (or whatever it may be better called), on which he patiently drags his load—a part of the household goods and furniture of the lodge to which he belongs. Two poles, about fifteen feet long, are placed on the dog's shoulder, in the same manner as the lodge poles are attached to the horses, leaving the larger ends to drag upon the ground behind him; on which is placed a bundle or wallet which is allotted to him to carry, and which he trots off amid the throng of dogs and squaws; faithfully and cheerfully dragging his load 'til night, and occasionally loitering by the way.—George Catlin, *Letters and Notes of the Manners and Customs of the North American Indians* (1833)

These dogs of the Puna Indians are a peculiar race (*Canis Ingae*, Tsch). They are distinguished by a small head, a pointed muzzle, small erect ears, a tail curling upwards, and a thick shaggy skin. They are in a half-wild state, and very surly and snappish. They furiously attack strangers, and even after having received a deadly wound they will crawl along the ground, and make an effort to bite. To white people they appear to have a particular antipathy; and sometimes it becomes rather a venturous undertaking for a European traveler to approach an Indian hut, for these mountain dogs spring up to the sides of horses and try to bite the rider's legs. They are snarlish and intractable even to their masters, who are often obliged to enforce obedience by help of a stick. Yet these dogs are very useful animals for guarding flocks, and they have a keen scent for pishacas [large rodents], which they can kill with a single bite.—J. J. von Tschudi, *Untersuchungen über die Fauna Peruana* (1844–46)

Although dogs, like humans, are products of both biology and culture, it is human culture that defines a dog's situation, its status and its place. But humans, like dogs, are constrained by the environment they inhabit. People must adapt to the possibilities their landscape provides. For hunting and gathering people, life centered on prey animals and the quest for highly dispersed sources of food. Dogs have fit well into such societies. As camp followers, hunters, and transporters, dogs have usually found places for themselves. The accounts of early visitors and later ethnographers describe some dog-owning hunting and gathering groups of the recent past, from the arctic to Tierra del Fuego.

Numerous accounts from early visitors to North America state that most native groups had dogs that resembled coyotes or wolves. Those dogs were ill-mannered, often hungry, and treated casually or harshly, and had more of a howl than a bark. Small barkless dogs were encountered on the Caribbean islands and in northern South America. In Mexico the Spanish found small hairless dogs, along with medium-sized yellow-haired dogs, for sale in markets. The Inca of South America bred four kinds of dogs. In his famous monograph on dogs, Harvard professor Glover Allen listed seventeen types of dogs living among American native groups at the time of contact between the Eastern and Western hemispheres. He divided aboriginal American dogs into the following categories: Eskimo, Plains Indian, Sioux, long-haired pueblo, larger or common Indian, Klamath Indian, short-legged Indian, Klallam Indian, Inca, long-haired Inca, Patagonian, Mexican hairless, small Indian or Techichi, Hare Indian, Fuegian, short-nose Indian, and Peruvian pug-nosed. He used skeletal remains, early historical accounts and ethnographies to produce this list, and his report, published in 1920, has remained the most complete document on native American dogs.[1]

Among the hunting and gathering societies in the Americas, there was great variety in how dogs were regarded—whether they were kept at all, were numerous or rare, or were pampered, given names, or trained to hunt. The way dogs were treated was connected to the affluence of the group in question and the benefit accrued by keeping dogs versus the cost of maintaining them. The groups discussed in this chapter never practiced maize agriculture or they gave it up to pursue buffalo on horseback.

North American Hunting and Gathering Peoples and Their Dogs

The arctic region of North America is home to peoples variously called Eskimo, Inuit, Iglulik, and Aleut, all more recent migrants from Asia than those who populated the rest of the Americas. Highly adapted to life in the frigid north, these people lived primarily on hunted sea mammals and caribou. Meat and blubber were eaten raw, the state in which they retain their vitamin C content. The vegetable stomach contents of slain animals provided additional nutrients. Seal parkas kept arctic people warm, and umiaks, kayaks, and dogs provided the means to move hunting gear and baggage in summer and winter.

Glover Allen describes the Eskimo dog as follows: "size large, appearance wolf-like . . . ; tail usually carried curled forward over the hip; teeth much smaller than those of the Wolf. Pelage thick, with a shorter under fur overlaid with longer hair which on the shoulders may be as much as eight inches long; tail bushy."[2]

The Iglulik hunted musk oxen with dogs.[3] Other arctic groups trained dogs to locate seal breathing holes. These dogs would also haul the meat back to camp. Before the Europeans arrived, the people of the arctic did not use a lead dog. Instead, dogs were strung out on a single trace with a human grasping the harness of the first dog and running with the team. Sometimes dogs were harnessed in a fanlike trace that was easier to release when polar bears or wolves came too near.[4]

The Caribou Eskimo did not keep many dogs because they had only caribou meat with which to feed themselves and their dogs. Dogs fended for themselves when not working and were fed only every other day in winter and never in summer. It was taboo to allow dogs to chew on bones. No Caribou Eskimo could bring himself to kill a dog or even touch the skin of a dead dog, but only puppies were treated with affection and petted. All dogs were named, often with the same names given to people. Families without dogs would pull the sledges themselves.[5]

A single harnessed dog hauls a baby seal in this Inuit winter hunting camp in Baffinland. All the dogs pictured have the tightly curled tails typical of indigenous arctic animals. Two dog sleds and a kayak are propped against an igloo on the left. From Charles Francis Hall's Life with the Esquimaux, *1860. Courtesy of the Rare Book and Special Collections Division, Library of Congress.*

North Alaskan Eskimos staked dogs outside even in winter, feeding them once a day. The dogs would burrow into the snow for warmth. Because people did not like it, walrus meat was the usual dog food. Fish was also an acceptable food for dogs. Whale meat was never fed to dogs, however, as this was believed to be "hateful to the whale." For the same reason, dogs were not allowed on the ice when men were hunting whales. Women trained the dogs, hitching them to the sled and calling them forward. When the dog moved the sled in the right direction, it was petted. A food reward was considered unnecessary. Children played with the puppies and were allowed to cry if a dog died. It was the custom, however, for adults to show no grief at the death of a dog, even a highly valued one.[6]

North Alaskan Eskimos thought that dogs were born without a soul but that giving a dog a name allowed a soul to enter it. On the rare occasions when a dog received a human name, it was taken into the house and fed better than the other dogs. A range of names was reserved for dogs and used by humans only for magic. If a family lost several children in a row, it might choose to give the next infant a dog's name. This, it was said, always worked to save the new child's life.[7]

The subarctic is a vast region stretching across North America, and most of its inhabitants relied almost exclusively on the hunting of large mammals for their livelihood. The people living in the eastern and southern part of the subarctic spoke a language belonging to the Algonquian linguistic family, and those toward the northwest spoke an Athapaskan language. The most important subsistence animal was the caribou, followed by the moose, mountain goat, sheep, snowshoe hare, migratory waterfowl, and fish. Many subarctic people lived in conical lodges and wore clothes made of caribou skins. The canoe was a vital form of transportation in summer, and snowshoes were used for travel through the deep winter drifts.

Most inhabitants of the subarctic had deeply felt proscriptions about eating dogs or allowing them to chew on the bones of certain animals. It was uncommon to use aboriginal dogs to carry loads. Instead, women would pull the small sleds. Families could afford to feed only one or two dogs. The native dogs were small and used for hunting bear, moose, caribou, beaver, and elk. Only after Europeans introduced larger, stronger dogs and Western technology, such as fishing gear and guns, did subarctic people keep dogs large enough to pull toboggans.[8]

Glover Allen has a description of the Hare Indian dog based on one nineteenth-century source and a single illustration. It is a "small, slender dog, with erect ears and bushy tail, feet broad and well-haired. Color white with dark patches."[9] Although a dog fitting precisely this description may have vanished, the Hare Indians, like others in the north, have a special and long-standing relationship with their dogs.

The ethnographer Joel Savishinsky wrote about this relationship with considerable depth and thought.[10] Although he refers to the Hare, whom he studied in the twentieth century, his insights may offer a glimpse into a past of which we have no record. As Savishinsky explains, the Hare are very involved with their dogs and talk about them more frequently than any other topic. The dog is an extension of the family, especially valued because it sees farther, hears more acutely, and has a sense of smell infinitely superior to that of humans. The dog's function is to supplement the human senses and thus increase human survival. To the Hare, their dogs' appearance and well-being reflects on their own image in the community. On the other hand, in a society that values self-control in responses toward other humans, it is acceptable to relieve frustration on one's dog with a kick or a sharp word.

In Hare society children and pups tend to socialize one another and be viewed with tolerant affection by adults. But female dogs are regarded as less desirable and may be killed at birth. Young female dogs that survive frequently receive less attention and less food than

The Hare Indian Dog possessed feet that spread out on the snow to keep it from sinking into the drifts. This helped the dog pursue moose, which sank with every step. The tail of the Hare dog did not curl as much as those of Eskimo dogs, and its long-haired coat was white marked with large patches of black or brown. After Walsh, 1879.

male puppies do. Hare boys also tend to be treated more affectionately and given a higher quality diet than are girls. As children grow older they learn to handle dogs and are given their own sled and harness to practice with the pups. Both child and animal soon learn that the adult world is filled with work and not play.[11]

The Pacific Northwest, with its plentiful supply of salmon and timber, provided its residents with riches unparalleled in other hunter-gatherer societies. Wealth, warfare, and elaborate rituals characterized the cultures of this area. Huge plank houses, war canoes, and totem poles were prominent displays of wealth, as were personal goods crafted with a sophisticated artistic style. The native groups of the Pacific Northwest were unusual in that they developed a highly stratified society consisting of hereditary nobles, commoners, and slaves in the absence of agriculture. In such a place a person could afford a pet, and a dog need not earn its keep.

Among the Nootkan, the great whalers of the Pacific Northwest, tamed crows and seagulls were the most popular pets, and young wolf and bear cubs were sometimes brought home and raised. Dogs were kept "for no particular reason except that the animals managed to survive and preferred human company to competing with wolves in the woods. Only rarely did the animals serve

White and black "wool" dogs join clan groups telling stories in a large plank house, the typical winter dwelling of northwest coast peoples. Female wool dogs were sequestered during estrous to keep them from breeding with hunting dogs. "Interior of a Clallams Winter Lodge, Vancouver Island," 1845–1848, oil painting by Paul Kane. Courtesy of the National Gallery of Canada, Ottawa, transfer from the Parliament of Canada, 1955.

any useful purpose."[12] Dogs were never eaten, for their flesh was considered poisonous. Frogs, snakes, ravens, and crows were taboo for the same reason.

Tlingit communities were built lining a ribbon of beach, with the steep and forested land serving only as a backdrop to a life spent facing the sea. Hunters went inland as little as possible and tried to teach their dogs to drive the deer to where they waited on the beach. The Tlingit also used dogs to hunt bear, elk, goat, and river otters, and to carry packs. The typical Tlingit dog was shepherd sized with long hair, a bushy tail, and erect ears. The Tlingit also kept a separate breed of "Tahltan bear dogs," fox terrier–sized dogs that were quick and fearless in holding a bear at bay until the hunter arrived. The highly prized bear dog may have been kept only by the Tlingit and some of the nearby Athapaskan groups. Bones of prey animals were tied around dogs' necks to improve their hunting skills, and the nostril of a puppy might be split with a bear bone to give it a keen scenting ability.[13] The Tlingit did not always treat the dogs well, but they viewed them as great allies, as this story illustrates: "There was a Flood, when all the people had to go to the tops of the mountains. They built walls of rocks around the tops, like nests. Some people had dogs. The bears came up after them. Those that didn't have dogs to chase the bears were all killed, but those that had dogs were saved."[14]

The Haida, who live to the south of the Tlingit on the Queen Charlottes Island, have a myth about a woman who mates with a bear. This story, known as the "bear mother myth," features a heroic dog named Maesk, perhaps the greatest hunting dog of the Americas. In this story an unmarried woman is kidnaped by a bear while picking berries. She is taken to his cave and becomes the mother to his two cubs. Meanwhile, her distraught father sends his oldest son, a famous hunter, to rescue her. When he returns, unable to locate her, the father sends his second son, and then his third son, all to no avail. Finally, in desperation, he sends his last son, who is still a child. But the child takes his dog Maesk. On hearing this news the bear husband weeps with grief. It is Maesk, he says, that all bears fear. The dog, with its keen nose, locates the bear. The dog, with the young hunter, kills the bear and rescues the woman.[15]

The potlatch, with its feasting, gift giving, and conspicuous consumption on a grand scale, was the ritual activity for which the northwest coast was most famous. Against this background were a number of elaborate rituals featuring mimetic and sleight-of-hand performances. For the Haida, the *'wi'łam,* or dog-eating performance, occurred near the end of the potlatch festivities. At the appropriate time the performers entered the dance-house single-file and marched around the fire, holding their hands outstretched. The leader held a

The heroic dog Maesk aids his master in killing a bear to save the woman and her bear children in this version of the bear mother myth. A Haida carver created the scene in argillite in 1890. Skidgate (sp. 248). Courtesy of the Royal Museum of British Columbia.

dead dog in his arms while singing a song. Afterward he ate or pretended to eat some of the dog's flesh. The other dancers followed the leader's example as the carcass was handed to each in turn until the end of the line was reached.[16]

In other groups—for example, the Kwakiutl and Coastal Salish—the dance was performed with living dogs and was referred to as the Live Dog Eating Ceremony. In this ceremony a dancer, after fasting for four days, had to catch and eat a live dog. According to ethnographer Philip Drucker, the meaning of this ritual lies in its ancestral association with wolves. By eating the dog the dancer becomes possessed by the wolf spirit, and this rite was the prototype for the more complex dancing societies that developed on the northwest coast.[17] In this case, the dog serves as a convenient stand-in for its wild wolf brethren. And the ritual or symbolic consumption of a fearsome predator to imbue oneself with that animal's power occurs elsewhere on the American stage.[18]

At the time of contact, California was inhabited by people of diverse cultural and linguistic origin living side by side but maintaining separate ways of life. Varied environmental zones also served to keep this cultural mosaic intact and people culturally distinct. In general, the California climate can be characterized as Mediterranean. The area's natural resources were rich, and agriculture was practiced only in the far south. Acorns were a staple in the diet, supplemented with deer, fish, rabbits, insects, and other gathered plants. Men generally wore no clothes summer or winter, and women wore very few. People built semi-underground round log and bark houses, or domed earth-covered dwellings. Sweat houses were used by men for ritual purification, and women were secluded during menses.

Apparently dogs were rare or absent in the area around San Francisco Bay.

Where present, dogs often received special treatment, being buried "like persons," given dog houses, and allowed to reside with owners.[19] To one Miwok owner, his dog was as worthy as "life itself," and he would have given this animal his last piece of meat.[20] A Yurok informant described the native dogs of California as collie-sized, spotted black and white, with erect ears and no bark. They were imported from the north in small numbers before European settlement.[21] Dogs were most commonly used to hunt rabbits and squirrels but were also used to chase deer to the shore. Elk were sometimes herded into ravines. According to a Yokuts man, small dogs—"about twelve inches high"—were trained to track rabbits to their burrow. The dogs would also pursue and catch gray squirrels. A larger dog would be used to hunt foxes. Some of the dogs were yellow, some coyote color, some had long, slightly woolly fur, and others were black and white spotted. They were fed acorn soup, bones, and the feet of rabbits and squirrels. Men would stay out all day hunting with their dogs, even in winter.[22]

Shasta Indians took great pains when training their dogs. They constructed dog huts behind their own dwellings and sang special songs to give dogs a keener scent and hunting power. The Shasta Indians also credit the dog with bringing them fire for the first time, sneaking a hot coal from the "fire-keepers" by hiding it in its ear.[23]

Three Mono groups, two Kern River groups, and five Yokut groups said they had never used dogs to hunt. But these people lived in the heart of dog-eating country.[24] As a rule, West Coast societies did not eat dogs, but these groups and others centered in the San Joaquin valley did. The southern Yokut raised dogs primarily for that purpose, considering dog meat a "special dainty," particularly when other meat was scarce.[25] The northern Yokut, who felt that dogs possessed immortal souls, viewed the southern Yokut dog-eating habits with distaste.[26]

A dog walks with a woman in front of earthen lodge houses, typical dwellings for California's Sacramento Valley. Entry into the house was through the roof. From Tribes of California, *by Stephen A. Powers. © 1976, The Regents of the University of California.*

Great Basin culture was characterized by a continual quest for food in a marginal environment. Simple lean-tos made of twigs served as shelter. Seeds, roots, and nuts supplemented by caterpillars, grasshoppers, rodents, lizards, and rabbits made up the bulk of the diet. Rare inclusions in this diet included deer, antelope, fish, and birds. People lived in small egalitarian bands, and ritual life was simple.

Even though the rock art of the Great Basin indicates an early relationship between dogs and ritualized hunting, ethnographic reports suggest that in fact dogs were not abundant throughout the Great Basin. The Ute and Southern Paiute did not use dogs for hunting at all. Northern Paiute informants said they had no "dogs" whatsoever (meaning dogs of European origin) but instead had small, scarce Indian dogs, whose ears stood straight up.[27] The Northern Paiute used dogs to hunt deer and mountain sheep, but only on rare occasions. The Shoshone regularly employed dogs to hunt mountain sheep but no other game.

Anthropologist A. K. Kroeber noted that giving dogs names, the normal practice elsewhere in North America, was not characteristic of Basin cultures. This lack of naming, he says, is "in line both with the general meagerness of Basin culture, and with the fact that dogs were of little importance there for

A lone dog accompanies a group of Gosiute at their campsite. Dwellings in the Great Basin were often just collected brush, as illustrated in this 1859 painting by H. V. A. von Beckh. From Civil Works Map File, Misc 120–2; Records of the Office of the Chief Engineers, Record Group 77; National Archives, College Park, Md.

hunting, food, transport, wool, ritual, or anything else."[28] Life was hard for these dwellers of the Basin, and dogs would have presented too much competition for the scant resources.

In the seventeenth century, wild horses arrived on the Great Plains, escapees from Spanish settlements to the south. Gradually some were captured and tamed by people farming the river valleys or by hunters from the north. With horses, these linguistically and culturally distinct peoples were able to move out onto the plains to hunt the buffalo. Horses transformed the way of life for these groups in two crucial ways. First, societies changed from being sedentary to being mobile, and second, they went from being poor to being rich. The role of dogs, who were important members of their societies before the arrival of horses, also changed.

If dogs were used for hunting among groups in the Great Plains and prairie areas in pre-horse days, little mention is made of it. Perhaps the prowess of the horse erased the collective memory of what tasks the dog performed in the old days. The Poncas reportedly used dogs to hunt beaver and muskrat. A group of men and dogs would move along a stream looking for beaver lodges and muskrat dens. When a lodge or den was located the dogs would dig it up, and the hunters would club the fleeing animal to death. Raccoon and other animals were also hunted with dogs.[29]

Before the horse, buffalo were typically hunted twice a year—in spring and in fall, after the crops had been planted and harvested. Hunting groups would go off for long periods in pursuit of the wandering herds, and, most probably, they took dogs with them. In fact, it has been suggested that pemmican technology, which developed three thousand years ago, provided a readily transportable dog food. Pemmican, which consisted of sun-dried strips of buffalo meat pounded fine and mixed with fat and dried berries, allowed hunters to travel farther in search of bison herds. It also enabled each family to keep the twenty or thirty dogs they needed to move their possessions.[30]

Dogs in the Amazon

The Amazonian tropical rainforest, covering 6 million square miles in eight countries, is not a homogenous zone but is regionally diverse. The two major environmental zones are the floodplains of the rivers, which make up 2 percent of the area and terra firma, the interfluvials, away from the floodplain, which consist of 98 percent of the area. The floodplains of the Amazon's great rivers provide a wealth of animal protein, including that from fish, turtles, and caimans, to those fortunate enough to live along the riverbank. In addition, annual flooding enriches the soil, allowing continuous and intensive agriculture. Permanent settlements and large populations existed on these floodplains by A.D. 500. In the interfluves the tropical soils are poor, and prey animals are widely dispersed and well camouflaged. Here, people must survive as best they can by hunting, gathering, and trading with river folk for agricultural produce. The human communities living in the forests are as heterogenous as the region's resources are diverse. Of the approximately two thousand languages spoken in the Amazon at the time of contact, two hundred remain.

Before the Europeans arrived, groups on the margins of the vast rainforest possessed dogs, but there is no evidence that people in the interior ever had them.[31] Dogs certainly were present in the Guianas and in the Orinoco Basin. Early chroniclers described the dogs they found in northern South America as being of "various colors" and the size of lap dogs. These dogs never barked; apparently they were mute. The people of the Orinoco River and Guiana all had words for *dog* in their languages, further proof of the aboriginal existence of these dogs.[32]

The Makusi of Guiana had domestic dogs but would also adopt a wild canid called a maikong. This "wild dog" probably was a crab-eating or pampas fox. A tame maikong was the most treasured possession of the Makusi. It was fed cooked flesh, fish, and ripe plantains. The Makusi said they liked to breed the maikong with their domestic dogs because the offspring made the best hunting dog.[33] In 1925 a female pampas fox reportedly gave birth to two litters fathered by a fox terrier hybrid,[34] but such an event must have been extremely rare. South American canids that have been tested have a different karyotype (the diploid number of chromosomes) from dogs and other members of the genus *Canis,* and the offspring of such crosses would usually be sterile.[35]

In the past, the best hunting dogs were bred by the Taruma and the Maiong-gong and then traded to other groups participating in a long-distance inter-tribal trade network in the Guiana highlands. In exchange they received curare poison from the Makusi, blowpipes from the Arekuna, hammocks from the Guinau, and fibers from the Waiwai.[36] The hunting dogs of the Taruma were given special care; in camp they were kept tied on platforms to prevent their feet from becoming infested with jiggers. Some dogs were called deer dogs or jaguar dogs in acknowledgment of their skill at flushing out these animals. Taruma dogs were most useful, however, in hunting tapirs and the two varieties of peccaries. After being located by dogs, tapirs tended to run to their favorite waterhole, where hunters waited with bows, arrows, and spears. Peccaries, when chased by dogs, tried to hide in hollow logs, trees, or holes in the ground where they could be easily trapped.[37]

The Waiwai, neighbors of the Taruma, received their first outside visitor, R. H. Schomburgk, in 1837. He reported them to be great hunters and famous among surrounding groups for their dogs. Although today the Taruma have disappeared, the Waiwai continue the Taruma traditions, including trading their well-trained dogs to other more distant tribes in the northwest and carefully tending these esteemed animals. Male dogs are kept tied on raised "post beds," and lactating bitches are provided with woven "nursery beds." Contrasting with these dogs are the village curs, which are mistreated, never fed, and left to fend for themselves on the margins of human activity.[38] A valuable hunting dog is buried or cremated, and its owner will weep at its demise, but other dead dogs are merely thrown into the forest.[39]

According to some, the Bororo, living on the southern rim of the Amazon, also had dogs of native origin. Unlike many interior groups who obtained dogs only after the European invasions, the Bororo show their dogs little affection. A hunting dog is not considered a valued enough possession to be counted as part of an owner's property after death. Most of the dogs of the Bororo are emaciated, half-wild, and vicious. On the other hand, the Bororo are very attached to their pet macaws. They play with the birds and premasticate their food for them. At death, ownership of a pet macaw passes to the decedent's heir.[40]

Amazonian peoples who had no tradition of keeping dogs were eager to obtain them once they understood the hunting abilities of the European imports.[41] Dogs improved hunters' efficiency in pursuing larger game through the rainforest, as is illustrated by the comments of some Waorani, a people of eastern Ecuador who acquired dogs only about fifty years ago. A Waorani, when asked "Did you eat collared peccary before you came into contact with the outside world?" typically answers: "How in the world would I have ever eaten collared peccary? We never had any dogs!"[42] Thus, these new hunting dogs allow the Waorani to obtain a food item that previously was beyond their reach.

The Achuar are Jivaro people living in the Peruvian Amazon. They value their dogs greatly, give them proper names, and feed them a carefully prepared diet of mashed manioc and sweet potatoes served in a tortoise shell. Dogs must observe food taboos just as humans do, and if they become sick they are given a medicine prepared for them from a special plant in the garden. The dogs, important in hunting, are owned and cared for exclusively by women. Women trade the dogs for other goods, and a very good hunting dog may be worth a

A dog sleeps peacefully in the foreground as a Puri family in their palm frond dwelling cook a monkey over a fire. The Puri, living on the east coast of the Brazilian Amazon, were visited early in the nineteenth century by the German prince Maximilian von Wied. He reported that the Puri obtained their dogs, which they called joare, *from Portuguese settlers. From Wied, 1820.*

dugout canoe. Dogs are raised with as much care as children, and, as privileged members of the household, they sleep on low platforms beside their mistresses.[43]

Dogs are ranked by the Achuar according to the type of animal they are capable of pursuing and killing. The lowest-ranking dogs are those that can catch only rodents, such as agoutis. Next come those who pursue armadillos. The more highly skilled will tackle peccaries, and the bravest will attack ocelots and even jaguars. Dogs are subjected to various training methods to help them improve their rankings. Pups are thrown into cold water and made to swim until the point of exhaustion to toughen them. Later, young dogs run with the pack to learn from their elders. When successful, dogs are given some of the kill to encourage them in the future. Meat is never fed to dogs in camp, keeping them eager for the hunt.[44]

The Achuar, not having had dogs before the arrival of Europeans in South America, had no word for the animal. They chose to call the dog *yawa,* a term that also refers to the jaguar. They added the term *tanku,* which means "tame or having the capacity to live with people"; tanku yawa is "tame jaguar." The Achuar also understand the similarity of the dog to another canid with which they share the forest, the bush dog (*Speothos venaticus*). They know that bush dogs hunt in packs and, through teamwork, are able to kill peccaries and small tapirs. Bush dogs are untamable, however, and hunt only for themselves. In hunting songs, dogs are metaphorically linked to bush dogs (*patukmai*).

> My *patukmai* dog, now that dawn is breaking, I set you on the game
> Now I make you bay
> Having unleashed you, I make you follow your prey.[45]

Dogs in Patagonia and Tierra del Fuego

In the 1.5 million square kilometers that make up the pampas, Patagonia, and Tierra del Fuego, people lived in small to medium-sized groups and hunted the guanaco (*Lama guanicoe*), one of the last survivors of South America's original array of wild camels. Deer were a secondary resource in places where they were available. Seals, sea otters, sea birds, and fish were important food sources in the far south. It was, however, the hunt for the guanaco that defined the cultures living in this immense stretch of territory. Just as the caribou defined cultures over vast regions in the north, these people literally lived and died by the guanaco. Patagonians were nomadic and had only *toldos* (lean-tos) as protection against the bone-chilling wind.

In "Dogs of the American Aborigines," Glover Allen describes the "Patagonian dog" as follows: "a medium-sized dog, as big as a large Foxhound, coat usually short and wiry, or longer and of softer texture; ears short and erect; color dark, more or less uniform, rarely spotted; dark brownish black, dark tan, or occasionally black; tail bushy. General appearance like a small wolf."[46] This dog apparently did not bark but occasionally would howl in a most melancholy fashion.

The Tehuelche were one of the groups living on the grasslands of Patagonia. They hunted guanacos and rheas. They had two types of dog, a variety that looked somewhat like a Scottish terrier, and a larger, woolly-haired breed. According to Robert Fitz-Roy, captain of the HMS *Beagle,* the Tehuelche had "many large dogs, of a rough, lurcher like breed, [that] assist them in hunting, and keep an excellent watch at night."[47] These dogs were silent hunters but would bark loudly at the approach of strangers. Tehuelche women would dry or smoke guanaco meat, then pound and mix it with rhea grease to make pemmican for winter use. This dried food may also have been fed to the dogs, as some suggest it was in North America.[48] After the arrival of the Spanish and their horses, the Tehuelche rapidly adopted the equestrian way of life and added horse meat to their diet. Dogs, however, were never eaten. Among the Tehuelche, where chastity was strictly observed for girls, it was considered "unlucky" for dogs to eat any part of the wedding feast.[49]

The Chono Indians were coast-dwelling people who lived just north of the Taitao Peninsula. Their diet consisted predominantly of fish, shellfish, and seals. Chono dogs were excellent swimmers, as were other dogs of Tierra del Fuego, and were trained to drive fish into nets. The Chono also bred small, long-haired dogs and used their hair to make short mantles. These mantles were of skin, woven dog's hair, bark, and down.[50]

Dogs were seen among the Ona, living at the tip of Tierra del Fuego, by the James Cook expedition of 1769. Later reports state that dogs were important in hunting the guanaco, the mainstay of Ona diet. Dogs also hunted foxes, which were highly valued for their fur. If the hunt was successful, the Ona fox hunter made an apologetic speech to the slain animal to appease the fox world and ensure good luck in the future. Dogs were never eaten, and the flesh of fox was usually taboo as well. When an Ona boy reached puberty he was required to spend some time in solitude, though he was allowed the aid and company of a dog, which must have eased his loneliness considerably.[51]

An Ona man holding a rod of skewered fish stands with his dog and canoe while a family group appears in a conical log dwelling behind him. Ona dogs were small and wiry with rough coats and bushy, drooping tails. From Fitz-Roy, 1839.

Fitz-Roy reported that Ona dogs were adept at cracking open mussels and other shellfish, and he also appreciated their hunting abilities. "On moonlight nights, birds are caught when roosting, not only by men but by dogs, which are sent out to seize them while asleep upon the rocks or beach; and so well are these dogs trained, that they bring all they catch safely to their masters, without making any noise, and then return for another mouthful."[52]

The Yahgan, who lived next to the Ona on the southernmost part of Chile's coast, used dogs to hunt otters, which were much sought after for their flesh and fur.[53] Yahgan dogs needed to be small so that they could ride with hunters in canoes from island to island in search of otters. They were the size of fox terriers and were fierce and strong. By one early account, the feet of these dogs were plainly webbed, a useful trait when trying to catch otters.[54] All had prick ears, though some had more shaggy coats than others. Even though they were untrained and ill-natured, Yahgan dogs happily joined the family fire and played with the children. Pups from a good hunter were in high demand, but no attempt was made to improve the breed by the selection of both parents. If a dog whined in its sleep, Yahgan men were delighted; if a dog dreamed of hunting, success was foretold for the morrow.[55]

The Yahgan language, which is not closely related to that of any neighboring group, contains a wealth of words to describe the activities of daily life. The Yahgan have many ways to express the act of blubber preparation and the process of biting and chewing. According to the dictionary compiled by the missionary Reverend Thomas Bridges in the 1870s, they also had verbs meaning "catching with dogs," "picking up as a dog would," "catching as a dog would," and "biting as a dog would." In addition, the hunting abilities of dogs are reflected linguistically among the Yahgan. The same word, *yösöl-aiamalim,* can mean "dogs," "hunters with dogs," or "hunters alone."[56]

It is not clear from Allen's discussion of Patagonian and Fuegian dogs to what degree and in what form these animals existed before interbreeding with European dogs. Ethnographers are equally equivocal in their conclusions about which groups had dogs and when and how they acquired them. However, archaeological evidence indicates that dogs may have lived among the hunters of the pampas, Patagonia, and Tierra del Fuego well before contact.[57] As further testimony about the existence and origin of pre-Contact dogs, Lothrop reported that all purebred native dogs of Tierra del Fuego were extinct in 1928 but that their characteristics could be seen in the dogs of the modern Indians. These ancestral traits are heights at the shoulder of eleven to twenty inches, broad skulls, sharp noses, erect ears, and black and white coloring with tan legs.[58] Dogs that fit this description were all over the Americas.

The Hunt and the Ritual of Hunting

Because there is no archaeological record of the effectiveness of dogs as hunters, chronicles and ethnographies provide the only window into such ca-

Dogs aid Moche hunters, who are using nets to pursue deer. Dogs are consistently present in hunting scenes that decorate Moche pots, suggesting that they were used regularly for such activities. For more examples see Donnan, 1982. Rollout drawing by Donna McClelland from photographs by Christopher Donnan.

nine employment in the Americas. However, a few examples do exist in which pre-Columbian dogs are depicted in hunting scenes. Both the Moche (A.D. 200–800) from coastal Peru and the Maya (A.D. 200–800) of lowland Mesoamerica used dogs to drive deer into nets.[59] Since these hunters were members of the nobility, such illustrations may have nothing to do with sub-sistence techniques of the population as a whole. A better example of everyday life comes from the rock drawings found in the Coso Range in Nevada and California, where artists sketched people hunting bighorn sheep with what clearly are hunting dogs. More than 14,000 design elements have been documented in the Coso Range series of petroglyphs. Half of those designs are of sheep, but 225 dogs are represented. The dogs have been drawn with short legs, slender bodies, and long curving tails, and some are shown attacking sheep. Figures dressed as shamans appear to be directing the hunt. These drawings date from 200 B.C. to A.D. 300 and are the earliest direct evidence of dogs aiding in hunt-ing.[60] In the nineteenth century the western Shoshone were still hunting bighorn sheep using dogs to drive the prey to a predetermined spot.[61]

Although animals that are unmistakably dogs are not as abundantly repre-sented elsewhere, at Dinwoody site 48FR43 in Wyoming, a human figure ap-pears with a dog on a leash! This drawing has been dated to A.D. 400.[62] Ethno-graphic reports indicate that both the Thompsons and the Interior Salish of the Western Plateau occasionally kept dogs on rope leashes when hunting to pro-tect them from injury. The main hunting strategy among these groups was to drive game into nets or entanglements, over cliffs, into creeks or rivers, or, in the case of bears, into trees. The dog's job was to chase the quarry toward places where humans lay in ambush.[63] The petroglyphs of the Great Basin area clearly point to an ancient tradition for the type of hunting observed by twentieth-century ethnographers. Hunting with dogs predates the arrival of European breeds.

Throughout the Americas, hunting was steeped in ritual and magic. Rituals involved the preparations that the hunters undertook to put both themselves and their dogs in the best frame of mind for pursuit of the desired quarry. Hunters did their best to avoid all types of behavior that might bring bad luck. In addition, magic was performed by shamans and medicine men to ensure that the spirits were mollified, appeased, and ready to put the animals where the hunters could find them.

Training a dog to be a good hunter often entailed one part benign ritual and one part torture. The most valued dogs of the Thompsons went through the same regimen as their masters before going hunting. They were steamed, sweated, and bathed.[64] The Micmac hunter mixed boiled meat, sulfur, and the ashes of birch bark with stock and a little raw meat. If the dog drank this mixture it would hunt well.[65] In South America, the Achuar give their dogs a powerful hallucinogen to help them contact the "disembodied twin world." It is believed that this drug provides dogs with the knowledge and skills needed to be a good hunter.[66] The Waiwai put pepper juice in a dog's eyes to increase its hunting prowess, and the Taruma held a dog's nose over an ant hill if it had trouble scenting animals.[67] The Shipibo give their dogs hunting "medicine," a magical sedge, to make them better hunters of the prized land tortoise.[68] After dogs were readied in these ways, humans had their own highly ritualized preparatory procedures. A myriad of behaviors, both human and canine, were understood to affect the success of any hunting venture.

In Labrador, as elsewhere, the hunter's magic must not be disturbed. The Montagnais people went to some lengths to prevent their hunting

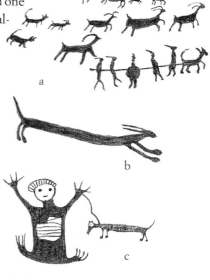

Rock art of the Great Basin, 100 B.C.–A.D. 200. a. Short-legged dogs aid a line of humans hunting bighorn sheep; b. a slender-bodied dog with a long, upsweeping tail; c. a dog being held on a leash by a rectangular-bodied human. Figures a and b are in the Great Basin representational style from big Petroglyph Canyon, the Coso Range, California; figure c, in the pecked style, is from Dinwoody site 48FR42, Wyoming. After Wellmann, 1979, and Francis, Loendorf, and Dorn, 1993.

dogs from chewing the bones of the caribou, telling visitors that it would make the dogs sick but privately holding the notion that caribou are sensitive to the ill-treatment of bones of members of their species. Caribou know that the dog has turned traitor to other animals in aiding man in the hunt. Throughout this northern area, skulls, especially those of beaver and bear, are cleaned and hung in trees to prevent dogs from defiling them and to induce the spirits of these animals to allow them to be hunted.[69]

The Micmac also took great care with the refuse from their post-hunt meals even though, when the following was recorded by a French Jesuit, the reasons for doing so had receded from their collective memories. The Micmac shaman Arguimaut explained to Abbé Maillard on Prince Edward Island, in about 1740, that "it was a religious act among our people to gather up all the bones very carefully, and either throw them in the fire (when we had one), or into a river where the beaver lived. I cannot tell you the reason for this, Father, for I do not know it. . . . [Our ancestors] told us that our domestic animals must never gnaw the bones because this would not fail to diminish the species of animal which fed us. None of the shamans [*puoinaq*], not even I, the foremost one (since I held the office before I was bathed in holy water) could give any reasons for these practices to our young people, who sometimes asked us questions on this subject."[70]

Throughout the Americas, people credited animals with having great magical power. They viewed the animals they hunted as their spiritual and mental equals, and often they traced their ancestry to some mystical animal being. In the arctic, as elsewhere in the northernmost latitudes, preparations for the hunt included magic and séances performed by shamans. Northern Alaskan Eskimos believed that walruses and seals were controlled by a hideous hag who lived in a cave beneath the sea and was guarded by walrus-headed dogs. To get this old woman to release the seals, the shaman had to visit her by means of a trance induced by hours of drumming and dancing. Once he had persuaded her, by any means available to him, to let the animals go, hunting improved.[71] For many Inuit people, the powerful and terrifying spirit Sedna was one of the primal forces of nature. Originally, as the ancient stories relate, Sedna was an Inuit woman who mated with a dog, became pregnant, and was isolated on a small island to have her dog children. Later, having been thrown into the water by her father, she retreated with great anger to the bottom of the ocean with her dogs. She was transformed into the Mistress of the Animals, and she periodically took her revenge by denying men a successful hunt.[72]

Frequently, a woman's sexuality and fertility were seen as dangerous and "of-

Inuit dogs helped in the hunting of seals and polar bears. Here, a harnessed dog pulls a seal from its breathing hole. Only if the powerful underwater spirit Sedna was appeased were seals available to hunters. From Charles Francis Hall, Life with the Esquimaux *(1860).*

fensive" to the animal prey. In addition, an animal would take umbrage if dogs were permitted to eat it. Only if the desired animal has not been "offended" by humans' previous treatment of its species while hunting, butchering, or eating it will the animal permit itself to be killed, butchered, and eaten again. Nowhere are such rules of etiquette more in evidence than among the hunters and gatherers of the subarctic of North America. Among the Rock Cree of the Churchill River in Manitoba, for example, the rules are clear. No woman who is menstruating can cross the path or establish eye contact with a hunter, or he will lose his power. In addition, a woman would upset an animal if she were to consume those "prestigious" parts of the beast reserved for hunters. Samuel Hearne, traveling among the Chipewyan and Dogrib, noted that menstruating women were not allowed to walk on the ice of rivers or lakes, or where fishing nets were set. Nor were they allowed to walk on any path where a slain animal had recently been carried.

Ethnographer Robert Brightman supplies a framework that he believes helps in understanding the logic behind such prohibitions among the Cree. He explains that the male activities of killing, hunting, and eating exist in parallel with the female biological activities of menstruation, conception, and birth. Men provide the group with meat, and women provide it with babies. Menstrual blood is analogous to the spilled blood of the animal. Giving birth and consuming food are also linked. The periodicity of the female cycle echoes the coming and going of prey animals. Bringing home the slain animal is the male equivalent of giving birth. It is unclear, however, whether the connections that Brightman makes between giving birth and hunting were also made by the Rock Cree.[73]

Cree dogs, though aiding in the capture of an animal, could not chew on its bones. This would be extremely offensive to the hunted animal, as dogs were considered dirty. If a piece of meat proved too tough for a hunter to chew, it had to be discarded into the fire and burned, because it was considered a very bad omen for a dog to eat any spit-out bit.[74]

The Interior Salish of Oregon expected failure for the hunter if men, women, or dogs were inappropriate in their behavior toward each other. An Okanagan invoked the soul of a bear killed in a hunt by chanting, "No woman shall eat your flesh; no dogs shall insult you." Okanagan women and dogs were not allowed to urinate near the men's sweat houses, and any dog caught urinating in the same spot as a woman was killed. The hunter's bond with his dog was weakened if he showed passion toward his wife. Thus, a dog would hunt for his master but could not chew on the bones of the prey that he helped to catch, and a woman could not have any contact with the hunter before the hunt or eat the animal's flesh after the hunt. These acts caused the hunter to lose his power.[75]

In the Amazon, prohibitions against woman, especially during menstruation, do not seem to have been as strict as among northern hunters. Many groups in the tropical forests practiced some horticulture, growing palm trees and other useful plants around their houses. Thus, they were less dependent on hunting than were groups in colder climates. Even so, some of the same type of concerns existed among tropical forest dwellers. For example, Waiwai women, when menstruating, take special care in what they touch and spend most of their time in their hammocks. Most *kworokjam* (spirits) fear and hate blood, so if a menstruating woman touches meat killed by dogs or young men, the kworokjam will transfer the killed animal's weakness to the dogs or the hunters. If this happens the dogs and men may never again hunt successfully. A dog who has been weakened can be invigorated in only one way: the woman who caused the accident must boil the bark of a certain tree with pepper and cassava juice and smear the mixture over the dog's entire body.[76]

Hunting was an important activity throughout the Americas, not only among people who grew nothing or had only house gardens but among farming people as well. A good hunting dog was greatly valued everywhere, although apparently not everyone had access to such animals. The differences that do exist seem to reflect changes in people's attitude as they shifted toward a more sedentary way of life.

Hauling Dogs

While men were out hunting with their loyal canine companions, the rest of the work fell to women. And some women were fortunate enough to have dogs to help them, as several early accounts point out. In 1724, the French soldier and trader Etienne de Bourgmont came across a party of Kansa moving camp. They had no horses, and all their possessions were loaded on dog travois and on the backs of the women.[77] On his trip across the northern Plains among the Assiniboin in 1738, another French explorer, Pierre La Vérendrye, noted that the women and dogs carried all the baggage and that dogs were often employed in carrying firewood, as it was not always available at the campsite.[78] In 1820, Sir John Franklin reported that the "greatest proportion of labour, in savage life, falls to women; we now saw . . . [the Cree women] conveying wood, water, and provisions. As they have to fetch meat from some distance, they are assisted in this duty by their dogs."[79]

In pre-Contact America, dogs carried loads by pulling a sledge or sled, wearing packs on their backs, or pulling a travois. The sledge was employed over

Two dogs pull the long, slender toboggan of a Saulteaux (Ojibwa) family traveling near Lake Winnipeg. The toboggan, introduced after the Conquest, soon became the universal form of winter transport from the St. Lawrence to the Mackenzie River. Color lithograph by W. Day after H. Jones, 1825. Courtesy of the Provincial Archives of Manitoba, Collection Red Settlement 14.

much of the arctic. Eskimo dogs were larger and stronger than the smaller hunting dog of the peoples of the subarctic, and more suited to hauling. In summer, when the animals could no longer pull sleds, arctic peoples used dog-packing. In the subarctic, dog-packing was used summer and winter.

The bags used for pack dogs consisted of two pouches made of skin that were cinched around the dog's middle and worn like saddlebags. The dog-pack seems to have been widespread among western Athapaskan people, but not among eastern Algonquian groups. The Tahltan, Carrier, Ahtena, Kutchin, Mountain, Slavey, and Beaver all used dog-packing transport.[80] Samuel Hearne noted that among the people he visited in 1772—the Chipewyan, Dogrib, and Yellowknife—dogs, "trained to that service," carried "their tents, and also their kettles, and some lumber." Dogs, in doing so, lessened the women's load by carrying "these articles only, which are always lashed on their [the dogs'] backs, much after the same manner as packs are, or used formerly to be, on pack-horses."[81] Sledges were constructed, according to Hearne, that were about eight to nine feet long and twelve inches wide. These sledges were pulled by people.[82]

In about A.D. 800, a group of Athapaskan speakers migrated from the western subarctic to the southern Plains. Along with northern cultural and linguistic traditions, they brought with them backpacking dogs. The archaeological record indicates that only small dogs were present in the Southwest prior to A.D. 800, but after this date larger animals appear among the faunal remains. This evidence confirms that the northerners brought their working dogs with them.[83] These immigrants later became known as the Navaho and the Apache. In 1599 a Spaniard named Zaldivar witnessed the nomads, probably Apache, with medium-sized shaggy dogs. "They drive great trains of them. Each, girt round its breast and haunches, carrying a load of flour of at least one hundred pounds, travels as fast as his master."[84] Another Spanish chronicler, writing in his journal in 1590, says, "These people [the Apache] had with them many loaded dogs, as is the custom in those regions, and we saw them loaded, a thing new to us, never before seen."[85]

It is doubtful that backpacking dogs could carry one hundred pounds for very long. A more reasonable estimate might be fifty pounds for a strong dog and thirty pounds for a less willing one. More weight can be dragged by a dog than carried, a fact well known to the people of the Plains. Hauling dogs needed to be big and strong, and people may have encouraged cross-breeding with wild canids to invigorate their stock.[86]

Early travelers on the Great Plains frequently remarked on the resemblance between native dogs and coyotes and wolves. Their impressions were that these native dogs were the result of cross-breeding. Although the reports are anecdotal, recent studies using discriminant function analysis have confirmed the existence on the Plains of dog-wolf hybrids since 8000 B.C. Six deliberately buried large canid skulls recovered from a pit feature at the Box Elder site in Wyoming were dated at A.D. 990. All of the canines and cheek teeth from the six skulls were broken and worn smooth, indicating that the animals had lived for some time after their teeth had been damaged. A similar dental pattern is found among Greenland Eskimo dogs, whose owners commonly hit their teeth with hammers and grind the jagged edges smooth with stones. This is done to prevent the dogs from chewing lines or biting handlers. The wear pattern from the Wyoming canids is consistent with such cultural modification, suggesting that the teeth of these wolf-dogs had been blunted to make the animals easier to handle.[87]

It appears that on the Plains, to a much greater degree than elsewhere, native dogs received frequent influxes of wolf blood—with or without with the connivance of people. In 1836, John Richardson reported that the "wolves and the domestic dogs of the fur counties are so like each other, that it is not easy to distinguish them at a distance. . . . The offspring of the wolf and Indian dog are prolific, and are prized by the voyagers as beasts of draught, being stronger than the ordinary dog."[88] According to several eyewitnesses, these hybrids were able to drag between fifty to a hundred pounds with a dog travois.[89]

The travois, from the French word *travail,* or work, consisted of two straight poles produced from tree trunks that had been dried and debarked. The poles were lashed together at their thinner ends with sinew. The thicker ends of the poles dragged on the ground, and the other ends crossed over the dog's back. The harness consisted of a broad strap across the chest and thongs running back toward the travois cross frame or basket.[90]

The Sioux, Cheyenne, Blackfoot, Comanche, and Pawnee were still using dog transport in the nineteenth century.[91] In fact, the Crow were the only Plains people who seem not to have employed the travois. All other groups used it to some extent, and it is estimated that a train of heavily loaded dogs could travel about five or six miles a day. Each family would have required between six and twelve dogs to move its belongings.[92] The hardest time to travel by dog train was in summer, when the dogs became easily overheated and needed frequent stops for water.[93]

Buffalo-Bird-Woman was a Hidatsa who told ethnographer Gilbert Wilson about her relationship with her dogs.[94] From her story a picture emerges of a

A dog pup is at the breast of the woman who leads a horse, carries a bucket, and has a child on her back. At far right, men are riding horses along the flank of the group. "Sioux moving camp." From Catlin, 1844. Yale Collection of Western Americana, Beinecke Rare Book and Manuscript Library.

well trained work animal highly valued by society as a whole and by women in particular. Dogs were trained and owned by women, and it was women's work that the dogs relieved. The hauling of firewood and of meat from distant kill sites was done with dogs, though horses might sometimes have been used for the latter. To produce good working dogs, Hidatsa women would select from a given litter three or four of the largest puppies. The rest would be killed to keep the bitch in good condition. Most male dogs were castrated. It took about four days to train a dog to the travois, with the woman coaxing and encouraging and gradually increasing the load. Four dogs were enough for the work required, and animals too old or too young to work were also kept in the lodge. When a dog died, it was thrown in the river. Dogs were never shot.

Two dogs are riding with Buffalo-Bird-Woman and her husband, who paddle one bull-boat and tow another loaded with meat and skins and the dogs' travois. On land, the dogs transport the bull-boat on their travois. Drawing by Buffalo-Bird-Woman's son Edward Goodbird. After Wilson, 1924.

Although European dogs had interbred with native dogs at the time this account was gathered, memories of dogs from the "old times" remained. The old dogs had "straight wide faces, heavy, but not short legs and ears that stood erect like those of a coyote . . . and their tails curved upward somewhat at the end, not like a coyote's which lies straight."[95]

The Plains way of life as represented in popular culture is inconceivable without the horse. One change allowed by the horse is that most characteristic of Plains icons, the tepee. When dogs alone were dragging the lodge poles, people were obliged to live in much shorter tepees. In some cases, rather than using tepees at all people may have stretched a buffalo skin over several upended dog travois to form a shelter.[96] Although they gradually were replaced as the primary beast of burden, working dogs continued to provide a service to Plains people that should not be undervalued.

Herding Dogs and "Sheep" Dogs

Seven thousand years ago, on a treeless Andean plain called the puna, human hunters and their wild camel prey were undergoing a transformation. The humans were shifting from hunting to herding, and the camels were being domesticated, becoming llamas and alpacas. Herding, or pastoralism, has an ancient history in Europe and Asia. Goats and sheep were domesticated in the Near East. Along with cereal grains, they formed the basis of the economy from which the great civilizations of the Tigris-Euphrates and Nile were built. In the Americas, only in the remote Andes were there animals suitable for such a destiny: members of the family Camelidae. The Inca used them as pack animals, for food, and, perhaps most important, for wool from which to make fine woven textiles. This Inca cloth was the currency of the Empire.

Dogs have been employed all over the world to help herders keep animals together, prevent strays from escaping, and keep away predators. Today the words "working dog" are synonymous with herding and guarding dogs. Early Western visitors to the Andes are frustratingly silent on the use of native dogs for this purpose. However, writing about Inca history in 1615, Inca chronicler Felipe Guaman Poma de Ayala does illustrate a young shepherdess with her llamas and dog. In addition, dog remains do occur at low frequencies at early puna archaeological sites.[97] J. J. Von Tschudi, traveling in Peru in the 1840s, was the first to put a name to the "Inca" dog, calling it *Canis ingae*. His description of these dogs (see epigraph) is of wild and snarling creatures that attacked foreigners and were often beaten by their owners. These Inca dogs, however, also used these same fierce qualities to vigorously defend their master's flocks and kill large rodents with a single bite.[98]

SESTA CALLE
CORO·TASQVE

A short-legged dog follows a young Inca girl and her llamas. Girls from twelve to eighteen years old worked as herders, gathered firewood, and made chicha *(corn beer). They wore their hair short. After Guaman Poma de Ayala, 1936.*

Traveling on the altiplano of southern Peru early in the twentieth century, Yale explorer Hiram Bingham noticed that children engaged in herding duties were often accompanied by long-haired dogs about the size of Airedales. The local people claimed these shaggy dogs, which they called *suncca,* were one of several kinds domesticated by the Inca. Unlike Tschudi, who described Inca dogs as fierce, Bingham proclaims them to be cowardly and given to slinking away.[99] Today, the Nunoa people, who have been herding on the altiplano for thousands of years, engage in labor-intensive agricultural activities while their young children and dogs take the herds out to pasture and bring them home again at night. As the way of life of the Nunoa has likely changed little since long before the Conquest, this relationship among children, dogs, and llamas may be equally ancient.[100]

The Coastal Salish men of the Pacific Northwest had their hunting dogs, and the women kept a separate breed of dog; its hair was used in the weaving of blankets. A woman's wealth was counted in the number of dogs she owned. These special dogs, with either thick white woolly hair or a long brownish-black coat, were sheared twice a year and kept on islands to prevent inter-breeding with hunting dogs. Each day women would paddle out to the dogs' islands with food and water. To produce the blankets, women combined sheared dog hair with mountain goat wool, adding goose down and the fluff of the fireweed plant, and then rubbed the fibers with white clay. Though most blankets were off-white, Salish nobles' blankets were patterned and colored.[101] In 1792, when George Vancouver anchored his British Navy expedition in Puget Sound, he took note of the woolen garments worn by the natives. His journal entry explains, "The dogs belonging to this tribe of Indians were numerous, and much resembled those of Pomerania, though in general somewhat larger. They were all shorn as close to the skin as sheep are in England;

and so compact were their fleeces, that large portions could be lifted up by a corner without causing any separation. . . . The abundance of these [the woolen blankets] garments amongst the few people we met with, indicates the animal from whence the raw material is procured, to be very common in the neighborhood."[102]

These woolly dogs, found only among Salish speakers of the central coast of the Pacific Northwest, had disappeared by the middle of the nineteenth century. The last recorded sighting of such a dog was made by a resident of Vancouver who, while attending a potlatch on the lower Fraser River in 1853, saw "one of the actors devour, or pretend to devour, alive, a small, white, long-haired dog of a species he had never seen before."[103]

The Zuni and the Chono of Southern Chile are the only other groups reported to have used dog hair in their weaving. In a letter dated April 17, 1540, Mendoza, a Spaniard, described the pueblo of Cibola, near the present-day town of Zuni: "In their houses they keep some hairy animals, like the large Spanish hounds, which they shear, and they make long colored wigs from the hair, like this one which I send to Your Lordship, which they wear, and they also put this same stuff into cloth which they make."[104]

Many Native American women depended on dogs to help them with their daily chores. Children and dogs often grew up in parallel social settings and learned that adulthood and work came early. Men, on the other hand, were preoccupied with the hunt, and with the spirits and magic needed for success. The hunting dog, with its superior senses and fearlessness, was very much a player in this male world of life and death. Dogs, then, have found themselves a useful place equally well in the society of women, children, or men.

"Native dog of the kind called 'suncca,' seen frequently in the Villcamayu Valley. One of the four or five kinds of dogs domesticated by the Inca. Apr. 14, 1915 — 11:50 A.M." reads the label from this Hiram Bingham photo. Courtesy of Peabody Museum of Natural History, Yale University.

A recently sheared dog sits beside a Coastal Salish woman weaving a blanket. The woman is incorporating the dog's coat as well as that of mountain goat into the textile. A cradled-boarded baby is propped against the loom. Painting by Paul Kane, 1845–1848. Courtesy of the Royal Ontario Museum.

Endnote

What are we to make of the prohibitions against women and dogs in many hunting and gathering societies in the northern latitudes? It is useful, perhaps, to imagine a triangle with Woman, Man, and Dog forming the three points. Work links Woman and Dog, Hunting links Man and Dog, and Sex links Man and Woman. When survival depends on a steady supply of large animals, as it does for many hunting societies, the rigidity of these links and separations is more carefully maintained. This framework provides a way of thinking about a world bounded by rules that can be understood in terms of oppositions and pairs. Myths and stories often explain and reinforce those rules. In the case of the Inuit spirit Sedna, the consequence of a female mating with a dog was the continuing disruption of male hunting endeavors.

In South America the structure takes a different turn. The Achuar believe that the dog, as the archetype of the domestic animal, stands at the intersection of nature and culture. And because the dog is cared for exclusively by women but is the province of men during the hunt, it is also viewed as forming a point of articulation between the world of men and the world of women. The Achuar way of explaining this articulation point is through the female spirit Yampani Nua, the Mistress of Dogs. Yampani allows women to use dogs but needs to be appeased. In myth, Yampani was a man who became female to satisfy male sexual desire at a time before there were women. Thus, Yampani—once a man but now a woman—is the perfect mistress of the animals who hunt for men but are under the control of women.[105]

3 *The Edible Dog*

One day I went to observe the market there, just to be an eyewitness and discover the truth. I found more than four hundred large and small dogs tied up in crates, some already sold, others still for sale. And there were such piles of ordure that I was overwhelmed. When a Spaniard who was totally familiar with that region saw [my amazement], he asked, "Why are you astonished? I have never seen such a meager sale of dogs as today! There is a tremendous shortage of them."—Fray Diego Duran, *Book of the Gods and Rites and the Ancient Calendar* (1576)

These Huancas were especially well-known for their strange cult of a dog, which was represented in all their temples. Indeed, they had such an immoderate passion for dog meat that they would have ruined themselves to obtain it, and we are told that we must look in one of these facts for the explanation of the other, that is to say, that their gluttony is at the origin of their religion. There is no feast more important for them than a dog banquet. And in their dances and peaceful festivals, as well as when they went to war, they blew on horns made of dogs' heads, which, they said, "gave them, who were worshipers of the Dog-god, as much pleasure as it gave fright to our enemies, who were unaware of him."—Garcilaso de la Vega, *The Royal Commentaries of the Inca Garcilaso de la Vega* (1609)

When the Indians [the Penobscot] determine on war, or are entering upon a particular expedition, they kill a number of their dogs, burn off their hair and cut them to pieces, leaving only one dog's head whole. The rest of the flesh they boil, and made a fine feast of it. Then the dog's head that was left whole is scorched, till the nose and lips have shrunk from the teeth, leaving them bare and grinning. This done, they fasten it on a stick, and the Indian who is proposed to be chief in the expedition takes the head into his hands, and sings a warlike song in which he mentions the town they design to attack, and the principal man in it; threatening that in a few days, he will carry that man's head and scalp in his hand, in the same manner. When the chief has finished singing, he so places the dog's head as to grin at him who he supposes will go second, who, if he accepts, takes the head in his hand and sings; but if he refuses to go, he turns the teeth to another; and thus from one to another till they have enlisted their company.—John Gyles (captured by the Penobscot in 1689), *Memoirs of Odd Adventures, Strange Delivrances, etc. in the Captivity of John Gyles Esq.*

In many societies the eating of dogs is taboo. Dogs, often regarded as members of the family, live in houses with people. Eating dogs has been equated by some with less than civilized behavior and has been linked with cannibalism.[1] The Aztec, who sold dogs in their food markets, also sacrificed and ritually consumed humans. From this it might be inferred that violent societies would include dogs in their diet while other more "civilized" societies abstain from eating them. To the Inca, for example, dog-eating was abhorrent, and humans do not seemed to have been cannibalized, either. Yet the Aztec, who certainly practiced blood sacrifice on a large scale, ought to be credited with artistic achievements far surpassing those of the more bureaucratic Inca. The Maya, also dog-eaters, were the only people in the Western Hemisphere to develop a complete writing system and also were the first, worldwide, to develop a calendar so precise that the historical events they recorded can be calibrated to the Gregorian calendar to the exact day, month, and year. In short, no clear or easy distinction can be made between dog-eating and dog-averse societies.

Dog-eating has been practiced throughout the world. Faunal remains indicate that dogs were consumed in Celtic Europe (450 B.C. to A.D. 50), both in ritual and domestic contexts.[2] More recently, dog-eating became common in eastern and southeastern Asia, the Pacific Islands, and Africa. While the Japanese no longer partake, the Chinese, Koreans, and Vietnamese continue to consume dog. Indeed, to this day, a quarter of the population of the earth regard dog-eating as not only acceptable but as a great delicacy. There are restaurants in Beijing that serve only dog dishes. The Chinese consider dog a food that should be eaten in winter or when traditional healers diagnose corporal misalignment. Dog-eating was widespread in North Africa during the Middle Ages when dogs were fattened on dates and sold for consumption in markets. Berbers continue the practice, forbidden to Muslims, to the present. Many Nigerians believe that eating dog meat can fend off evil magic and increase sexual potency.[3] Hawaiian chiefs reserved dog feasts for themselves and would roast dogs wrapped in large leaves in holes dug in the sand. These dogs were known as *poi* dogs because they had been fattened on taro roots.[4]

Among some groups living in the Philippines, dog meat is considered the most appropriate food to serve visiting politicians.[5] In 1904 a group of Bontoc people from northern Luzon in the Philippines were imported to St. Louis for the World's Fair and put on display. Twenty times a month, at set times, Bontoc men would kill a dog, burn off its hair over a fire, grill or boil it, and eat it.[6] The well-bred ladies and gentlemen of St. Louis lined up to watch this spectacle, the most popular exhibit at the fair. The "civilized" and the "barbarian" met and viewed each other over a fence in St. Louis that year.

The Bontoc men at the World's Fair were putting on a show rather than illustrating their "normal" way of life. In point of fact, because a dog's nature is quite different from that of pigs, cattle, sheep, and goats, the most common domestic protein suppliers, and its association with its owner more personal, people have often created mystique and ritual around its consumption. In the Americas, an occasion of some importance was usually required to justify the "sacrifice" of a dog.

We cannot know, with any certainty, how important dogs actually were in the diet of most groups of people, even when ethnohistoric records exist. Nor can we know how frequently dogs were eaten or for what reason. But, based on existing evidence, we can make some generalizations about why some groups avoid eating an animal that other groups view as food. In many Native American societies eating dogs was forbidden. The Hare would rather have starved than eaten their dogs. The Dogrib, being descended from a dog, of course did not care to consume a relative. In fact, this prohibition seems to have been in place as often as not. Stanley Tambiah explains why many societies have regarded dogs as inappropriate food:

> The dog, by virtue of the fact that it lives in the house and has a close association with man, has a metonymical relation to human society. The taboo on eating dog has a metonymizing role; it cannot be physically eaten

and incorporated because it is in a sense already incorporated into human society. But at the same time the dog is considered degraded and incestuous and thus stands for the antithesis of correct human conduct. This degradation to a subhuman status is used by the villager to perform a metaphorical transfer on the basis of analogy. Man imposes on the behavior of the dog the concept of incestuous behavior, thereby attributing a human significance to the sexual behavior of dogs.[7]

Dogs were too similar to humans to be eaten, yet they were too lascivious to be considered food. Complex projections of human behavior onto dogs keep them off the menu. The question is under what circumstances do the rules change? Or were there ever any rules in the first place? Are we looking at cultural eccentricities, at barbaric versus civilized behavior, or at a spectrum of behaviors and attitudes, all in some sense explicable when viewed in context? Does putting dogs on the table tell us anything at all about the human lifestyle or ideology of the people cooking and eating this all-too-human animal?

Roughly speaking, Native American societies can be divided into three camps, one for groups who expressed an aversion to eating dogs, a second for those who ate dogs at ceremonies or as a subsistence food, and a third for those who had no dogs or so few dogs that eating them was not an option.

Dog-eating was rare among nonagricultural groups and more common among agriculturalists. Animal remains from middens at archaeological sites provide silent testimony to ancient meat consumption. Distinctions between the ceremonial eating of meat versus everyday diet are important to grasp but hard to establish in the archaeological record. I look at the evidence where it exists, extrapolate to fill in the gaps, and present a working hypothesis about whether or when dogs were eaten. I focus on farmers, from the near and distant past, who lived in diverse social situations, from small autonomous agricultural villages to tribute-paying communities living under the control of vast and far-removed empires. Everyone in these societies—whether slave, peasant farmer, merchant, noble, or monarch—had maize in common as a staple food. And all had dogs.

Shifting Subsistence Strategies in the Americas

The procurement and consumption of animal protein, and particularly animal protein from large bodied-mammals, has been a prevailing concern throughout human history.[8] Once humans developed weapons capable of "killing at a distance" (that is, atlatl darts), hunters were able to target and specialize in the largest available prey.[9] If the biggest animals dwindled in number relative to the number of human predators seeking them out, hunters would tend to move on to the next largest meat package until that category of mammal became scarce as well. In parallel with this shifting subsistence pattern there also was increasing reliance on gathered foods and, in some areas, the eventual cultivation of a narrow suite of food plants.

There were three centers for the domestication of plants in the New World: the highlands of Mesoamerica, the Andes, and the Eastern Woodlands of North America. In the Eastern Woodlands a complex of starchy and oily seeds showed signs of changes in form, consisting of increasing seed size, at about 3500 B.C. Some kind of squash has been identified at Koster, Illinois, at 5000 B.C. In the Andes, domesticated beans and peppers have been recovered from such sites as Pachamachay and Guitarrero Caves in Peru, which date to 3500 B.C. In the highlands of Mesoamerica, squash was found at numerous sites starting at 3000 B.C.[10] The domesticate that was going to change the face of America, *Zea mays,* made its first appearance in the Tehuacán Valley in 2750 B.C.[11] In the highland valleys of Mexico, the stage was set for the agricultural revolution.

These changes in subsistence are well documented in archaeological sequences in Mexico's Tehuacán Valley and reflect a mounting reliance on cultivated crops. Such shifts in subsistence strategies had enormous consequences for the societies involved. The transition from a highly mobile to a relatively sedentary lifestyle was the first key change. This was followed by a shift from small egalitarian bands to stratified and complex societies, which in turn led to a change in settlement patterns from small dispersed human populations to large urban aggregations. Choosing farming as a way to make a living was the most critical of decisions. Why these revolutionary changes occurred only in some areas continues to be a question of tremendous significance and interest. A related question concerns the rise of "pristine" civilizations in six areas of the world: Mesopotamia, Egypt, India, China, Mesoamerica, and the Andes. These independent developments all had an agricultural base.

Our story presents only one feature of these greater issues: How did dogs adapt to major societal changes? Because of their ubiquity among group-living humans and because the way they are treated provides a unique insight into a culture, dogs can be used as a point of reference for cross-cultural comparisons. The dog is one window on the dramatic transformations of American prehistory and serves to illustrate the diversity and continuity of communities of the near and distant past. What were the circumstances under which dogs came to be regarded as an appropriate food species? How has this affected their other functions in human societies?

Although dog burials were usually documented by early archaeologists, food refuse was not always recorded, nor were the remains quantified. Moreover, the presence of dogs has a serious impact on the faunal remains at any site, so that most small bones, including those of dogs, would have been chewed beyond recognition, if not by humans then certainly by fellow canine scavengers.[12] Ethnographic accounts mention that dogs were frequently denied access to favored prey animal remains, and, in any case, the higher preservation rate of these larger bones inflates their numbers relative to smaller ones. Thus, faunal remains collected from midden areas do not contain an unbiased record of what people were eating. In addition, local informants, understanding European repugnance to eating dog flesh, may have underreported their own taste for it. How often were they reciting what they thought the "white man" wanted to hear? All of these difficulties must be kept in mind when evaluating the narrative and archaeological data.

The earliest Mesoamerican remains of domestic dogs, dating to 3000 B.C. or perhaps a bit later, are from the Tehuacán Valley. At this time cultivated plants were beginning to be exploited by people in the long-inhabited valley, and the population was growing.[13] During the next 2,000 years there is abundant evidence that dogs were used for animal protein to supplement dwindling wild resources. Canid faunal remains increased through time, and by 600 B.C., dogs were routinely eaten in farming villages on the valley floor. By 150 B.C. the number of people living in the valley had risen dramatically; population estimates range from 20,000 to 30,000. Now both turkeys and dogs were being eaten by the people of the Tehuacán Valley.[14]

North of Tehuacán, in the Basin of Mexico, the urban center of Teotihuacán possessed, in A.D. 100, the largest building in the New World. The volume of this building, named the Pyramid of the Sun by the Aztec, was more than 1 million cubic meters. At the time of its construction the city's population numbered 80,000.[15] Dogs were common at Teotihuacán, as evidenced by faunal remains and buried animals recovered from the site. Except for jackrabbits and cottontails, dogs were the most prevalent medium-sized mammals in the middens. However, as butchery marks were rare, it is difficult to tell whether the dog bones recovered from midden contexts represent food refuse. Deer made up only 20 percent of the fauna, indicating that deer meat was scarce in urban Teotihuacán. Migratory fowl, domestic turkey, fish, and turtles were much more likely to be part of the dinner menu.[16]

Olmec and Maya Farmers

Starting in 1500 B.C. and lasting until around the birth of Christ, the Olmec people built ceremonial centers in the rich riverine lowlands of Veracruz and Tabasco. Highly productive agricultural zones on the floodplains and nutrient-poor soils in the interior resulted in concentrated populations along the river-banks. The craftsmen at the Olmec centers of San Lorenzo and La Venta pro-duced the colossal heads and large-headed sculptures of crying babies for which the Olmec are famous.

The Olmec ceremonial center of San Lorenzo (1200–900 B.C.) was located on the Coatzacoalas River, 60 kilometers from the coast of Veracruz. Over 50 percent of the vertebrate portion of the faunal remains from San Lorenzo came from fish and reptiles. Deer were rare, making up less than 8 percent of the to-tal count. Medium-sized mammals, particularly dogs, accounted for 35 per-cent of the midden material. If only mammals are considered when calculating bone frequencies, nearly 70 percent of the refuse consisted of dogs.[17] Several other Veracruz sites of a somewhat later date show a similar high incidence of dogs' remains, coupled with heavy exploitation of marine resources. Faunal expert Elizabeth Wing argues that in coastal Veracruz "the degree of human dependence on dogs for food as reflected in these data is quite comparable to the dependence on domestic animals throughout Neolithic and even up to me-dieval times in Europe and the Near East."[18] At this particular time and place in the Americas, dogs were eaten more regularly than any other mammal.

Located to the south of the Olmec and ranging from the highlands of Guatemala to the Yucatan Peninsula, the Maya started to develop the hall-marks of their civilization around 250 B.C. The massive, stepped pyramids, the precise calender, the written language, and the highly complex art style all were born among the competing city-states that today are collectively called the Maya.

Well before the Olmec developed their distinctive art style, the Maya low-lands were populated with farming villages. As the Maya continued to expand and intensify their agricultural activities, the habitat for game animals was greatly reduced; by the late Classic Period (A.D. 600) the region was probably completely deforested.[19] By this time many in the population were subsisting almost solely on maize.[20] As Sophie Coe pointed out in *America's First Cuisine,* the Meatless Maya model is certainly plausible because of the Mesoamerican method of processing maize. "Nixtamalization," or cooking with lime, in-creases the nutritional value of maize which, eaten in conjunction with beans, provides a balanced diet.[21] On the other hand, ethnographic information tells us that even though poor, Maya eat animal protein only on festival days, having meat for such ritual occasions is considered important. Meat was probably equally desired in the past.[22] Therefore, it is reasonable to assume that domesticated and husbanded animals were seen as solutions to a lack of wild resources in the pre-Columbian Maya economy.[23]

It is Maya women who raise animals for festivals today. It has been argued that, if in the past women also raised dogs to provide meat for ceremonial consumption, their own standing in the community would increase. Classic Maya figurines of women with small dogs support the notion that women raised dogs. Moreover, faunal records indicate that the Maya had developed a focus on dog meat as early as 1000 B.C.[24] Further evidence that dogs were actively husbanded in Maya areas comes from some results of carbon isotope analysis of dog bones recovered from Classic Period sites. All the dogs tested had a very high reading for maize consumption. Dogs could obtain maize only by being fed it by people or by scavenging the remains of household meals.[25] For reasons not entirely clear, dog-eating appears to decrease through time in some areas while remaining steady or increasing in others. Each of the Maya sites described below had different locally available resources that may explain the varying degrees of dog consumption.

Cuello, an inland site in northern Belize, had a long sequence of habitation—1000 B.C. to A.D. 300. During this so-called Maya Formative Period, Cuello had a dispersed egalitarian social organization with a central precinct for the ritual life of the community. Politically, Cuello was marginal to the emerging centers at Tikal and El Mirador. Maize, squash, and beans were cultivated.[26] The dominant vertebrate fauna in midden remains were deer, dog, and freshwater turtles. Other exploited animals included large rodents, peccaries, and turkey. Cuello faunal remains reveal a stability in the exploitation of animals

Maya woman with cooking pots and a small dog, Jaina Island, Western Yucatán, A.D. 600–900, height 19 cm. Courtesy of the Yale University Art Gallery, Stephen Carlton Clark, B.A. 1903, Fund.

A Tzeltal Maya couple in front of a cornfield holding a small tan short-haired dog, a Batz'il tz'i *(a true dog, or Indian dog), in 1971. Photograph courtesy of Eugene Hunn.*

through time, from 1000 B.C. to A.D. 300.[27] Indications that dogs were eaten are evident not only from the quantity of their remains but also because dog bones were mixed with other food remains and showed evidence of processing. In addition, most of the dogs were roughly a year old at the time they died, suggesting that the animals were allowed to obtain their full growth before being slaughtered.[28]

Cerros was a late Formative Maya trading community located on the shore of Corozol Bay in northern Belize. The site consists of a ceremonial center on the coast, as well as residential and nonresidential structures extending inland. The most important resources for these coastal people were fish, followed by dog and deer. Areas identified as elite residences or ceremonial centers at Cerros contained a higher percentage of all types of terrestrial fauna than did the nonelite areas, supporting the idea that deer and dog were considered appropriate to those of higher status.[29]

In the Formative, the people living at Seibal, on the Pasion River in Guatemala, ate dogs more commonly than they did during the Classic period. Faunal remains from the earlier period show a greater proportion of dog (18 percent) to deer (29 percent) than do those later in time, when the amount of deer bones (50 percent) was much higher relative to all medium-sized mammals (11 percent).[30]

In the late Classic, Seibal was a flourishing ceremonial center with an elite precinct and smaller structures densely distributed along the river. Intensive agriculture was practiced using ditched fields and terraces. Deer and turtle were the most important vertebrate resources, though a variety of forest animals were eaten at least occasionally. Remains from low status and peripheral localities show that turtle was more likely to be eaten in these areas than were terrestrial species. The overall frequencies of faunal remains from middens indicate that the elite had more access to meat than did commoners. Hunting was probably a highly ritualized affair, and some deer may have been tamed and herded.[31]

The same pattern occurs at Altar de Sacrificios, which was also situated on the Pasion River. In the Formative period dogs made up 18 percent of the midden remains and deer only 9 percent.[32] By late Classic times deer were 70 percent of the fauna and 24 percent were medium-sized mammals, most of which were not dogs. This small late Classic sample represents, for the most part, elite activity.[33]

Fauna collected on the island of Cozumel dates mostly to the Post-Classic (A.D. 800–1200). Cozumel was a coastal trading community with a ceremonial center and residential areas that have no clear-cut status differentiation. Fish, crab, and turtles were, however, usually associated with residences; mammals were more common in burial and ceremonial contexts. Over time there was an increase in the remains of dogs, opossums, and rabbits, and a decline in peccaries and iguanas. Deer were always very scarce.[34]

One piece of information not readily extracted from analysis of the faunal remains is what segments of the population were eating the meat.[35] Was meat consumed weekly, monthly, or rarely? Routine meat consumption may have been a perquisite of the rich, with poorer classes eating only what farmers could raise in their own backyard.[36] Patterns of flesh consumption reflect both availability and preference, but processes of obtaining, preparing, and eating meat were steeped in myth and ritual. Hunting deer was closely connected with a good harvest among the Maya.[37] Blood was the most precious and life-renewing liquid. To consume an animal was to absorb its essence, and to sacrifice an animal allowed for renewal and rebirth.[38] Although the actual amount of meat consumed by either the average laborer or the upper classes cannot be known, the importance placed on the ritual act of its consumption could have far outstripped its dietary significance.

The Great Aztec Market

To the north of the heavily populated Basin of Mexico, groups of nomadic hunters roamed vast regions too dry for agriculture. Farmers from the Basin called these people the Chichimec, which means "dog people."[39] At the beginning of the thirteenth century a group of these Dog People came from the north to settle on the already crowded shores of Lake Texcoco. This particular Chichimec group, the Mexica, claimed an origin in Aztlan, the place of seven caves. After several unsuccessful attempts, the Mexica finally located permanently on an island at the marshy edge of the lake. In 1325 the Mexica, better known as the Aztec, founded their capital, Tenochtitlan.[40] Beginning their rise to power as paid mercenaries, the Aztec soon used their skills as warriors for their own military expansion. In just a hundred years they became expert at extracting massive amounts of tribute from the thirty-eight provinces under their control in the Mexican Highlands. They were also involved in extensive long-distance trade with other independent polities. The population of Tenochtitlan is estimated to have grown to 150,000 to 200,000 people, and the Basin of Mexico itself was home to 1 million people when the Spanish arrived in Mesoamerica.[41]

Because the Aztec state was in full flower when Hernando Cortés landed on the shore of Mexico in 1517, and because of the historical bent of a Franciscan friar, Fray Bernardino de Sahagún, we know much more about the Aztec than we do about other cultures in pre-Spanish America. The Spanish were overwhelmed by the splendor of Tenochtitlan. In a letter to the king of Spain, Cortés reports, "This great city of Tenochtitlan is built on a salt lake. . . . It is entered by four artificial causeways. . . . The city is as large as Seville or Cordoba. Its streets are very broad and straight. . . . The city has many squares where they are always holding markets. One of these squares is twice as large as that of Salamanca, and is surrounded by arcades where there are daily more than sixty thousand souls buying and selling. . . . There is a street for game where they sell all kinds of birds, such as chickens (turkeys), partridges, quail, wild ducks, fly-catchers. . . . They also sell rabbits, hares, venison, and small dogs which they castrate for the table."[42] And, in much the same vein, Bernal Diaz del Castillo, who was a foot soldier in Cortés' army, writes, "Let us go on and speak of those who sold beans and sage and other vegetables and herbs in another part, and of those who sold fowls, cocks with wattles, rabbits, hares, deer, mallards, young dogs, and other things of that sort in their part of the market, and let also mention the fruiters and the women who sold cooked food, dough and tripe in their own part of the market."[43] This Great Market was so large and crowded with people that to see it all would have taken two days. Diego Duran, a Dominican monk (see epigraph), speaks of 400 dogs for sale as being a low number at a market he visited in 1581.

According to Sahagún, some Aztec specializing in the breeding of dogs for the market were especially good at it. "And thus they said: if he bred dogs, he whose day sign was the dog,[44] all would mate. His dogs would grow; none would die of sickness. As he trafficked in them, so they became as [numerous as] the sands. . . . It was said: 'How can it be otherwise? The dogs share a day sign with him. Thus the breeding of dogs resulted well for him.' He sold them all. . . . Also owners and breeders of dogs became rich, and the price of dogs was so high, because they were eaten and needed by the people in days of old. . . . When dogs were sold, they seemed to have greater jowls and mouths; they were judged, sought after, and coveted; whatever kind would be taken, whether short haired or long haired."[45]

Sahagún also reports how dog was prepared for state functions. "And then he [the merchant making the feast] provided turkeys, perhaps eighty or a hundred of them. Then he bought dogs to provide the people as food, perhaps twenty or forty. When they died, they put them with the turkeys which they served; at the bottom of the sauce dish they placed the dog meat, on top they placed the turkeys as required."[46] Of course this dog and turkey stew was only one of the many dishes prepared for the Aztec nobility. Sophie Coe has researched the extensive list of ingredients incorporated into the elaborate meals of Aztec lords. Cooks had access to eight varieties of maize, twelve types of beans, innumerable seeds and grains, seven different chiles, tomatoes, mushrooms, agave, edible cactuses, fruits, domestic ducks, waterfowl, fish, algae, and cacao beans with which to make chocolate drinks. Coe also points out, however, that moderation in everything was an important Aztec principle. Fasting and reflection were necessary to properly balance feasting and celebration.[47]

In contrast, members of the lower classes would eat about three pounds of maize a day made into tortillas. With tortillas they also might consume some beans, peppers, or other vegetables. On feast days they would have a slice of dog meat or, more rarely, venison. This diet was supplemented with fish, reptiles, and insects.[48] The "carnivorous beasts of prey" that the Aztec elite kept in a "zoo" were fed dog meat as well as the bodies of sacrificed human captives.[49] Bernal Diaz also informs us that the Spanish, when on the move, were not adverse to canine food. "Still short of food," he says, "they dined off baby dogs from the nearby town. They were about twenty miles from Tlaxcala."[50]

South American Dog-Eaters

The Santa Elena Peninsula in Ecuador contains a long archaeological sequence of occupation, with hunting and gathering giving way to farming. From 6500 to 5000 B.C., people hunted, gathered, and harvested marine animals. Agriculture was adopted by the Valdivia people in about 3000 B.C. During this period reliance on marine resources increased; at the same time, the exploitation of terrestrial animals decreased dramatically. The Valdivians cultivated cotton, gourds, canavalia beans, and maize.[51]

The demands of cultivation often interfered with seasonal hunting rounds, and the new farmers may have faced dietary stress caused by a lack of protein. At Loma Alta, an inland Valdivia site, excavators recovered an unusual number of human fetal remains, which may indicate protein stress. And, unlike the preceding periods, when no dogs were recovered, the burned bones of domestic dogs were found in middens.[52] These charred remains indicate that these early cultivators ate dogs. As in the Tehuacán Valley, dog bones start appearing in the refuse at the same time that agricultural debris does.

By 2500 B.C., people living along the coast of Peru were shifting, as they had already done on coastal Ecuador, from an economy based on collecting wild plants, hunting, and harvesting shellfish to more intensive use of marine resources and the cultivation of cotton and squash. After 1800 B.C., irrigated agriculture was practiced on a significant scale, and the types of plants grown increased to include pepper, beans, peanuts, avocado, and, somewhat later, maize. In the highlands, at the center of Pacopampa (1800 B.C.), rainfall agriculture was supplemented with hunted game, mostly white-tailed deer. Dogs were occasionally eaten at Pacopampa and were present at Kotosh and Chavin, but in small numbers.[53] Overall, very few dog remains have been found at sites of this period in Peru's prehistory, suggesting that either dogs themselves were rare or that they were common but not regularly eaten or buried.[54]

By A.D. 500, with irrigation farming well established, the Moche of Peru's north coast had used warfare to develop into a small but powerful state. Moche society was characterized by a regional hierarchy of administrative monuments, elite residential complexes, and workshops producing finely crafted ceramics and metalwork. The best evidence of diet for the Moche comes from the large ceremonial center of Pampa Grande, a 5.5-square-kilometer site located on an extensive alluvial piedmont at the neck of the Lambayeque Valley, occupied from A.D. 570–670. Domesticated camelids, llamas and alpacas, were by far the most common animals, accounting for about 85 percent of the identified bones. Bones of domestic dogs were the next most frequently recovered from midden contexts, followed by guinea pigs. Apart from the abundance of dog remains at Pampa Grande, butchery marks on the bones suggests that the dogs were eaten: 3 percent of the camelid bones (N=3761) have cut marks on them, and 7 percent of the dog bones (N=241) do.[55]

Before 1438 the Inca (the term refers both to the group and to the ruler of the group) were a small ethnic group living in the highland valley of the Urubamba River. They were marginal to the complex major Andean societies at this time. The Chimú Kingdom encompassed 1,000 kilometers on Peru's north coast, the Aymara kingdoms were centered on Lake Titicaca, and in the Central Sierra was a powerful ethnic group known as the Huanca. But in 1438, with the ascension to power of the Inca ruler Pachacuti, this remote Andean group launched into an expansionist campaign that quickly resulted in the creation of a vast empire, 4,000 kilometers long. Even without the wheel, money, or a true writing system, the Inca still could administer with great efficiency all the peoples that they conquered. The Inca worshiped the sun; the center of their universe was their capital, Cuzco. The heyday of the Inca empire was brief, its end signaled by the civil war between the Inca Atahualpa and his brother Huascar, and by the simultaneous arrival of Francisco Pizarro on the shores of Peru in May 1532. Pizarro captured Atahualpa and demanded a room full of gold for his release. Atahualpa, thinking the Spanish of little serious threat to his rule, had Huascar killed. Once the ransom was paid, however, Atahualpa was himself killed by the Spanish. With a puppet Inca replacement, the conquistadors marched into Cuzco on November 15, 1533. The conquest of Inca Peru was well under way.

A Spaniard, Pedro de Cieza de Leon, who traveled through former Inca territories in 1548–1550, has left the following description of the abundance he found: "Throughout these valleys the Indians plant corn, which yields two crops a year, and in abundance. In certain places they plant yucca [manioc] which is used to make bread, and for beverages when they lack corn. They also raise potatoes, and a great many beans, and other edible roots. . . . Guava trees grow in profusion, and cassia, alligator pears, sour-sops, caimitos, and pineapples of the native variety. Around their houses one sees many dogs, different from those of Spain, about the size of terriers, which they call *chonos*. They also raise many ducks, and in the woodlands of the valleys there grow carob beans, not as large as broad-bean pods."[56]

The Inca justification for their conquests was their wish to share their superior way of worshiping the sun and other sky spirits with other, less "civilized" groups. War preparations were elaborate: signs and portents were crucial. After sacrificing dark-colored llamas, priests would choose some black dogs,[57] which they would throw down in a flat place and kill. Certain people were required to eat the meat.[58] We do not know who those people were, but the Inca claimed, when questioned by the Spanish, that they never ate dogs. Moreover, the Inca prohibited this dietary option to those living in their empire who, under their own jurisdiction, might have been of a mind to exercise it. They referred disparagingly to their neighbors who did eat dogs as *alcomicoc* (dog-eater) and used the verb *allqochay* (to despise or insult) with its derogatory reference to dogs.[59]

Writing from Spain in 1609, the Inca Garcilaso de la Vega seems to have been prone to embellishment when he wrote of the many victories of the Inca and of their civilized behavior. Indeed, he was an old man remembering the events of his childhood when he wrote, with such flourish, *The Royal Commentaries of the Inca*.[60] Garcilaso may have not been entirely accurate when he talked about the Huanca, rivals of the Inca (see epigraph) who both ate and worshiped the dog. Other early chroniclers make no mention of dog-eating by the Huanca, but Guamán Poma de Ayala, most well known for the number of illustrations that he produced, had something to say on the subject. Among the wealth of detail in a several-hundred-page letter to the king of Spain, Guamán mentions that the Yauyo Indians and *some other tribes* sacrificed dogs and also ate them as a usual part of their diet. The Yauyo were neighbors of the Huanca. As he says, "They [the Yauyo] had to implore their idol not to be alarmed at the sound of barking made by these miserable animals. Although dog-eating is now considered barbarous, some of these people still risk punishment by carrying on the old custom."[61]

The Huanca lived in the Xauxa and Yanamarca valleys of the upper Mantaro River in Peru. Although the different groups of the Huanaca spoke the same language, they probably were organized into competing chiefdoms. These valleys, about 200 miles from Cuzco, had been heavily populated since A.D. 1000. In about A.D. 1300 the Huanca built impressively large (up to 100 hectares) nucleated and fortified sites on ridges bordering the valley floor. Smaller settlements on the valley floor were part of a well-defined settlement hierarchy. The area supported large numbers of inhabitants and possessed environmentally diverse zones. The higher areas were ideal for llama and alpaca herding. The lower slopes and valley floor were intensively cultivated using ridged and terraced fields. These features have been documented archaeologically and are clearly visible in aerial photographs.[62]

It was into this prime valley, in 1460, that the Inca, Capac Yupanqui, marched his army. According to Garcilaso and Guamán, he met 30,000 Huanca, known to be bellicose and with the reputation of skinning alive all those they captured in combat. It must be remembered that the Inca hated the Huanca, referring to them with the doubly derogatory epithet *guana alcomico* (guanaco [wild camel] who eats dogs). The two enemies met on the battlefield,

An early map of Peru showing the Inca Empire Tahuantinsuyu, *the Land of the Four Quarters:* Cuntisuyu, Chinchaysuyu, Antisuyu, *and* Collaosuyu. *At the center was Cuzco, the sacred capital of the Inca. Also marked are the ethnic groups, including the Huancas, whom the Inca fought and eventually subdued. The dog-eating Huancas are located in the Xauxa River Valley in the northwest corner of the map. Reproduced in 1907 for Sir Clements Markham and the Hakluyt Society, Cambridge, for* History of the Incas, *by Pedro Sarmiento de Gamboa (1572).*

and the Inca prevailed. Showing clemency, they ordered no looting, released their prisoners, demanded the fortifications be removed and divided the population into three provinces. And, of course, the Huanca had to pay tribute to Cuzco.[63] Finally the Inca decreed that the Huanca must give up the nasty habit of eating dogs. Neither could they worship the dog; they were enjoined to make trumpets for their ceremonies out of deer heads rather than those of dogs.[64]

Did the Inca-centric chroniclers malign the Huanca by calling them dog-eaters? Again we turn to the faunal remains. From the pre-Inca settlements in the Mantaro Valley we see that hunting, which was strictly controlled during Inca times, would have provided only a small portion of dietary protein, even in this earlier period, because of the high population density. Researcher Catherine Sandefur analyzed the faunal remains from thirty-one residential compounds, belonging to both the elite and the commoners, in six Huanca towns from two time periods. The Huanca got their animal protein from a few species, with camelids supplying 88.7 percent of the meat by weight. Deer, dog, and guinea pig were the other important species. Reliance on small mammals relative to large ones increased through time for commoners, but the ratio remained stable for the elite. Over time, the overall consumption of dog increased; in both phases commoners ate dogs more frequently than did the elite. Butchering marks on some of the bones and their placement in the middens leaves little doubt that dogs were eaten. And, contradicting the intent of Inca administrative might, dog consumption actually increased after the Inca conquest.[65] While the Huanca may no longer have flaunted their fondness for dog, they certainly continued to partake. Indeed, they may also have continued to worship their dog-eating deity, Huallallo, though well out of the Inca's watchful eye.

Dogs of the Caribbean

The islands of the Lesser and Greater Antilles were colonized by horticulturalists from northern South America starting in about 500 B.C. With them they brought their dogs and their crop plants: manioc and sweet potato. Arawaks and later Caribs moved from the mainland and the Guianas onto the islands of the Caribbean sea. When Columbus arrived in the Caribbean in 1492 he found, throughout the islands, small dogs that did not bark but rather chortled, howled, or whined. The Taíno, the first people Columbus encountered, called this mute dog *aon*.[66]

The early chronicler Acosta, writing in 1590, declared, "Of real dogs there are none in the Indies, save certain animals resembling little dogs. . . . So fond are they [the Indians] of their little dogs that they deny themselves of food and water in order to give it to them; and when they go on a journey they carry the little dogs with them on their shoulders or in their arms."[67] Another chronicler confirms that the natives had little dogs, which were "dumb, and served for the amusement of the ladies, who carried them in their arms. They were also used in hunting, in starting up other animals, were good to eat, and were a great resource to the Spaniards in the period of their first famine."[68] During this first famine of 1494 the Spanish consumed so many of these dogs that the *aon* went extinct before the Taíno did.[69]

It is possible that there were actually two very different dogs in the Caribbean. One type was the small, fattened *aon*, which the population ate occasionally to compensate for the dearth of terrestrial protein available on the islands. The second dog is the one found buried in human graves and whose canine teeth were perforated and used for men's necklaces; this dog was larger,

A Micmac hunting camp. Two hunting dogs rest on the shore. One dog rides in a canoe and another is in the water retrieving a fallen fowl. Wearing "traditional" (for the eighteenth and nineteenth centuries) high-peaked hats, two women help paddle the canoes and a third cares for a baby. The Micmac birch-bark canoe was large enough to carry five or six people with all their dogs and baggage. Micmac Indians. *Anonymous oil, c. 1820–1830. Courtesy of the National Gallery of Canada, Ottawa.*

A white dog decorated with red paint and ribbons for the Iroquois Sacrifice of the White Dog Ceremony signaling the beginning of a new year. For the Iroquois, white was the color of purity and faith. White Dog Dream. *Egg tempera and acrylic on handmade paper with ribbons attached, 1985, G. Peter Jemison.*

An Assiniboin hunter on snowshoes is aided by four dogs as he pursues a wounded buffalo. Watercolor, 1833, Peter Rindisbacher (1806–1834). Courtesy of the Amon Carter Museum, Fort Worth, Texas.

An Assiniboin woman attaches a travois to her dog. Three other travois lean next to a tepee, and a loaded animal walks in the background. Nearby a child plays with a dog as big as he is. "A Skin Lodge of an Assiniboin Chief." Aquatint after Karl Bodmer from Wied, 1843. Yale Collection of Western Americana, Beinecke Rare Book and Manuscript Library.

The Great Aztec Market with dogs for sale in the top left corner of the scene. A pottery dog on wheels can be seen in the center, and a dog is in someone's hands in the lower right. In the background are the pyramids and canals of Tenochtitlan. Portion of a mural by twentieth-century Mexican artist Diego Rivera. Courtesy of the Instituto Nacional de Bellas Artes y Literatura, Mexico.

The New Fire Ceremony. Dead warriors carrying blue dogs light the new fire in a ceremony held at the end of each fifty-two-year cycle of the Calendar Round. In the time of the Fourth Sun, the gods turned the sole remaining two people into dogs for starting the first fire, and thereafter dogs were associated with the most important Aztec ritual, the New Fire Ceremony. Codex Borbonicus. Courtesy of Beinecke Rare Book and Manuscript Library.

Two dancing puppies from Colima (A.D. 300). The puppy at left has pronounced vertebrae, often a Meso-american symbol for death. The dogs' ears are intact. West Mexican dog effigies do not have the cropped or ragged ears that Toltec, Aztec, and Maya dog effigies do. These dogs, meant to guide the dead, may not accurately represent what living dogs of the time looked like. Photograph by William K. Sacco.

A man's face is encircled by the gaping mouth of a canid with large canine teeth. This animal has the squat body of a dog but it may be a coyote, an animal asso-ciated with warrior cults. Human and animal have merged in this burnished plumbate ware effigy jar from central Mexico. A.D. 1200. Toltec. Courtesy of Instituto Nacional de Anthropologia e Historia, Mexico.

Two "smiling" dog pots with similar squat body forms. These effigies may represent the mute eating dogs of the Caribbean and the small dogs given to DeSoto during his march through the south. The "weeping eye" spouted vessel at right is from Tennessee (A.D. 1400), and the monochrome short-tailed dog is from Puerto Rico (A.D. 100). Drawings by Susan Hochgraf. After Brose, Brown, and Penney, 1985, and Roe, 1995.

more of a hunter than the smaller dog, and not eaten. Although no large land mammals lived in the Caribbean, ethnographic reports indicate that the Taíno and the Island Caribs used dogs and torches to pursue hutias. Hutias, now extinct, were rodents found throughout the Caribbean; they are the most common mammal found in archaeological contexts.[70] These larger dogs apparently persisted into post-Conquest times, and even today, throughout the Greater Antilles, mixed breed dogs known as *satos* retain characteristics of pre-Columbian dogs in their brindled coats.[71]

The remains of three dogs and two or three humans were found in the midden of the Hacienda Grande Village Site, in Puerto Rico, dating to around A.D. 100. Their presence in the midden does not prove or disprove that either species was eaten. One immature dog, however, was complete except for its skull and tail. Whether this dog was part of ritual activity, a food offering, or a pet is impossible to say. However, elsewhere at Hacienda Grande, a dog mandible that had a straight cut mark on its right ramus was recovered; the nature of this mark is the result of intentional working of the bone rather than of butchering. Dog bone and teeth seem to have been valued as material for ornamentation in a place where the bones of large land mammals were unavailable.[72]

The largest sample of Caribbean dogs comes from the Sorcé site (0-A.D. 500) on Vieques, a small island just east of Puerto Rico. The Sorcé midden yielded the remains of at least twenty-two dogs. Seven of the dogs were buried, apparently with their legs tied together. The rest of the dog remains were scattered throughout the midden. One percent of the canid bones were charred. All of the Sorcé canids were roughly the same size, and there was a high incidence of congenital and traumatic tooth loss. Elizabeth Wing concluded that a mandibular premolar (P4) was frequently removed during the dog's life.[73] Dogs recovered from archaeological sites on Barbados are consistently smaller than those from Vieques, as is one dog from the Dominican Republic, indicating that between islands, at least, dogs of different sizes existed.[74]

Dog-Eating in North America

At times, dog-eating occurred in Mesoamerica to such a degree that dogs were an important subsistence item.[75] In South America, archaeological evidence supports the early historical accounts that, among some groups, dogs were eaten.[76] In North America such conclusive evidence is found only in the historic period—that is, after the Conquest. Dogs were eaten before this time, we presume, because of the occasional cut mark or burned bone, but, if faunal remains are to be relied on, rarely. And yet there is reason to think that dogs were a more popular part of the cuisine than the remains suggest. This information comes not from the ground but from the pens of chroniclers. By piecing together the evidence one can conclude that the agricultural people of North America were not averse to dog flesh but, as elsewhere, preferred bigger meat packages, particularly deer.

The only existing reports that people of the Eastern Woodlands actually raised dogs for consumption comes from members of Hernando DeSoto's North American expedition. DeSoto landed in Tampa Bay in 1539 and left a wide wake of destruction and misery during his five-year meandering march from Florida to the Mississippi River. During those years DeSoto's six-hundred-man army lived off the land and was always hungry. They depended on locals to provide them with all the food they needed, either in friendship or by theft. "And because they lacked meat so badly, when six hundred men with DeSoto arrived in any town and found twenty or thirty dogs, he who could get one and killed it thought he was not a little agile."[77] Rodrigo Rangel, DeSoto's personal secretary, made the following mention of these aboriginal dogs: "The Indians came forth in peace and gave them corn, although little and many hens, and a few little dogs, which are good food. These are little dogs that do not bark, and they rear them in houses in order to eat them."[78] The "Gentleman from Elvas" recorded that when DeSoto and his men reached Ocute, the "cacique [chief] sent him two thousand Indians bearing gifts, namely, many rabbits, partridges, maize bread, two hens, and many dogs, which are esteemed among the Christians as if they were fat sheep because there was a great lack of meat and salt."[79] At Guaxuale, the point farthest north in their journey, the Spaniards were given three hundred dogs, according to DeSoto. The Gentleman from Elvas also mentions these three hundred dogs but says that the Indians claimed not to eat dogs themselves.[80] If three hundred dogs were provided to DeSoto and were being raised for consumption by Indians, this would be in striking parallel to Mesoamerica, and the reference to little dogs that do not bark is a refrain also heard in South America and the Caribbean. In North America these little dogs are mentioned only in passing by a few chroniclers, so that their existence and numbers remain a mystery.

If one were to look in the archaeological record for these little dogs raised for eating, the best place to start is with the Mississippian cultures (A.D. 800–1400) that had all but disappeared before DeSoto's arrival. The term Mississippian is used for those agricultural societies existing in the Mississippian River drainage and in the southeastern United States. They were characterized by fortified mounds and plaza ceremonial centers. Distinctive features of these cultures include large populations, segregated and elaborate mortuary areas, and intensive maize farming. Before the Mississippian period, maize had not been an important food crop in eastern North America, in contrast with Mesoamerica and South America, where it became a staple well before the birth of Christ.

The largest Mississippian center was Cahokia, located in the American bottom part of the central Mississippi River Valley in the present state of Illinois. The population of Cahokia numbered in the thousands, if not in the tens of thousands, and the settlement covered thirteen square kilometers and contained more than one hundred mounds.[81] Deer were far and away the most important animal resource for all Mississippian people; of identified skeletal elements at Cahokia, 60 percent were deer. Migratory waterfowl, making up 29.7 percent of the identified specimens, were an important protein source as well. Dog bones, some with butchery marks, were present in Cahokia middens in greater numbers than those of other small and medium-sized mammals, with the exception of squirrels.[82] There were also several dog burials at Cahokia, one of which was in a cemetery for high-status individuals.[83]

Perhaps a better place to look for edible dogs is Florida. If these little dogs were imported from Mexico via the Caribbean, Florida could have been the port of entry. Again, as with many parts of this story, the case for the importation of these dogs is largely circumstantial. First, Mesoamerican crops such as maize, beans, and squash had made it to the southeast. Second, the central plaza and temple mounds with structures on top of Creek towns suggests a Mesoamerican influence. Dogs were imported into the Greater Antilles, a sixty-mile boat trip from Florida. Of course North American dogs would have been present throughout the southeast, but evidence exists for the trade in hairless dogs between western Mexico and Peru.[84] Hence the importation of Caribbean animals to Florida should be considered as a possible source for these dogs.[85]

DeSoto's hungry hordes found small dogs along with maize and beans in the deserted town of Ocale on the Withlacoochee River on their march north from Tampa Bay.[86] In Florida, the archaeological evidence for the consumption of dog is stronger than for the rest of the southeast. Much of the excavation of Florida's extensive mound sites was done in the nineteenth or early twentieth centuries, and, consequently, quantitative information about dog remains is limited. However, dogs were clearly encountered with some frequency in burial mounds and shell middens.[87] Two early sites from east Florida's Orange Plain Period (2000–1000 B.C.) contained large quantities of dog in a context consistent with food remains. At South Indian Field, 437 fragments of dog bones were recovered, all from the earliest excavated levels. Adding further credence to the idea that these dogs were eaten is the high incidence of juveniles in the sample.[88] At the Cotton Orange Period Site in Volusia County, dogs were "as common as deer," but no figures are reported.[89]

If it is true that smaller dogs were eaten and that larger ones were kept for hunting, finding differently sized but fully adult dogs from the same time period might suggest such a division of duties for the southeastern dog. At the late Prehistoric Cushing

Two Timucua men smoking meat in order to preserve it. One carcass, which appears to be a dog, is shown on the wooden scaffold with several fish, an alligator, a snake, a deer. The Timucua, living in Florida, were the first people to greet DeSoto when he landed in Tampa Bay in 1539. Engraving by Theodore de Bry in Americae Pars II *(Frankfort, 1594).*

Site at Marco Island in southeastern Florida, the remains of five dogs were part of the refuse debris. Four of the dogs were small, but one individual was substantially larger.[90] Dogs of two sizes have also been reported from the late Prehistoric Site of Belcher Mound in Louisiana.[91] The written reports of the earliest visitors to these areas of considerable human complexity and diversity are necessary to flesh out the scanty and dispersed evidence available from the bones of American dogs.

North American Maize Growers

The Natchez of Louisiana, with a population of about six thousand, had a social organization that was unique, at least for North America. Although not a true state, this community had a king who was called the Great Sun. He was treated with the same awe as were Aztec and Inca monarchs. He was considered sacred, could never be touched or looked at, and wore a large headdress. When the Great Sun died, many of his subjects were killed to follow him to the Next World. Early visitors to the Natchez claimed that in addition to the Great Sun, there were other Suns who inherited their positions. Below the Suns were the Nobles and the Honored People, and below them was a group called Stinkards. Although only the Suns inherited their positions, a Stinkard could aspire to become an Honored Person by merit. Strict rules regulated marriage between groups.[92]

The Natchez were visited by the Frenchman Le Page du Pratz in 1758, and he had some intriguing comments about the Great Sun, his followers, and Natchez dogs. The Natchez prepared for war by singing death songs and dancing, followed by ritually consuming dog and venison. They would roast a large dog whole. The meat of the dog symbolized the care with which a Natchez warrior would follow his chief, and the deer symbolized the speed with which they would move.[93]

Le Page du Pratz reports, "The flesh-meats they usually eat are the buffalo, the deer, the bear, and the dog."[94] He also says, "In their meals they content themselves with maiz prepared various ways, and sometimes they use fish and flesh. The meat that they eat is chiefly recommended to them for being wholesome; and therefore I have conjectured that dog's flesh, for which we have such an aversion, must however be as good as it is beautiful, since they rate it so highly as to use it by way of preference in their feasts and ceremonies."[95]

Du Pratz makes a curious remark that may have some bearing on our larger story. He says, "The wolf is not above fifteen inches high, and of proportion-

A hunter holds a small short-tailed dog on a leash outside a southeastern temple. This Acolapissa Temple, similar in design to that of the neighboring Natchez, was topped by three great wooden bird effigies pointing east. The interior was divided into two small rooms, one of which contained the Eternal Fire. A woman and child are on the other side of the temple. Pen and ink sketch by French artist Alexandre de Batz, 1732–35. Courtesy of the Peabody Museum, Harvard University. Photograph by Hillel Burger.

able length. He is not so brown as our wolves, nor so dangerous; he is therefore more like a dog than a wolf, especially the dogs of the natives, who differs from him in nothing, but that they bark."[96] Du Pratz's Louisiana "wolf" may have been the larger breed of dog gone feral, a dog-coyote hybrid, a dog-wolf hybrid, or a coyote-wolf hybrid.

The Natchez told Du Pratz that the only way to hunt turkeys was with a dog. If a hunter chased the bird it would quickly outrun him, but if a dog were in pursuit the turkey would fly up into a tree. There it would remain, making no attempt to leave, as the hunter shot at it with a bow and arrow. Although the Natchez hunted other animals, no mention is made about their methods, including any use of dogs.

Among Northeastern agriculturalists, only the Huron seem to have eaten dogs regularly. According to a Jesuit chronicler, dogs were raised for consumption "like sheep." He goes on to say that Huron dogs "howl rather than bark, and all have upright ears like foxes, but in other respects all are like the moderate-sized mastiffs of our [French] villagers."[97] Dog feasts were prepared to celebrate Huron marriages, during dances, when entertaining visitors, to prevent misfortunes foretold in dreams, or to cure the sick. On appropriate occasions, the Huron *arendiwane,* or medicine man, would prescribe that a dog feast be held as part of an elaborate three-day curing ceremony. One Huron woman was so sick that she saw demons and felt herself to be on fire. A Jesuit priest described the incident: "When she related this, all those present concluded that it was, without doubt, the Demon Aouterohi who caused her sickness. Many feasts were made for her recovery; and, among others, one day when she was very sick they made a feast of a dog, in consequence of which, according to their story, she felt wonderfully well,—and also, because she began to open her eyes while the dog was still alive on the coals, they thought that this medicine was operating, and that she already felt some effects from it."[98] During another curing ceremony a young man met a spirit which so upset him that he became insane. "As a remedy, two dogs, one of which he held especially dear, were killed and a feast made."[99]

The Delaware sometimes claimed they did not eat dogs, but when Henry Hudson paid some Delaware a visit they "killed at once a fat dog, and skinned it in great haste, with shells which they got out of the water," which suggests some familiarity with dog cuisine.[100] For their feasts, venison generally was the meat of choice. Dogs were ejected from the areas where the ceremonies were to take place, and feast remains were burned to keep the dogs from eating them. Allowing dogs to eat ceremonial remains would have been a sign of disrespect.[101]

The Iroquois, like many others in the Northeast, feasted on dog meat before going to war. William Fenton describes the symbolism of this rite as follows: "War feasts were far from acts of piety. Seeing the kettle and the steaming platters of dog meat, which symbolized the broth and the flesh of captives that they would later drink and eat, transported the beholders into fits of rage and fury as they mentioned their enemies in songs and compared them to dogs. 'In fact they give no other names to their captives,' remarked Lafitau (1724, 2:189). The most distinguished warriors present received the heads of dogs boiled in the kettle; the head was the symbol of the feast, as it has remained for two centuries."[102]

The Iroquois practiced another ritual in which the dog figured centrally, the annual Sacrifice of the White Dog, which signaled the beginning of the New Year. Unlike the war feast described above, the sacrifice was the highest act of piety, according to Lewis Henry Morgan, the first American ethnographer, in *League of the Iroquois*.

> To approach Ha-wen-ne'-yu in the most acceptable manner, and to gain attention to their thanksgiving acknowledgments and supplications in the way of his own appointing, was the end and object of burning the dog. They hung around his neck a string of white wampum, the pledge of their faith. They believed that the spirit of the dog hovered around the body until it was committed to the flames, when it ascended into the presence of the Great Spirit, itself the acknowledged evidence of their fidelity, and bearing also to him the united thanks and supplication of the people. . . . They used the spirit of the dog in precisely the same manner that they did the incense of tobacco, as an instrumentality through which to commune with their Maker.[103]

Mohawk Chief Thayendanegea (Joseph Brant), who, along with other Iroquois, fought with the British during the American Revolution. Beside him is his dog, an aboriginal breed that the Iroquois raised and traded with neighbors. These Iroquois dogs typically had sharply pointed muzzles and slender bodies. Oil painting by Wilheim von Bercy, 1807. Courtesy of the National Gallery of Canada.

Dog sacrifice was a key feature of White Buffalo Dance of the Fox of the upper Midwest. This dance was still being performed in 1924, when this account was recorded. There was, according to this witness, one attendant for each dog to be killed. The ritual started as each dog was walked around the wickiup (lodge) four times. The first dog was clubbed to death facing east, the second facing south, the next toward the west, the last facing north. The rest of the dogs (no number is mentioned) were "strewn on the high scaffolding at the west end of the summer house."[104] These additional dogs were eaten by the assembled crowd, while the four cardinal dogs remained in place until the end of the ceremony, when they too were eaten. The Illinois and Miami had White Dog ceremonies similar to that of the Iroquois, and the Sauk and Potawatomi had dances in the same vein as those of the Fox.[105]

The Winnebago, like other Midwestern peoples, knew the prestige value of feast-giving, and the host had to make elaborate preparations before the festivities. The feast giver and some of his clan members went hunting to procure meat for the feast—typically deer—and then built a lodge to hold the feast. Others brought dogs and tobacco as their contribution to the festivities. The dogs were killed, singed, then boiled. The meat was then mixed with dry corn. The same method was used to cook the deer. After the food was consumed, tobacco was smoked, speeches were given, songs were sung, and there was dancing. Often this procedure was repeated; the ceremony might last as long as four days.[106]

A Winnebago dog was sacrificed with enhanced ceremony if the feast was given to appease either the Thunderbird or Disease-Giver, both spirits having particular connection with dogs. In this case the dog was strangled and a pouch of tobacco placed around its neck. The dog would then receive an apology from its slayer and be laid to rest in front of the sacred war bundle facing south, toward the home of the Disease-Giver. What follows is a transcription of an oral text of a Winnebago informant on the preparations for the War Bundle Feast.

> When they decide to use a dog [as a sacrifice] they take the greatest care of it from its infancy upward. With great kindness do they rear it. They never strike it when rearing it. Just like their own child they treat it. They take great care of its food. They love it very much, just as they love their own children. Thus is the dog loved. If they are going to sacrifice it, then before they kill the dog they make the following preparation and the man who is to make the sacrifice speaks thus: "My younger brother, you are to go to the south; to the Disease-Giver you are to go. There you will live better than here. War powers and life we wish to have and that you should ask for."[107]

The Native Americans of the Southwest did not have the tradition of eating dogs ritually. Much of their storytelling is centered on the trickster coyote and not on his domestic cousin. The coyote was the "unheroic" hero who fumbled through tale after tale, usually losing his life at the climax of each one. This bumbling coyote trickster, which brought various types of bad luck to people, nonetheless was viewed by them with affection.

*Unidentified midwestern tribe participating in dog feast ceremonies. The dogs
pictured are long-haired with dark and light patches of fur. After Young, 1890.*

The southern Athapaskans, the Navaho and the Apache, by their own accounts had an aversion to eating dogs. Sometimes dogs were used to hunt rabbits, squirrels, turkey, and quail.[108] The Eastern Navaho felt that dogs came
from the gods, although in general the Navaho did not hold dogs in very high
esteem. An Apache informant said that his village had had only one dog during his childhood and that, in the past, dogs had not been numerous. The typical Apache dog had yellow patches over each eye and white on each paw. To
the Apache the yellow symbolized the sunset and the white the morning light,
indicating that the dog was expected to protect the people both day and
night.[109]

For the Hopi, the first dog was brought from the North by a member of the
Willow clan when the Hopi still lived in their original settlement at the foot of
the second mesa.[110] Visiting the Hopi village of Moquis in 1881, John Bourke
stated that the village had a "superabundance of growling, worthless dogs" and
that the Hopi were "by no means adverse to a good mess of stewed pup."[111]
Hopi Don Talayesva, writing his autobiography early in the twentieth century,
describes killing a stray bitch and then raising one of her puppies. This puppy
became a good hunter that dug rabbits and prairie dogs out of their holes. Don
Talayesva named him Moonlight because he was yellow.[112]

The dogs of the Pima, at the time when Frank Russell observed them early
in the twentieth century, were gaunt and hungry and suffering from the same
scarcities that plagued their human community. Older Pima said that originally

all dogs had resembled coyotes. Their main function was to warn villagers of the approach of enemies.[113] Hopi dogs also gave warning to the village of Moquis at the approach of a coyote.[114]

Dogs have been in the Southwest for a long time. Among the oldest are those recovered from all occupation levels at Ventana Cave in Arizona. In the Southwest, archaeological evidence indicates that people and dogs first lived in the cave at about 2000 B.C. As a rule, dogs were used as food more often and buried less frequently in later times. Changes in the environment, including decreasing precipitation and declining wild animal populations, may well have been responsible for changes in the dog's function within its human community. Grasshopper Pueblo, Arroyo Hondo, and Canyon de Chelly, all in Arizona, are three sites at which the evidence suggests that dogs were eaten.[115] At Grasshopper Pueblo (A.D. 1300–1400), 803 skeletal elements definitely attributable to dog were recovered. The remains were scattered across the three major room blocks of the pueblo and belonged to dogs of two sizes; 5.35 percent (N=43) of the dog bones have cut marks resulting from either meat or hide processing. One small dog was buried in a room adjacent to the pueblo's main *kiva* (circular ceremonial center).[116]

Hopi Snake Dance at the Pueblo of Hualpi, Arizona, 1881. Five small hairy dogs watch the proceedings in the foreground. This ceremony was performed in even-numbered years to ask the snake deities for plenty of springwater and rain. Members of the Snake Clan gather their "elder brothers," including rattlers, wash them ritually, and dance, holding them in their mouths. From Bourke, 1884. Yale Collection of Western Americana, Beinecke Rare Book and Manuscript Library.

The Mimbres were a farming people who lived in a small area in the south-west corner of New Mexico. From A.D. 800 until 1100, Mimbres potters created black-on-white bowls with complex geometric designs and distinctive figures. Several of these bowls have dog figures on them. One shows a dog with some wood gatherers, another illustrates a hunter patting one of two panting and eager dogs. A third bowl is decorated with two Mimbres figures placing a rope around a dog's neck.[117] Although the hallmark of Mimbres art lies in its abstract qualities, these scenes suggest that dogs accompanied people on gathering trips, were used for hunting, and received some training. Whether Mimbres people ate dogs is unknown.

Buffalo Hunters of the Plains

The Plains people who had moved from the east, from the Great Lakes, from the forests of Minnesota, and from the rivers of the Mississippi, brought with them the traditions of the sacred dog feast, which originated on the east coast. Some Great Plains groups apparently ate dogs on a more regular basis than in the east. Joseph Berlandier made the following record of people he encountered in 1830: "Like the Plains Lipans (Kiowa-Apaches) they eat a species of small dog, specially fattened, which is the staple of their diet. It is because of this practice that the Comanche call them Chariticas, which in their language means 'dog eaters.'"[118] Archaeologist Melburn Thurman argues that these Chariticas were Athapaskan speakers who have since disappeared or been absorbed into other groups. He believes that at least two groups called "dog eaters" existed on the Plains in

A Mimbres black-on-white bowl circa A.D. 1100. A dog plays with a bee. Open bowls such as this were by far the most common vessel form made by Mimbres potters. When figures were represented, as in this case, the center of the bowl became the focal point and the sidewall served as a frame. Even within the abstract and geometric regime of Mimbres visual organization, the relationship between bee and dog has been captured. Photograph by William K. Sacco. Courtesy of the Peabody Museum of Natural History, Yale University.

the eighteenth century.[119] The other group, the Algonquian-speaking Arapaho, were called *sari tiqats* (dog-eater) by their abstaining and disdaining Shoshone and Paiute neighbors.[120]

The Hidatsa, whose dogs were better trained than the "wild and surly" dogs of their enemies the Sioux, ordinarily did not eat dogs.[121] To them the dog was sacred, and its flesh was taboo. When the Hidatsa learned the Grass Dance from the Santee Sioux in the 1870s, they also adopted the practice of eating dog during the ceremony.[122] Thus, they belatedly joined a wide group of ceremonial dog-eaters on the plains.

George Catlin told of a feast prepared in his honor when he visited the Sioux of the Upper Missouri in 1833. First, Catlin and his friends were treated to dancing, ball playing, horse racing, and wrestling for several days. This was followed by a great feast with 150 men sitting in a large semicircle. Six iron kettles and many serving bowls were in the center of the group. After speechmaking and tobacco smoking, the lids to the pots were opened, revealing dog stew. Although it smelled good, Catlin said, he and his friends ate only enough to be polite. However, they had been witnesses to an event of great solemnity and sacredness. The Sioux, who could have provided plenty of buffalo meat for their guests, chose instead to honor them by killing their best and most faithful companions. The Sioux, by making a sacrifice of their favorite dogs, did their guests the greatest possible honor.[123]

The Oglala Sioux still participate in sacred dog feasts. Dog meat, to the Oglala, is a spiritual delicacy rather than a gastronomic one. In the *yuwipi,* or curing ritual, the medicine man invokes the spirits of the Thunder People to join the ceremony by offering dog stew and tobacco. The singers intone: "Great Spirit, pity me: I want to live, that is why I do this. They stand in place in the sky: These, the Thunder People, stand in place. Over here they are eating dog. In the west, the Thunder People are eating dog. Sacredly, they are eating dog."[124] For them, dog meat is the medicine that keeps people well.

Among the Assiniboin, an individual wishing to succeed at a particular endeavor invoked the aid of Wakoñda, the Creator Spirit. To do this a person destroyed an object of value, killed a dog, made a feast, and invited neighbors, "by whom the flesh is eaten and small portions thrown on the ground as a respect to Wakoñda."[125] The Ponca had a Reach-in-the-Boiling-Kettle Dance in which, bare-handed, they pulled a dog's head out of a bubbling cauldron.

The Cheyenne ate dog only as a sacred food during ceremonies that required "nonnatural" meat. The *Massaum* (the sacred Wolf Ceremony) was one occasion when dog (puppy) meat was ritually consumed. During this ceremony dancers assumed the roles of the sacred wolves—the male red wolf and the white female wolf. Both were master hunters. In addition, the red wolf represented thunder and the red star Aldebaran, and the white wolf stood for the earth spirit and the white star Sirius.[126] For the Cheyenne, the dog was the most distant animal from the wolf. Its meat was considered "contrary" to other animal flesh. However, the Cheyenne valued their dogs greatly and believed that to eat them nonceremonially would be a grave offense against the spirits.[127]

The Pawnee, like the Huron and the Sioux, used dog meat in curing rituals. In one ceremony the healer offered dog meat to the gods, to Mother Earth, and to the animals, and gave dog ribs to the sick and the rest of the meat to the others partaking of the feast. In historical times, the Pawnee had large numbers of dogs. Charles Murrey reported in 1835, while he was traveling with the South Band Pawnee, that their encampment contained four thousand dogs, seven animals for every tepee.[128]

Cut and charred dog bones at protohistoric and historic Pawnee archaeological sites indicate that dogs were eaten both as a staple and in feasting episodes. At the site of Barcal (A.D. 1700–1750), in central Nebraska, 38 percent of the mammalian faunal remains were dog. Large and small-sized dogs were represented in the sample.[129] The mammal fauna from the Omaha Big

A dog feast given by the Sioux to honor George Catlin and his fellow travelers. "Each guest had a large wooden bowl placed before him, with a huge quantity of dogs' flesh floating in a profusion of soup, or rich gravy, with a large spoon resting in the dish, made of buffalo's horn." From Catlin, 1844. Yale Collection of Western Americana, Beinecke Rare Book and Manuscript Library.

Encampment of Piegan Blackfoot near Fort McKenzie, Montana, in summer 1833. Numbers of dogs crowd around the group of humans and horses in the center of the picture. The Blackfoot saw their first horse in about 1730, and because it was enslaved to men, as was the dog, they called it "Big Dog." Detail of a lithograph from an original drawing by Karl Bodmer from Wied, 1843. Yale Collection of Western Americana, Beinecke Rare Book and Manuscript Library.

Village site, also in Nebraska, was 30 percent dog,[130] and the Arikara Buffalo Pasture site in South Dakota yielded 18 percent dog from its middens.[131]

Dogs probably served all Plains people as a hedge against starvation. A Piegan Blackfoot remembered a time when the buffalo disappeared and bad weather prevented his people from using horses: "That was the winter when we ate only dogs."[132] In pre-horse days, eating dogs may have been even more critical in preventing starvation during hard winters. Keeping dogs may have been an important adaptive strategy among the peoples of the Plains.[133]

Endnote

Although hunting and gathering people generally did not consider dog an appropriate food and agriculturists did, actual culinary practices across the Americas were extremely diverse. Cultural perceptions and practical considerations were equally involved in attitudes toward dog-eating. Here are some observations from which readers may draw their own conclusions. Dog-eating was more widespread in Mesoamerica than elsewhere in the Americas. Dog-eating was common among Algonquian speakers and not reported among any northern Athapaskan speakers.[134] Hunting with dogs was more prevalent in the northeastern woodlands than in the south, although agriculture was established in both places. Among the Maya, dogs were more likely to be eaten by the elite, but among the Huanca, commoners ate more dog. Both the Huanca and the Arapaho were called "dog-eaters" by their neighbors, the Inca and the Shoshone. This was not a compliment. Iroquois men ate dogs to increase their valor in war. The Huron and Pawnee ate dogs to cure diseases. The Sioux made a dog feast to honor a visitor. Some raised "eating dogs," castrating them and fattening them on maize. Others ate dogs only when there was no other food. In both North and South America, dogs were heterogeneous in form and function. Skilled hunting dogs were treasured, village mongrels ill treated, and small dogs were pets, were eaten, or both.

4 *Dogs in the Land of the Dead*

They [the Huron] believe that souls are immortal, and that when they leave the body they go at once to dance and rejoice in the presence of Yoscha and his grandmother Ataensiq, taking the route and way of stars, which they call *Atiskein andahatey,* the path of souls, which we call the Milky Way or the Starry Scarf. . . . They say that the souls of dogs go there also by way of certain stars which are near neighbors to the soul's path, and which they call *Gagnenon andahatey,* that is to say, the path of the dogs.—Father Sagard-Theodat, *The Long Journey to the Country of the Hurons* (1632)

. . . yet do they [the New England Algonquians] hold the immortality of the never-ending soul, that it shall pass to the South-west Elysium . . . at the portall whereof they say, lies a great Dogge, whose churl-ish snarlings deny a Pax intratibus, to unworthy intruders: Where-fore it is their custom, to bury with them their Bows and Arrows, and good store of the Wampompeage and Mowhackies; the one to affright the affronting Cerbens the other to purchase more immense prerogatives in their Paradise.—William Wood, *New England's Prospect* (1634)

And also they [the Aztec] caused him to take a little dog, a yellow one; they fixed about its neck a loose cotton cord. It was said that it would take [the dead one] across the place of the nine rivers in the place of the dead. . . .

And this, it was said, all arrived with Mictlantecutli. And when

the four years had ended, thereupon [the dead one] went to the
nine places of the dead, [where] lay a broad river.

There dogs carried one across. It was said that whosoever went
to pass looked over to a dog. And when it recognized its master,
thereupon it threw itself into the water in order to carry its master
across. Hence the natives took care to breed dogs.—Fray Bernardino
de Sahagún, *General History of the Things of New Spain: Florentine Codex, Part
IV* (1547–1575)

The archaeological remains of dogs occur in several distinct categories. The
presence of disarticulated skeletal elements in midden deposits suggests that
dogs may have been eaten and thrown out with other food remains. Sometimes
dog bones were made into tools such as awls or spatulas. At other times dog
teeth were pierced to be used as jewelry. Occasionally an entire dog was carefully buried, either with humans or alone, or as part of a ritual offering. The
methods of disposing of dog remains varied greatly across cultures and through
time. The investment of effort and energy required to bury a dog signals an
event of some significance to the people involved. Why did some people bury
their dogs? How were such burials related to their beliefs about death? Ethnohistoric accounts indicate that dogs have played a part in conceptions of the
afterlife in many cultures. This widespread association of dogs with death may
be relevant in understanding the archaeological record of buried dogs.

Myths that connect the dog with the afterworld have two basic themes. In
one, the entrance to the "next world" is guarded by a fierce dog that attempts
to keep souls out. In the other, a dog guides dead souls on their journey to the
next world. Variants of these ancient themes are found all over the world. In
the Middle East and Europe, the most famous guardian of the gates is perhaps
Cerberus, the three-headed dog who guarded the entrance to the Greek underworld Hades. The guardian dog is also found in the myths of India, Rome,
Iceland, and among the Celts, the Finns, and the Koryaks of Siberia. A well-
known canid guide for the dead is Anubis, the Egyptian jackal-headed god who
led the departed out of the tombs and across the desert to the land of the dead.
The dog as guardian or guide is found in the myths of the Americas as well.

People everywhere have perceived the dog as straddling this world and the
next, linking nature and culture, sky and earth. The Dog Star, Sirius, has been
identified with canines from China to Mexico, and is associated with the heat
of the dog-days of August throughout the Northern Hemisphere. At this time
of the year Sirius lies on the eastern horizon just before sunrise and is connected

to the opening of the gates of the dead. This Dog Star guarding the beginning of the day is akin to the dog guarding the passage to the next world. In Indo-European traditions, paths of the dead lie in the night sky, where celestial dogs are stationed at perilous heavenly crossroads.[1] The Dog Star and other celestial canine travelers have equally strong associations among people in the Americas. Such similarities across great distance and cultural isolation are striking, and this convergence cannot be solely the result of some worldwide dispersion of ideas and worldviews. In good measure it also reflects the nature of the real-life dog, which willingly and eagerly guides, guards, and leads its human master or mistress. It is understandable that these qualities would be transferred intact to the afterworld. Using much the same logic, people buried a whole range of goods for the use of the dead on their journey. These stories also serve to justify the affectionate feelings people had for their dogs. Knowing that dogs passed judgment on human beings in the next world was a good reason to treat dogs well in this one.

Dogs have frequently found themselves as voyagers to the land of the dead, both in the flesh and in effigy. Moreover, mythical dogs often reside on the Other Side. A dog in a grave may have considerable symbolic significance, though the dog's presence may simply reflect the affection an individual had for that particular animal. In either case, the dog was selected for special attention and becomes worthy of note.

Travelers Among the Stars and Across Difficult Waters

Four extraordinary carved bones were found in the Tomb of Hasaw-Ka'an-K'awil, ruler of the Maya city of Tikal in the late Classic. Two of the bones have scenes of a canoe trip with two paddlers, Stingray and Jaguar, and five passengers: an iguana, a spider monkey, the Maize God, a parrot, and a dog. The second pair of bones shows the canoe and its passengers plunging under water. One of the hieroglyphic texts translates as "Hasaw-Ka'an-K'awil canoed 4 katuns [80 years] to his passing." The phrase "star-over-earth" appears in the second text, along with a date. Mayanist Linda Schele and her colleagues have determined this date to be September 16, A.D. 743. At midnight on this date in Tikal, the Milky Way would have stretched across the sky from east to west, looking very much like a celestial canoe. In the hours after midnight, the Milky Way "canoe" would seem to sink in the same way that the canoe sinks on the incised bone.[2] These scenes combine many mythical elements from the corpus that connects dogs to death, but in a unique way. A journey through a watery

| Stingray | Iguana | Spider | Maize God | Parrot | Dog | Jaguar |
| Paddler | | Monkey | | | | Paddler |

In this remarkable scene the twin paddler gods, Stingray and Jaguar, are transporting the Maize God to the Underworld in a canoe. Along for the ride are an iguana, a spider monkey, a parrot, and a dog. Drawing of design taken from a carved bone recovered from the tomb of Hasaw-Ka'-K'awil, located beneath the Temple 1 at Tikal, Guatemala. Drawing courtesy of Linda Schele.

substance, movement from the world of the living to the world of the dead, is a familiar story. The concept of souls traveling along the Milky Way recurs as well. The Maya, however, have combined the water and the sky journey into one image.

The Huron, like the Maya, envisioned a sky journey as well as a water passage after death. They believed that once a person arrived in the Village of the Dead, life went on pretty much as it had before. People possessed, in Huron ideology, two souls. After death, these souls hovered near the corpse until the great Feast of the Dead, which was held every twelve years or so. After the feast all the souls were finally released. One of a person's souls was reborn and the other left for the Village of the Dead, which lay in the direction of the setting sun. The souls traveled along the Milky Way on a path slightly different from the one used by dogs (see epigraph). On the way they met the Head Piercer, who would draw out their brains. Next they encountered a fierce dog on a log that lay across a raging river. Many were so frightened by the dog that they fell into the water and were swept away. After many months, successful voyagers reached the village to find their status in life unchanged by death.[3]

The soul of the Delaware also traveled along the Milky Way, but the goal was to reach the twelfth heaven and join the creator. A bridge along the Milky Way was guarded by dogs who had died. These dogs allowed only good souls to pass, those souls that had treated dogs well.[4] The Seminole, like the Hurons, saw in the sky the "dogsway" which is smaller than the "spiritway" (the Milky Way), the path human souls must travel to reach the Other World. At a point along the journey the dogsway and the spiritway joined and dogs and owners continued together to the City of Good Souls.[5]

Fierce dogs, slippery logs, the Milky Way, raging rivers, deep lakes, and peril-filled voyages are often-repeated themes in American myths about the afterworld. Central Inuit myths include a guard dog at the entrance to Land of the Death, as does a myth of the Taulipang of Guiana. In Taulipang belief the soul travels along the Milky Way, where dogs stand in judgment of human behavior.[6] In many cultures the Milky Way is considered to be a river, and the river of the underworld is transformed to a sky journey by the Taulipang, the Seminole, the Huron, and the Maya.

The Cherokee tell a story of a little dog that came from the north and stole cornmeal from a bowl. After the theft was discovered, the dog was whipped, and it ran off howling and spilling meal from its mouth. To this day the Cherokee call the Milky Way *Gi:li'-utsûñ'stăn ûñ'yĭ* ("Where the dog ran").[7] For the Shawnee, neighbors of the Cherokee, the land of the dead was simply the place where the creator, Our Grandmother, lived, and it was like Earth in every way. Our Grandmother had only her grandson and her little dog as her permanent associates. The souls of the dead and the unborn were with the Shawnee creator only temporarily. On rare occasions Our Grandmother has visited Earth, but always in the company of her dog and grandson.[8]

When a Shipibo of the Peruvian Amazon dies, three souls leave his body, and one of these souls journeys to a big lake. After arriving, this soul encounters a spirit known as Master of the Dogs, who lives in the Village of the Dogs (*Ochiti ni jëma*). If the soul has been cruel to his dogs in life, feeding them only bones and no meat, the Master of the Dogs feeds the soul only meatless bones.[9] In the Andes, some groups believe that a soul meets a pack of black dogs on the journey to *Upamarca* (the Silent Land).[10] The Menominee, from the North American Midwest, told of a huge dog guarding the land of the departed. The only way across the raging water was by means of a slippery log. Evildoers and dog mistreaters would, it was believed, fall into the stream and be swept down the rushing waters forever. If a soul was able to get past the dog, it would join the spirits who had gone before and, with them, have plenty to eat and play lacrosse for all eternity.[11]

In the middle of the sixteenth century Friar Ramón Pané was commissioned by Christopher Columbus to investigate the beliefs of the Taíno people of Hispaniola in order to better convert them to Christianity. Thanks to his efforts and his understanding of the Taíno language, we know about the dog *zemi* (spirit) called Opiyél-Guaobirán. Opiyél means "spirit of those absent" and is derived from *Opía,* the "inverted spirits of the dead." According to Pané, this zemi was "four-legged like a dog" and ran through the forest at night.[12] This "guardian-gatemaster" dog sat at the edge of a lake and controlled access both in and out of the dark realm of the nonliving, a place called Coaybay.[13]

The Cora live in western Mexico and have a myth that goes as follows: Long ago the people followed the trail of a dog up a high mountain in order to escape the rising flood. The dog beat a drum to cause the water to swell up in waves. Most of the people who were able to reach the summit died of starvation while waiting for the water to recede. The few who survived are believed to be the ancestors of mankind. The dog then disappeared into a large lake, and the wandering souls of the dead visit this dog on their way to their final resting place.[14] In Central America, the Miskito included in their burials a small canoe and a dead dog for the use of the deceased. In their worldview, a dog paddled a soul across a large river in a canoe to get to the underworld.[15] The Talamanca also believed that a dog would ferry them across a stream after death.[16] In southern Mexico the journey to the underworld consisted of two paths, with good souls following a straight and narrow path while bad ones followed a wider path. All souls would arrive at a river where a dog would come—or perhaps not come—to take them across.[17]

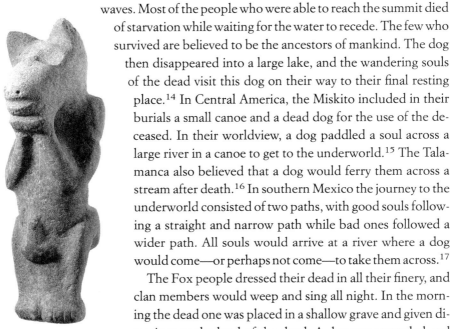

A stone sculpture of the Taíno dog spirit Opiyél–Guaobirán. This spirit of the afterworld holds its front paws under its chin. It was discovered in the Trois-Rivière Valley of northwest Haiti, where it was buried with a ten-inch pointed stone roller and a stone parrot. Courtesy of the Peabody Museum of Natural History, Yale University.

The Fox people dressed their dead in all their finery, and clan members would weep and sing all night. In the morning the dead one was placed in a shallow grave and given directions to the land of the dead. A dog was strangled and hung on a post to serve as guide.[18] Father Biard reported in 1611 that a large feast (*tabagie*) was prepared for a dying Micmac. "While it [is] being prepared, those who are present exchange gifts with him in token of friendship; dogs, skins, arrows, etc. They kill these dogs in order to send them on before him into the other world. The said dogs are afterwards served at the tabagie, for they find them palatable."[19] The Wintu of California placed the deceased's dog in his grave,[20] and the Tehuelche of Patagonia dispatched hunting dogs to be buried with their masters.[21] The Tlingit of the Pacific Northwest disposed of their dead by removing a plank from the rear corner of the house and carrying the deceased through it. Immediately after the corpse was re-

The conical structure to the right is a Tehuelche tomb, around which a ditch has been dug. Beside the tomb are two stuffed horses on stick legs that have recently been killed. When Tehuelche hunters died most of their horses and dogs were killed to accompany them to the afterworld. Other dogs rest in front of a toldos (windbreak dwelling). After Fitz-Roy, 1839.

moved a dead dog was thrown through the same opening. This was done, according to an informant, so that the dog could protect the deceased from the many animals that might beset him on his journey.[22] On the other hand, the Tlingit believed that the souls of the wicked traveled with the souls of dogs, ending up in dog heaven, where they would be transformed into dogs.[23]

Alexander Henry, an English captive among the Ottawa in the 1760s, recounts this story about the injury and death of a young girl. While the child lived, large feasts were made to the Master of Life, that he might save the child. Dogs were sacrificed and hung on poles to try to please this supreme being. After the child died her body was placed on a scaffold to keep it from the wolves until it could be moved to the family's burial place. The body was put into a large birch bark–lined grave, along with an ax, a pair of snowshoes, some other shoes, a small kettle filled with meat, and some beads. Her mother cut a lock of her daughter's hair to keep with her until her own death. The Ottawa, according to Henry, also sacrificed dogs to the *manito* (supernatural being) of the water during storms while they were in their canoes on Lake Michigan. "On our passage we encountered a gale of wind, and there were some appearances of danger. To avert it, a dog, of which the legs were previously tied together, was thrown into the lake; an offering designed to soothe the angry passions of some offended Manito."[24]

The Maya called their underworld Xibalba, a word derived from *xib,* which means "fear, terror, and trembling with fright." As we have seen, death involves a journey, and often this journey is filled with danger. The underworld of the Maya was filled with terrible creatures, the most awful of which were the nine Lords of the Night, or the Lords of Death (see illustration). In Xibalba, fantastic and composite animal deities dwelled with the death gods. Fourteen such supernaturals encircle a late Classic painted vase from the Naranjo region of the Maya Lowlands.[25] Most of the creatures are wearing eyeball-studded death collars. In addition, the skeletonized primary Death God has stingray spines in his penis for ritual bloodletting. Seated behind him is the God of Suicide by Self-Decapitation, who vomits blood over an enema syringe. Lying on his back is the Fat God. Surrounding this trio are various oddly constructed animal spirits. Dog deities also inhabit this world. A torch dog looks back over its shoulder at its flaming tail. This is the dog that brought fire to the Maya. Below the Fat God sits a group of three dogs with flint blades in their ears bearing the name *sak ox ok* ("white-three-dog"). These dogs occur elsewhere in Maya iconography and will be discussed later. Here they occupy Xibalba, the scary, watery world through which a soul must struggle to emerge safely on the other side.

In the Aztec worldview, death was necessary for life to continue. Death was chaos, evil, and darkness, but it was also a major force in nature and the pre-

Polychrome Maya vase with fourteen supernatural beings of the underworld. The three dogs (bottom row, right) and the torch dog (middle row, center) have scalloped ears typical of canines. Note, however, that the fire peccary (bottom row, center) has canine ears as well. The tapir (top row, right) has jaguar spots and tail. The monkey (middle row, far right) has rabbit ears. Rollout photograph K927 © Justin Kerr, 1980.

The Earth's Surface

The Place of Water
Passage

The Place Where the
Hills Clash Together

The Place of the
Obsidian Mountain

The Place of the
Obsidian Wind

The Place Where
Banners Are
Flourished

Where Someone Is
Shot with Arrows

Where People's
Hearts Are Eaten

The Place of the Dead,
Where the Streets Are
on the Left

The nine levels of the Aztec underworld. Note that a dog's head occurs both on the second level, "the place of water passage," and on the eighth level, "the place where people's hearts are eaten." Dogs were considered ferrymen across rivers as well as "biting animals." Redrawn by Susan Hochgraf. After the Codex Vaticanus A, folia 2r.

condition for life. The Aztec believed that human blood must be spilled each day to ensure that the sun would rise the next morning. If a person died a violent death, however, either in war or as a human sacrifice, he or she would go to live with the sun as compensation for losing life in this world. Thus, in Aztec thought an individual's manner of death determined where the soul would reside after death. If, for example, an Aztec drowned, he or she would go to the place where Tlaloc, the god of rain, dwelled. An individual dying an ordinary death was in for much more of an ordeal. This person was destined to go to Mictlan, which lay beneath the cold desert to the north of Tenochtitlan. There the soul would wander for four years among the nine layers of the underworld. The Aztec cremated a dog to be sent with the dead one to serve as guide for the journey. According to the Codex Vaticanus A, a picture book from the early colonial period (1566–89), this journey started with the soul crossing a river, "the place of water passage" (see p. 101). A dog's head is drawn there to indicate that the animal waits to ferry the soul across the water. After crossing the river the soul crossed "the place where the hills clash together," then passed by "the place of the obsidian mountain," "the place of the obsidian wind," "the place where banners are flourished," "the place where someone is shot with arrows," "the place where people's hearts are eaten," also depicted with a dog's head, and the ninth level is "the place of the dead, where the streets are on the left."[26] After four years the soul would reach the place of the nine rivers and, once across the rivers, disappear forever.[27]

A blue dog is attached to the mummy bundle of a dead Aztec warrior to guide the warrior's soul on its journey to live with the sun. The masked warrior, wearing the aztaxelli, *the forked heron-feather ornament, is being serenaded by two singers, who also play the drums and a rattle. Redrawn by Susan Hochgraf. After the Codex Magliabecchiano XIII 3, folia 72.s.*

The future of a dead Aztec warrior was much more ceremonially impressive and altogether brighter than that of the ordinary soul, who had four years of wandering and oblivion to look forward to. In the Magliabecchi Codex, sheet 60, a bundled corpse wears the head ornament of a dead warrior. Food and an alcoholic beverage have been provided for his journey, and a blue dog that will guide and accompany him in the land of the dead is on his lap.[28] Musicians sing to the dead warrior and beat on drums.

One also shakes a rattle. Such was the proper sendoff for an Aztec warrior slain in battle.

In the reality of Aztec life, a mortuary bundle of a dead warrior such as the one shown here would have been taken to the foot of the main temple at Tenochtitlan. Servants were sacrificed, and food, drink, and flowers were provided to make the warrior's trip more pleasant. A reddish-colored dog was killed and placed on the bundle to help the deceased cross the waterways he would encounter. The warrior, the servants, the provisions, and the dog were burned with copal and torches. The Aztec believed that the soul was transmitted by fire and was then liberated by it.[29] This may have eased the journey of the dead one, but it destroyed the evidence for archaeologists.

Buried Dogs in North America

Although most arctic people are relative newcomers to American shores, dogs have always been essential for human survival in this unforgiving land of ice and snow. Archaeological evidence for the importance of this partnership exists in the form of an Archaic cemetery from Port au Choix, Newfoundland (2340 B.C.), where two large dogs were buried with a man and a woman. At the later site of Ipiutak, Alaska (150 B.C.), five dogs were interred with humans. Although the Newfoundland dog crania appear somewhat more massive than those from Alaska, both show affinity with Siberian dogs. It is also true that there is considerable variation in size among these prehistoric dogs of the "Eskimo" type.[30]

As far as we know, the first dogs to be deliberately and carefully buried come from the Archaic site of Koster (6400 B.C.), in the Illinois River Valley (see table 4.1, p. 122). At Koster, at least three dogs were placed on their sides in shallow pits just large enough to accommodate their bodies. None of the skeletons show any evidence of having been cut or burned. One dog had a grinding stone and a clam shell near its cranium.[31] At Rogers Cave in Missouri a small male dog with an unusually robust mandible was buried in a prepared grave in about 5500 B.C.[32]

The site of Eva, dated at 5000 B.C., is located in Benton County on the banks of the Tennessee River. Along with the 198 human burials recovered from this site were the remains of eighteen dogs. Four of these dog burials were associated with humans, and fourteen dogs were buried alone. In addition, the numerous disarticulated dog bones collected from disturbed burials suggest an even higher number of interred dogs.[33] Two of the dog burials are of special

The earliest dog burials in the Americas are the three found at the Archaic site of Koster in the Illinois River Valley. Each animal was discovered lying on its side in a shallow pit. Grinding stones were found beneath the skull of the dog pictured above. Photograph by D.R. Baston, Center for American Archeology.

interest. First, the skeleton of a small, curled-up dog was found underneath the skull of a human. A projectile point, a turtle shell rattle, a rattlesnake vertebra necklace, several awls, and an antler tine also accompanied this thirty- to thirty-five-year-old male. Second, a very large dog, without association with humans, was found buried with two splinter bone awls and a large stone pick.[34] Both animals probably were highly valued hunting dogs since the first was buried with a man who was also accompanied by special grave goods, and the second had burial goods of its own.

The Lamoka people lived in western New York state from 4000 to 2500 B.C. and hunted, fished, and collected for their sustenance. Deer were the most important resource, although fish were important as well. At the Frontenac Island Lamoka site in Cayuga County, William Ritchie and his team from the Rochester Museum unearthed thirteen dog burial sites. Uniquely for Archaic dogs from New York state, Ritchie reports two sizes of dogs, one noticeably larger than the other. At the Geneva site, however, only the smaller type of dog was represented. [35] But the presence of the three large dogs from Frontenac Island as well as the large Eva dog show that Archaic Eastern Woodlands dogs were more diverse than some researchers have suggested.[36] Seven of the buried dogs were associated with human burials. Almost all the dogs lay curled in a sleeping position. An immature large dog was part of a burial cluster that also contained two infants, two adult females, and two adult males. Burial 23 at Frontenac Island is particularly touching as it contained an infant with an oyster valve pendant on its chest. On top of the infant an immature dog of the small breed was buried. Because of the presence of white ash and charred bark in the burial, it is assumed that both dog and child had been cremated.[37]

Although no dog burials were uncovered at the type site at Lamoka Lake, some canid elements were found in the refuse. In this case the dogs may have been eaten. In addition, perforated dog canines, probably parts of dog-tooth necklaces, were found. Also common to this site were probable dog coprolites containing identifiable fish vertebrae. Ritchie claims that dogs were held in high esteem among Lamoka people, judging from the treatment they received at death. As a companion to the Archaic hunter, he argues, dogs would have been useful not only in tracking animals but also in fending off wounded animals that decided to charge their attackers.[38] On the other hand, the hunting skills of Archaic dogs are only inferred from burials such as those of the Lamoka people. It is possible, for example, that dogs were valued because they protected the campsite against unwanted animals or humans but were not taken on hunting trips. Whatever the case, some dogs were carefully buried in human cemeteries.

The Indian Knoll was one of many shell heaps that lined the Green River in west-central Kentucky. These shell middens represent former habitation sites for Archaic people (3000 B.C.) of the Eastern Woodlands. William Webb of the University of Kentucky excavated many of these mounds in Kentucky and Alabama between 1937 and 1957 with the help of labor supplied by the Works Progress Administration (WPA, enacted in 1935). Before 1937, archaeology in Kentucky had been done on a part-time basis by Webb and a colleague, and was paid for by Webb himself. In 1937, Webb received $75,000 for archaeological work. By 1940, 1,750 skeletons were excavated and repaired, 48,000 artifacts were discovered and catalogued, and 37,000 photographs were taken.[39] It was, ironically, the Depression and Kentucky's high unemployment rate that led to the excavation of and publishing about the greatest quantity of dog burials that the Americas has ever produced.

Indian Knoll contained twenty-one dog burial sites. Eight dogs were buried alone in their own graves. Three adult men and three adult women were buried with dogs. Also buried with dogs were two boys, aged seven and nine. Two dogs were included in two separate graves, one of a one-year-old girl and another of a girl who died at age three. In total, 880 human skeletons were excavated from Indian Knoll; 275 of the graves also contained artifacts, most commonly in the form of shell beads.[40] Dogs buried by themselves probably died of natural causes, but dogs buried with people, particularly children, may have been dispatched to accompany the departed to the land of the dead.

The Read Shell Midden, located downriver from Indian Knoll in Butler County, Kentucky, contained 247 human burials and 63 more or less complete dog burials. The ratio of dogs to humans was much greater at the Read site than at any other locality under discussion. Another difference at this site is that none of the canids was associated with a human burial. In some cases dogs were interred directly in the shell debris and covered with more debris. In other cases dogs were buried in a pit in the same manner as humans. For the most part, burial goods were limited to personal articles and were not commonly found in the mound.[41] The excavation of Carlson Annis Mound, also on the Green River, revealed 390 human and 28 dog burials. Three of the dogs were associated with human skeletons. As with the other mounds, the humans had been placed in round pits and were sometimes buried with shell beads and gorgets, awls, clothespins, and hairpins.[42]

The Pickwick Basin of northern Alabama on the Tennessee River was the location of a number of Archaic shell mounds excavated by William Webb and others as part of a Tennessee Valley Authority Project, preceding the construction of a major dam. At the Perry Site, unit 1, 141 humans were recovered, along with 20 dogs. The dogs occurred at all depths of the mound, and two dogs were buried directly under a human skeleton at this site. At unit 2 of the Perry Site, 16 dogs were buried. Although dogs were found in other mounds along the river they were mentioned only as being scattered through the middens.[43]

At the Lambert Farm Site in Warwick, Rhode Island, a group of late woodland people (around A.D. 1000) performed some sort of ceremonial activity that left the curious feature discovered in the 1980s. A dense, circular deposit, 1 meter in diameter and 65 centimeters thick, consisting of oysters, clams, and scallops, some whole and some broken, overlay the skeletons of two five-month-old dogs. The entire feature was constructed as a mound and contained large burned rocks, ceramics, local and exotic lithics, bone fragments, and a steatite platform pipe.[44]

A sandy bluff on Flushing Bay, across from LaGuardia airport in Queens, New York, was once the location of a late woodland village and cemetery. The site was exposed during a bulldozing operation to obtain fill for the marshy area that was to become home for the 1939 World's Fair. One of the four pits unearthed by the bulldozer had a fill of black earth, ash, and shell, with noticeable stratification. In addition, there was a lens of red-stained soil. Under these layers a headless, tailless dog was buried. Three shells—an oyster, a clam, and a scallop—were lying by the dog's spine. In a row between its legs were three unmodified stones, and near its neck was its charred mandible with fire-split teeth. The remains of another animal, possibly a weasel, also decapitated, was located near the dog's rump. Four large marker stones were in the pit as well.[45] The Lambert Farm dog burials and the one from Flushing suggest ritual behaviors. The inclusion of the same three types of shells, the evidence of fire, and the buried dogs would seem to link these sites, despite their considerable distance from one another.

Northern Arizona's White Dog Cave is approached by a tortuous ravine and a steep talus slope. It is a large cave measuring 120 feet at the opening and 70 feet deep. Because of the dry climate the contents of the cave are remarkably well preserved. The cave served as a storage room and burial ground for the agriculturalists, usually referred to as Basketmakers, who farmed the valley floor at around A.D. 100. Round graves were dug into the hardpan floor, and the bodies of humans, with some of their most cherished possessions, were lowered into the ground. Cyst 24 contained the mummies of two adults, a male and female, and the remains of an infant. Each adult corpse had been clothed in a fur string robe and wrapped in two large woven bags. Underneath the bodies were bundles of feathers and skin containers, and nearby were digging sticks and baskets of food. Lying near the male body was the mummy of a long-haired white dog about the size of a collie, and near the woman was a smaller dog with black and white spots.[46] The small dog was the size of a fox terrier but was more stockily built and possessed a short, heavy muzzle. Glover Allen refers to this Basketmaker dog as a "short-nosed Indian dog" and reports that similar dogs have been found in Virginia, California, and Peru.[47]

The remains of two adult humans and an infant plus two dogs in a single grave suggest that the family dogs were killed when their owners both died and placed with them. We have no way of knowing whether Basketmakers thought that the dogs would be helpful in the Next World, but dog remains were not found in the middens, at least around the first century A.D. Basketmaker dogs, it seems, were not usually part of the menu for dinner.[48]

In the 1890s, Clarence Moore traveled the inland water passages that parallel the Georgia coast and examined and reported on fifty mounds. With regard to Mound D on Ossabaw Island, Moore reports that "one curious feature was the presence of numerous skeletons of dogs, which were not found in fragments, but interred in their entirety. These dogs, therefore, evidently

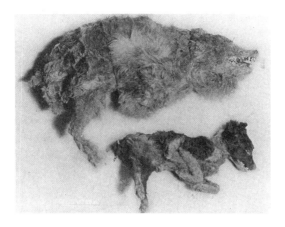

The two dog mummies recovered from White Dog Cave, Arizona. Both have erect ears and bushy tails. The muzzle of the larger dog is narrow and pointed, whereas the small dog's face is relatively short. Basketmaker people sometimes wove dog hair into string to make the fur cloth used to wrap the dead. Courtesy of the Peabody Museum, Harvard University. Photograph by Hillel Burger.

had not served as food. Curiously enough, however, the dogs did not lie with or near human skeletons, as one would expect had they been slain and buried with their masters, but were accorded internment by themselves. In no mound of the coast of Georgia have burials of dogs approached those in Mound D, though occasional ones—always represented by entire skeletons—have been met with."[49] Moore recorded finding ten buried dogs in this mound. The mound was made up of sand with layers of oyster shell. It contained human burials, ceramic vessels, and worked bone. Some of the more finely made ceramics suggest a Savannah II provenence, though this is not certain.[50] The Savannah II period is Middle Mississippian in age, but the coastal fishing cultures of Georgia were slow to adopt cultural trends from the west.

Mound D presents an interesting subject for study. Dogs, buried separately with no discernable ritual intent, may have enjoyed a particularly high status on Ossabaw Island. This status resulted in the considerable human effort of burying dogs at death. Rather than being seen as necessary to conducting humans safely to the next world, dogs were allowed to live out their lives and, on dying, were buried "like people." They were on their way, perhaps, to the same after-death destination as humans.

Cahokia (A.D. 1000–1400) was the largest of the Mississippian centers, and its elite seem to have received the most elaborate sendoff at death. Although Cahokia tombs do not contain gold, turquoise, or jade, as do important tombs in Mesoamerica and Central and South America, they were clearly constructed for high-status individuals. Unlike average people, elites were buried en masse in mound structures with large amounts of imported material. Ceramic cooking vessels were common in nonelite burial areas but rare among the upper classes. In Cahokia society those clear demarcations between the classes were carried on into death. In one of the elite burial mounds at Cahokia, Wilson Mound, a single dog was buried along with the carefully disarticulated, cleaned, and arranged remains of nearly a hundred people and great quantities of marine shells and beads.[51] Although the most common fate of dogs was to end up in middens at Cahokia,[52] this lone animal in Wilson Mound, for reasons that we can never know, received special treatment at death. For other dogs at Cahokia, life was a pretty risky business.

At Moundville, another massive Mississippian site, no buried dogs were recovered among hundreds of human remains. Some canid elements were in the middens, however.[53] Two dogs were buried at Etowah, none at Hiwassee Island, and none in the Pickwick Basin.[54] Buried dogs, having been common in the Eastern Woodlands during the Archaic,[55] were seldom found during the Mississippian time period.[56] This paucity of canine burials can be best understood as a consequence of the increasing importance of agriculture and the lessening dependence on hunted game. Dogs were no longer playing a critical role in the high-stakes quest for food and were therefore suffering a loss of stature within their human community.

Buried Dogs in Mesoamerica

In Mesoamerica, the greatest numbers of buried dogs, both skeletons and effigies, come from sites in the western Mexican states of Colima, Nayarit, and Sinaloa. Indeed, probably the best-known effigies from the entire pre-Columbian world are the red and well-rounded ceramic dogs from Colima. Although not found in their original contexts, it is believed that these dogs were created to be placed in large shaft tombs among the offerings for deceased kin. Ceramic dogs engaged in sleeping, scratching, sitting, standing, playing, and dancing are the most common forms in Colima art. Maria Gomez de Ahumada of the Museum of History and Archaeology of Colima states that 75 to 90 percent of Colima tombs contained ceramic dog effigies.[57] Why did the potters of Colima make so many dogs? Even though ceramic dogs from Colima are usually referred to as *los perros cebados* (fattened dogs), we should not assume that they were food offerings for the dead.[58] Instead, the fascination that Colima people had for dogs seems to hinge on their abilities as otherworld guides.

A naked and presumably dead woman has been wrapped securely on a pallet with an arch above her head. At her feet are two dogs. Such a pallet may have been used to lower corpses into the shaft tombs of western Mexico. The dogs here are in their most protective role. Colima, western Mexico. Ceramic, 12.1 cm. Courtesy Yale University Art Gallery, Stephen Carlton Clark, B.A. 1903, Fund.

A number of Colima sculptures show what appear to be warriors holding shields and weapons in their arms with dogs perched on their helmets. In one piece a seated figure holds two rattles and wears a headdress with a forward-projecting horn. Behind the shoulders of this individual are dog figures with their bodies presented in high relief and their heads projecting laterally. Peter Furst argues that these Colima "warriors" are shamanistic in nature and that the enemies they face are supernatural rather than corporal. These figures, he feels, are guardians of the human soul and the dead. They join dogs as guides for otherworld journeys, a role more familiar to the canines.[59] Even though virtually all the tombs in western Mexico have been looted or disturbed, it seems clear that these ceramic dogs, along with an assortment of other pottery animals and people, were intended solely for funerary functions. They were made to be buried.

In the Marismas Nacionales, located just north of Colima in Sinaloa, nine estuarine sites have yielded Mesoamerica's richest source of buried dogs. From A.D. 700 to 1300, western Mexican people buried at least sixty-seven dogs. In addition, they buried four racoons, an armadillo, and an offering of six deer skulls. These burials, as well as those of humans, were found in midden refuse. Elizabeth Wing has analyzed the dog remains, and her results are intriguing for several reasons. First, the dogs ranged in weight from 7 kg to 14 kg, with the smallest dogs coming from the Rincon de Panal site and the largest coming from Panales. Dogs varied from to site to site in terms of their body build as well. This suggests to Wing that at seven of the Marismas sites dogs were quite heterogenous and perhaps living in small, isolated populations. The second intriguing piece of information to come out of this study is that many of the dogs had had their canines and incisors intentionally broken. Sixty-four percent of all the canines recovered from these sites showed this pattern. Some of the raccoon teeth were damaged in the same way.[60]

Dog effigies or dog skeletons were sometimes included in human burials at Teotihuacán, but because of their rarity they must not have had the symbolic connotations that they did at Colima. Of the 284 burials containing some type of grave good excavated at Teotihuacán before 1978, six contained dog skeletons and one had a dog effigy pot in it.[61] However, there was another development at Teotihuacán that has implications for the story of the American dog. The great Central Mexican deity Quetzalcoatl, the feathered serpent, made his first appearance at a temple at Teotihuacán. When the Temple of Quetzalcoatl was built (A.D. 250–450), Teotihuacán was the largest and most important center in Mesoamerica. The temple itself was located in the Ciudadela, which was the heart of the city geographically, politically, and culturally. The facades of this temple were elaborately carved with serpents, snails, and shells. Human burials, presumably sacrificial, were placed at each corner and along each axis of the building. The graves contained 1, 4, 8, 9, 18, or 26 individuals, all men of warrior age, usually with hands joined. Obsidian blades were arranged around the heads of these victims, and some wore pendants made from human and dog mandibles.[62] The placement of graves at the Temple of Quetzalcoatl formed an integral part of the architectural plan of the building, either along its central axis or at its cardinal and intercardinal points. The dog mandibles were part of the warrior regalia and served to announce the wearer's bravery and valor. This temple required the dearest of sacrifices: members of the warrior class.

Kaminaljuyu, a key trading center for obsidian, was located in the Guatemalan highlands. Around A.D. 400 it was operating under a sphere of influence far to the north, Teotihuacán: whether by conquest, migration, or emulation, Teotihuacáno form and style were abundantly present in the architecture and in the tripod polychrome ceramics that were part of the burial goods of Mounds A and B. The excavation of Mound B produced a structure that was a diminutive version of the Pyramid of the Sun at Teotihuacán. The homo-

Plan of Burial 2 from Kaminaljuyu. Note the dog skeleton (62) in northeast corner of the tomb. Note also 60, a jaguar skull with pyrite eyes; 61, a dog skull; 63, peccary tusks; 65, an eagle skull. Pyrite mirrors, jade beads, ceramic vessels, and flaked tools are also shown on this plan. The remains of a litter can be seen in the south end of the grave. After Kidder, Jennings, and Shook, 1946.

geneity of the contents of the ten excavated elite burials suggests that the two mounds were built over a short period of time, perhaps less than a century. The burial goods from the graves, which have Maya affinities as well as links to Teotihuacán, included jade beads, pyrite plaques, obsidian blades, shells, grinding stones, cylindrical tripod vessels, and pitchers. All the burials had a variety of ceramics numbering from eight to thirty-six pieces. Jaguars, dogs, and turtles were the most common animals included in the grave inventory. Dog teeth or skeletons were recovered from seven of the ten excavated graves.[63]

In Burial 2, in addition to a complete dog skeleton in the northeast corner, another canid skull was placed northwest of the main human skeleton. A jaguar skull with inlaid pyrite eyes was set just south of this individual. A small cat skull was lying beside his right foot, and two white-lipped peccary tusks were located in the northwest quadrant of the grave. The skull of a raptor, probably an eagle, was lying near a series of tripod pots. A ceramic sleeping dog effigy, in the thin orange style of the Basin of Mexico, was another ceramic offering placed in this tomb.[64] A litter and suitable human bearers were also in the grave, undoubtedly to carry the central occupant on his underworld journey; his dog would be his guide. The placement of the dog skeleton in the northeast corner of the grave was, I believe, of symbolic importance. The Maya believed that dogs were associated with the north and with the rains that come from that direction. Among the Aztec, the north was the place of the cold obsidian wind and Mictlan, the land of the dead.

Dogs on the Isthmus of Panama

The site of Sitio Conté, located on the Pacific side of the Isthmus of Panama, was unimpressive when first discovered. Pot shards were strewn over the eight acres of the site, but major architectural features were absent. Yet beneath the ground, in sixty graves, was the elaborate paraphernalia of chiefs bent on taking masses of personal property to the next world. Grave 1 was one of the richest of the graves excavated by Samuel Lothrop in 1931. It consisted of a deep (ten feet) rectangular hole with nine turtle carapaces at the bottom. Four large capstones were placed over the carapaces. On top of the stones the principal skeleton was seated on a stool and surrounded by 180 pottery vessels, plates, carafes, and bowls. He had on or beside him 58 articles of personal adornment, including sixteen nose

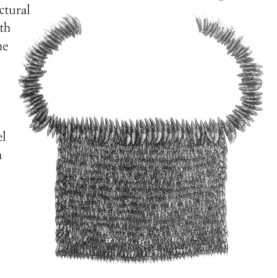

Restored dog-tooth "apron" from Grave 1 at Sitio Conté on the Isthmus of Panama. This garment, originally backed with leather, is covered with the split molar and carnassial teeth of dogs. The tie strings are adorned with canine teeth. Width 23.4 cm. Courtesy of the Peabody Museum, Harvard University.

pendants and 24 other objects made out of gold. He also had two necklaces made of dog canine teeth and an apron covered with dog molars. The three other males buried with this man had relatively few adornments and no dog-tooth necklaces.[65]

Such lavish burial goods may reflect a "contingent" political system in which a leader's power was transitory, gained through temporary advantage in warfare. Such societies do not build permanent architecture, but leaders indicate their status through displays of wealth.[66] Status, in this case, seemed to include wearing jewelry fashioned of dog teeth. One might infer from this that dogs themselves may have enjoyed some status on the isthmus and were likely to be hunting dogs rather than eating dogs. To investigate this suggestion further, we will take a brief look at what written sources report about dogs in Panama.

Traveling in Panama in 1681, Lionel Wafer, like most Europeans remarking on the dogs of the natives, did not have many kind words for them. "The Dogs they have are small, not well-shap'd, their Hair rough and straggling, like our Mungrels. They serve only to bark and start the Game, or by their barking give notice to the Hunters to shoot their Arrows. They will run about in this manner from Morning to Night; but are such meer whissling Curs, that 2 or 300 Beasts started in a Day, they shall seldom kill above two or three; and these not by running them down, but by getting them at Bay and besetting them, till the Hunters can come up with them."[67]

Even though the inhabitants of the Isthmus were agriculturalists, dogs do seem to have had important roles in hunting strategies. Hunters used nets, snares, traps, and pits and organized game drives with dogs and grass fires.[68] And, in Panama, canid remains of any type are rarely recovered from middens; this suggests that dogs were not eaten.[69] The dog-tooth apron that adorned the old man buried in Grave 1 at Sitio Conté, and Wafer's description of hunting trips—"They take with them one or Two Dogs apiece, to beat about"[70]— show some special sentiment toward dogs that did not exist somewhat farther north.

Buried Dogs of South America

No remains of domestic dogs have been found in excavations of Santa Elena Peninsula sites inhabited by the fishing and gathering Vegas people (6500–5000 B.C.). However, a wild canid, the desert fox or zorro (*Dusicyon sechurae*), must have had significant symbolic importance among these early people. In one Vegas burial three piles of fox teeth were placed around one human skeleton. The number and types of teeth in these piles indicate that at least twenty-seven foxes were represented in this burial.[71]

The Valdivians, later occupants of the Santa Elena Peninsula, had constructed a large agricultural village at the site of Real Alto by 3100 B.C. The houses at Real Alto were substantial, with mud plastered walls and thatched gabled roofs. Two of the buildings, located on the central plaza, were larger than the rest and had ceremonial functions. The Fiesta House was constructed on a natural rise. The contents of refuse pits in its floor indicate that feasting was one of the main activities in the Fiesta House.[72] Also excavated from beneath the floor were three buried dogs that may have been special offerings made at various times in the structure's history. Jorge Marcos, an excavator at the site, speculates that dogs were used principally for hunting and would thus have been valuable offerings. Although dogs were eaten at the inland Loma Alta site, here they seemed to have enjoyed higher status.[73]

On coastal Peru a dog was buried with ears of corn at Paloma,[74] and another dog, dating to 1000 and 500 B.C., was discovered on the Paracas Peninsula wrapped in a Chavin-style textile.[75] Although the Paloma dog burial was of later date than the site itself, a lone canine tooth that probably belonged to a dog was also recovered among the other Paloma faunal remains dating to 3000 B.C.[76] From 500 B.C. to A.D.100, a series of coastal sites have also yielded the remains of buried dogs. On the Paracas Peninsula the tradition of burying dogs wrapped in textiles continued. The people of the Paracas culture placed their dead in a sitting position and wrapped them in many layers of cloth. These woven and embroidered textiles were sometimes elaborately decorated. The Paracas "mummy bundles" were placed in deeps pits or cisterns with internal (in the bundle) or external grave goods. Sometimes a dog was included in the tomb, either wrapped as humans were or with a rope around its neck. A pair of puppies was found in one grave. Each of the buried dogs was associated with a human mummy bundle.[77]

On the central coast of Peru, the Lighthouse Site in the Supe Valley has produced a number of high-quality ceramics and textiles.[78] One of the burials at this site had many goods associated with it, including textiles, netting, twinned basketry, a feather headdress, an intricately carved gourd, and a thin piece of beaten gold. In addition, this burial of an adult male contained the foot of a llama tied with a cord and the mummified head of a small brown-haired dog.[79] The offerings of dog's head and llama foot are curious, since the rest of the cadavers were not present in the grave.

The Salinar people in the Viru Valley on Peru's north coast interred their

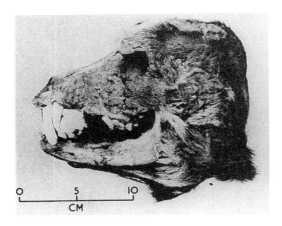

The Lighthouse Point dog's head is covered with a thick, long amber brown coat of hair. Its snout is blunt and broad. The dog approximates the size of Allen's so-called Inca dog rather than the smaller "Peruvian pug-nosed dog." The head was the only part of the dog found in the grave of a male human. After Willey and Corbett, 1954.

corpses in an extended position wrapped or covered with textiles. Great stone slabs were used to form a crude sarcophagus. The dead wore ornaments, and a piece of beaten gold was sometimes put in their mouths. Gourd bowls were filled with meat, pumpkin seeds, maize, land snails, and molluscs and placed around the body. Red powder was deposited in special receptacles or placed around the grave in chunks. Round stones, rough quartz, and pieces of chalk were included. A dog was sometimes placed at the dead person's feet.[80]

The Castillo de Tomaval, a fortified adobe monument in the Viru valley, was occupied by the Gallinazo people at the end of the first millennium B.C. During the Gallinazo occupation at least one dog was buried with an unusual amount of care and attention. The dog mummy, still possessing its yellow hair, was discovered in a small room of the Castillo de Tomaval. The dog was wrapped in several pieces of cloth making a bundle about 60 centimeters long. This bundle was lying on a plaited fiber mat along with a piece of copper, two small gourd bowls, two sections of wood, and few shards, and some fish bones. The buried dog and offerings were not associated with any human burial. Another buried dog was recovered but without offerings at Castillo de Tomaval. Llama bone fragments were found scattered throughout the site, but no canid remains were recovered except for the burials.[81] The yellow-haired dog mummy was clearly special and may have been an offering to the gods.

In Andean Peru, the dog's closest association has been with lunar deities. During a lunar eclipse people feared that the moon was sick and would soon die and fall upon the earth, causing its destruction. According to the Inca chronicler Garcilaso, to prevent this, people would "tie up their dogs, both large and small, and beat them hard to make them bark and bay at the Moon, for, they said, at one time, dogs had rendered great service to the Moon, and ever since then it had special affection for them; for this reason, they thought, if the Moon heard them baying for her, she would awaken from the dream in which illness held her a prisoner."[82]

On the north coast of Peru the dog frequently was used with felines and the lunar deity in motifs for ceramics and other decorative mediums.[83] Moon worship was more important on the coast than in the highlands and the dog's status was higher there, too.[84] At least all indications point in that direction. It seems that the dog's fate was closely linked with that of the Moon. Of course the flesh-and-blood dog could be eaten without damaging this relationship.

In 1985, William Alva discovered the first unlooted tombs of Moche rulers at Sipán. These tombs have no equal in the Americas for the quantity of precious metals recovered, for the skilled workmanship revealed, and for the amount and variety of grave goods contained. Among the hundreds of items adorning the Moche leaders were gold masks with lapis eyes and shell teeth, necklaces of gold and silver peanuts nine centimeters long, and gold and turquoise ear spools with minute movable parts.[85] In Tomb 1, dated at A.D.

DÉSOLATION des PERUVIENS pendant L'ECLIPSE de LUNE.

Two Peruvian men beat tied-up dogs to make them bark during a lunar eclipse. It was thought if the moon heard the barking of dogs it would wake from its dream and not fall to earth. The people and buildings appear more Greek than Andean in this early illustration from Bernard Picard, Ceremonies et Cotumes Religieuses des Peuple Idolatres de Tous les Peuples du Monde, *vol. 2 (1723). Courtesy of the Yale Center for British Art, Paul Mellon Collection.*

300, amid a vast store of accumulated wealth, was the skeleton of a dog. We will return to this intriguing dog in the next chapter.

In Tomb 2 at Sipán, in addition to the centrally placed and adorned adult male, was a ten-year-old without adornment and two youths between 15 and 17 years old. A small cane coffin was found at the foot of the principal figure. It contained a child, between eight and ten years old, lying on its back. The child was wearing a copper headdress. Thirteen gourd bowls and a ceramic stirrup bottle were also in the cane coffin. On top of the child was a dog, and by his feet was a snake.[86] The Moche envisioned the serpent as the mediator of the opposing forces of good and evil, and of male and female. The serpent also united the sun and ocean.[87] This powerful snake, playing such a key role in Moche iconography, was carefully buried with the dog and child; what symbolic meaning do these three beings have? Or, perhaps the dog and the snake were the child's pets, and, since the child was to accompany the Moche Lord to the next world, he was allowed to take his animal companions.

Burial themes with complex and esoteric imagery decorate some Moche vases. A rollout drawing of a vase schematically illustrates the two parallel dimensions of the living and the dead by juxtaposing pyramid steps with burial shaft. Above the burial shaft on the right are two strange-looking figures, called Wrinkle Face and Iguana by Christopher Donnan.[88] Each holds ropes to lower

A dog's skeleton was placed on the body of a ten-year-old child in a cane coffin situated at the feet of the principal occupant of Sipán Burial 2. A snake, a ceramic bottle, and some gourds were also included in the coffin. Note also the decapitated llama lying to the left of the boy's coffin. Painting by Percy Fiestas. Photograph by Guillermo Hare.

In this Moche burial ceremony scene, Wrinkle Face, wearing a fox headdress and accompanied by a dog, and Iguana, dragging a reluctant llama, prepare the grave. At some distance a naked woman, who may represent the doctor of the deceased, is pecked by birds. Rollout drawing of Moche bottle by Donna McClelland from photographs by Christopher Donnan.

the casket into the ground. Iguana is holding a reluctant llama that will probably be part of the grave offerings. A spotted dog waits at Wrinkle Face's feet. Wrinkle Face has snakes exuding from his belt and a doglike creature on his headdress. The dog and snake images paired here with "Wrinkle Face" may have symbolic content similar to that of the dog and snake paired with the boy in the coffin in Sipan Burial 2.

Dogs were buried in the highlands as well as on the coast in Peru. Dog burials were recovered from Rosamachay (200 B.C.) and Wishgana (500 B.C.) caves in the Ayacucho Valley.[89] A dog carefully wrapped in a leather pouch was buried at the base of a wall in the upper levels at Telarmachay Cave. The burial (from phase II, 200 B.C.) postdates the earliest dog fragment recovered from the cave (from phase V inf 4800–2700 B.C.) by 3,000 years.[90]

The Inca believed that virtuous people went to live with the Sun in the "upper world" after death. With the Sun one always had plenty to eat and drink. People who did not lead exemplary lives on earth went to the interior of the earth, where they were forever cold and had only stones to eat. The nobles, however, went to live with the Sun, regardless of their behavior on earth. Souls of the dead might linger on earth, however, and would thus need food offerings. Souls also liked to have their skeletons brought out from their tombs to witness festivals.[91]

Apparently dogs did not appear in the otherworld of the Inca, but "the howling of a dog foretold the death of a relative."[92] Unfortunately, no undisturbed elite graves have been found, so that we do not know for certain whether a dog was placed in the grave of an Inca to provide guidance into the next world. To find buried Inca dogs we have to travel away from Cuzco to the enormous administrative center of Huanuco Pampa, where several dogs were buried,[93] or to the mountain retreat of Machu Picchu.

The Inca site of Machu Picchu, discovered by Hiram Bingham in 1911 and excavated by the Yale Expedition of 1912, is located in the Urubamba drainage system of the southern highlands of Peru. It was occupied by Inca elite and various retainers and servants until shortly before the Spanish conquest in 1532. As the Inca themselves would have been buried in the sacred city of Cuzco, the

The Rock Shelter Terrace, located on Machu Picchu Mountain, elevation 9,500 feet, some distance from the Inca city, was described by excavator George Eaton as the most magnificent place of burial at Machu Picchu. Beneath the large rock overhang the residents of Machu Picchu buried a woman with her pottery vessels and her small dog. After Eaton, 1916.

people buried in the more than 100 caves and rock shelters scattered near the ruins of the city must have been retainers, herders, and farm laborers who managed the estate for their Inca landlords. The caves and rock shelters frequently contained multiple human burials, as well as ceramic and metal grave goods mixed with both altered and unaltered nonhuman bone. A variety of fauna was collected from the graves, but llamas and alpacas were the only large animals present, making 99 percent of the faunal sample.

The most impressive of the burial locations was the rock-sheltered terrace, which was reached by two short flights of stairs and was overhung by a large natural flat-faced boulder. On this terrace the expedition found the remains of five individuals. On the east end of the terrace, George Eaton found a bone bodkin and a saucer handle, beautifully modeled in the form of a llama head. In the principal grave was a woman in a contracted position, several complete pots, some bronzes, and textiles. A small dog had been buried with this woman, and its entire skeleton was recovered. This is the only instance in which a complete animal skeleton was found, perhaps indicating the extreme care that was taken with its burial. In many cases human and nonhuman material was simply placed on the cave floor and not buried.[94]

Dog remains were found in seven of the caves. There are no cut or burn marks on these bones, and only a small portion of the camelid bones show such traces.[95] The alpaca and llama herders of Machu Picchu may have used these dogs to help in their herding activities.

Endnote

There are far easier methods of corpse disposal than placing an animal in the ground and covering it. For example, after the death of a dog, the Hidatsa either threw the body into the river or left it in the woods.[96] On the other hand, a valuable hunting dog may have rated an internment of its own. A pet in life could become a guide and companion in death. In the land of the dead, where fierce and judgmental dogs patrolled, some souls were sent down raging rivers. In the Huron language, *Gagnenon andahatey* means "path of the dogs," a celestial route running parallel to the Milky Way. The Maya envisioned the Milky Way as a canoe with a dog passenger that sinks and disappears beneath the water. For the Mexican Cora, the Caribbean Taíno and the Amazonian Shipibo, a deep otherworld lake was controlled by dogs. The Dog Star was in the sky, the dog was ferryman on the river, the child was comforted by the puppy, and the Colima dogs danced. Such was the land of the dead in the Americas.

Table 4.1. *Dog Burial Sites*

Site	Date	Description	Reference
Koster (Illinois)	6400 B.C.	3 buried dogs	Morey & Wiant, 1992
Rogers Cave (Missouri)	4700 B.C.	1 buried dog	McMillan, 1970
Eva (Tennessee)	5000 B.C.	18 dogs buried with or near humans	Lewis & Lewis, 1961
Frontenac Island (New York)	4000–2500 B.C.	13 dogs buried with or near humans	Ritchie, 1945
Geneva (New York)	4000–2500 B.C.	7 buried dogs with or near humans	Ritchie, 1980
Real Alto (coastal Ecuador)	3100 B.C.	3 dogs buried in ceremonial setting	Marcos, 1988
Hiwassee Island (Tennessee)	3000 B.C.	8 buried dogs with or near humans	Harrington, 1922
Read Shell Midden (Kentucky)	3000 B.C.	63 dogs buried with humans in shell heap	Webb, 1950b
Indian Knoll (Kentucky)	3000 B.C.	21 dogs buried with humans in shell heap	Webb, 1946
Carlson Annis (Kentucky)	3000 B.C.	28 dogs buried with humans in shell heap	Webb, 1950a
Perry Site, Pickwick Basin (Alabama)	3000 B.C.	36 dogs buried with humans in shell heap	Webb & DeJarnette, 1942
Port au Choix (Newfoundland)	2340 B.C.	2 large dogs buried with an adult man and woman	Tuck, 1970
Paloma (central coast, Peru)	<1000 B.C.	Intrusive buried dog with corn cob	Benfer, 1984
Paracas Peninsula (south coast, Peru)	600 B.C.	Dog buried wrapped in Chavin-like textile	Engel, 1960
Paracas Peninsula (south coast, Peru)	500–100 B.C.	8 dogs buried in cemeteries with mummy bundles	Tello and Xesspe, 1979
Lighthouse, Supe (central coast, Peru)	500 B.C.	Dog mummy head buried in human grave	Willey and Corbett, 1954
Salinar Sites (north coast, Peru)	500 B.C.	Dogs buried with humans	Larco Hoyle, 1946

Table 4.1. (Continued)

Site	Date	Description	Reference
Telarmachay (Highland Peru)	200 B.C.	Dog buried in leather pouch beside wall	Lavallee, 1977
Castillo de Tomaval (north coast, Peru)	200 B.C.	Wrapped dog mummy with offerings	Strong and Evans, 1952
Ipiutak (Alaska)	150 B.C.	5 dogs buried with humans	Murie, 1948
Rosamachay (Highland Peru)	150 B.C.	1 buried dog	Wing, 1986
White Dog Cave (Arizona)	100 B.C.–A.D. 100	2 dog mummies in burial cave with humans	Guernsey and Kidder, 1921
Teotihuacán (Basin of Mexico)	A.D. 200–450	13 dog burials; dog mandibles in ceremonial setting	Sempowski and Spence, 1994
Sípan (north coast of Peru)	A.D. 300	2 dogs buried in royal tombs	Alva and Donnan, 1993
Kaminaljuhu (Guatemala)	A.D. 450	Complete or partial dog remains in 10 elite tombs	Kidder, Jennings, and Shook, 1946
Flushing (New York)	A.D. 600	Headless dog buried in mound with shells, marker rocks, and ash	Lopez and Wisnjewski, 1956
Marismas Nacionales (West Mexico)	A.D. 700–1300	67 dog burials; several raccoon burials	Wing, n.d.
Lambert Farm (Rhode Island)	A.D. 1000	2 dogs buried in mound with shells, burned rocks, ceramics	Kerber, Leveille, and Greenspan, 1989
Grasshopper Pueblo (Arizona)	A.D. 1400	1 dog buried near Great Kiva	Olsen, 1990
Cahokia (Illinois)	A.D. 1100–1500	1 dog buried in elite mound; several in other contexts	Milner, 1984; Parmalee, 1957, 1975
Hiwassee Island (Tennessee)	A.D. 1100–1500	No buried dogs	Lewis and Kneberg, 1946
Pickwick Basin Sites (Alabama)	A.D. 1100–1500	No buried dogs	Webb and DeJarnette, 1942

(continued)

Table 4.1. (Continued)

Site	Date	Description	Reference
Moundville (Alabama)	A.D. 1100–1500	No buried dogs	Welch, 191
Ossabaw Island (Georgia)	A.D. 1100–1500	10 dogs buried with humans in mound	Moore, 1897
Etowah (Georgia)	A.D. 1100–1500	2 dogs with tails curled over back buried in temple mound C	Van der Schalie and Parmalee, 1960
Huanuco Pampa (highland Peru)	A.D. 1450	3 or more buried dogs	Wing, 1988
Machu Picchu (highland Peru)	A.D. 1490	Dog buried with woman, dog elements in burial caves	Eaton, 1916; Schwartz, n.d.

5 *Molded, Carved, and Painted Dogs*

It is a dog with no hair at all; it goes about completely naked. It sleeps upon a cape, which covers it. Thus do they produce a *xoloitzcuintli:* when it is still a puppy, they cover it with turpentine unguent, so that its hair falls out absolutely everywhere. Thus its body becomes bare.—Fray Bernardino de Sahagún, 1547–1575, *General History of the Things of New Spain: Florentine Codex, Part IV*

This was to observe a festival and in it to execute a dance on very high stilts, and to offer him [the Lacandón Maya god *Yax Cocah Mut*] dogs made of pottery with bread on their backs, and the old women had to dance with these dogs in their hands, and to sacrifice to him a little dog with a black back and which was a virgin. And those who were devout had to draw their blood and to anoint the stone of the idol *Chac Acantum* with it.—Bishop Diego de Landa, *Relación de las Cosas de Yucatán* (1566)

The tenth sign, which belonged to the tenth day of the month, was Itzcuintli, which means Dog. This sign was held to be fortunate and happy. Those born under it were omened bliss and felicity. They were to be courageous, generous, likely to ascend in the world, men with many children, overflowing with plenty, lavish, prodigal, fond of having enough to give away, enemies of poverty, friends to those who ask favors, always willing to comply.—Fray Diego Duran, *Book of the Gods and Rites and the Ancient Calendar* (1576)

In this chapter I examine how Native Americans represented "dogness" in their ceramics, sculpture paintings, books, and words. Even the smallest difference in the dog's portrayal—its size, the position of its body, the expressiveness of its face, its juxtaposition with other components of the scene—serves to convey a unique message. The language used to describe dogs also reveals much about the describer. Because these renditions and descriptions were created by pre-Columbian artisans and scribes for a pre-Columbian audience, they are among the best primary source materials on the multifaceted role of dogs. Dogs were conceived as archetypes, as stand-ins, as symbols, and as companion animals. Of course we cannot know what was in the mind of the beholder or the creator of a piece of art, but we can turn for help to numerous scholars whose labors lend valuable insight into the symbolic complexity of pre-Columbian artistic expression.

A gigantic line dog with its elongated penis and nipple was created by the Nazca as an invocation for rain and fertility to Illa-kata, the mountain deity thought to control the water needed for irrigation farming. Dog geoglyph on the high arid plain above the Nazca River, Peru. Photograph courtesy of Banco de Crédito del Perú, Lima.

Pre-Columbian dog representations were crafted in many mediums and on different scales, from the gigantic (measured in tens of meters) outline of a dog on the Nazca Plain to the one-centimeter-long gold dog pendant created by Sitio Conté craftsmen. Also from Sitio Conté comes a small smiling "begging" dog carved from serpentine with gold caps on its feet and tail.[1] The Chimú of Peru crafted dog vessels from silver. The Maya portrayed a crouching dog of shell with jade inlay and a ceremonial flaked flint dog. A wooden dog's head has been recovered from the Caddoan site of Spiro in Oklahoma, and a steatite "great pipe" carved in the shape of a dog was found in the Middle Woodland Copena Mound on the Tennessee River. Among the murals painted on the residential palaces at Teotihuacán are some doglike creatures of power and force. Of all these pre-Columbian dog creations, perhaps the most remarkable is on a woven mantle recovered from a grave on the Paracas Peninsula on the southern coast of Peru. This mantle has a frieze around its borders of ninety small embroidered human figures sewn in twelve different colored threads. One of these figures holds a black and white dog in one hand and a dart in the other, and wears the headdress of a dog. The figure is less than eight centimeters high.[2]

From crudely made to supremely crafted, drawn, sewn, molded, or carved, whether a toy or a deity, domestic and wild dog images have been recovered throughout the Americas. Each reveals some aspect of the relation between dogs and people. They also tell us what real-life dogs looked like and how dogs fit into the society in which they resided.

The Dogs of Altar de Sacrificios

The polities that developed a class of full-time artisans are the most fertile places to look for representations of dogs. An inquiry into the manner in which dogs were portrayed within and across cultural boundaries yields some intriguing results. Our first example is the sample of dog representations from the Maya site of Altar de Sacrificios during the late Classic period. Altar de Sacrificios and other lowland centers had experienced considerable population increase during the late Preclassic. At that time several thousand people were living at Altar, and there had been an increase in the number and size of public buildings. For the first time, archaeologists detected status differences by studying the burial goods encountered. By the late Classic period the Maya lowlands were home to as many as 10 million people who were integrated culturally, linguistically, and economically.[3] Rulers of competing polities vied for

Throughout pre-Columbian America, dog images were crafted out of a variety of materials and at different scales. a. Mesoamerica, crouching dog, shell with jade inlay, Maya, 14 cm. After Berjonneau, Deletaille, and Sonnery, 1985. b. Central America, begging dog, serpentine, gold caps, Coclé, 3.5 cm. After Lothrop, 1928. c. South America, man holding dog, cotton embroidery, Paracas, 8 cm. After Harcourt, 1962. d. North America, dog with curled tail, ceramic, Mississippian, 4 cm. After Webb and DeJarnette, 1942. Drawings by Susan Hochgraf.

control of smaller centers. These larger centers were able to support an array of craft specialists, including potters, woodworkers, stone masons, flint and obsidian workers, bark-cloth makers, and manuscript painters. In the late Classic there was both a demand for well-crafted goods and a system to provide these items.

During the 1959 to 1963 field seasons, excavations conducted by the Peabody Museum at Harvard University yielded a wealth of ceramic figurines and flaked stone objects. Turtles, frogs, crocodiles, lizards, felines, monkeys, pigs, coatimundis, and owls, turkeys, and other birds are all represented in the small figurines and whistles found at Altar. Maya men and women in varying styles of clothing and hair are common. Dog images were also crafted by the artisans at this site. Among the Altar figurines are two full-figure dogs with collars lying in similar positions. One of the heads has pronounced wrinkles on its face. A headless sitting animal with an exposed backbone and ribs is probably a dog. Such skeletal representations had underworld connotations in Mesoamerica.[4] There are figures of Maya women holding small dogs and another headless figure with a dog in one hand and a cup in the other. In addition, a Maya man sports a large dog headdress. A chipped stone dog was also uncovered.[5]

Several recurring themes are expressed in these figurines. Sometimes a dog is just a dog—in other words, a pet or food item, or both. Such dogs are the resting dog figures and the ones being held by the women and the headless figure. These are the dogs of everyday life, domesticity, and the hearth—the woman's sphere. These "ordinary" dogs illustrate the variation in the physical appearance of pre-Columbian dogs. The wrinkled faces of some of the Altar dogs, an artistic convention used elsewhere to denote that these were hairless dogs, may represent this type of pre-Columbian dog. The small size of some Maya dogs is also revealed when they are portrayed with human figures.

More complicated is the deployment of dogs as symbols. As we have seen, dogs can serve as stand-ins for certain human qualities or can link different realms. They can also be omens or totems. Canine characters can be "borrowed" by deities and humans alike. The layers of meaning and abstraction of canid depictions are wide ranging, but nowhere do they reach the level of complexity and variability attained in literate Mesoamerica. At Altar de Sacrificios these abstract attributes were captured by one of the great masters of Maya vase painting. In a scene full of movement this artist has created a large bird with a boa around its neck hovering above a death god with flint knives at his elbows and knees and in his hand. One of the Hero Twins holds fire in a seated position over a jaguar in a bamboo cage. Another god is playing a shell trumpet over a waterlily jaguar. Three human dancers have evoked this otherworld scene; one delicately dancing man wears a dog headdress (see p. 158).[6] Only recently have Maya epigraphers been able to decipher what was going on in this scene, to which I return at the end of the chapter. At this single Maya lowland site we can demonstrate that whenever human artists created canine images they were also conveying messages. The created dog is always a "metaphorical dog," and it is for those metaphors that we search.

A Chronology of the Ceramic Effigy Dog

By far the most common medium for the expression of "dogness" is the pottery effigy. The earliest clay dog figures were found at Tlatilco, a site in the Basin of Mexico dating to 1200 B.C. Tlatilco was a village agricultural society where the deceased were buried with numerous small clay figures, including dogs.[7] The earliest hollow ceramic dog effigy found anywhere in the Americas was a product of the Chorrera culture, a descendant of the Valdivian tradition, on coastal Ecuador (sometime before 500 B.C.). This brown-and-white spotted sleepy-eyed standing dog is a technically sophisticated spouted and bridged whistling bottle. Anthropologist Donald Lathrap believes that Chorrera dogs from Ecuador were the inspiration for all the clay canines found later at the western Mexico site of Colima. "The Mexican hairless was bred as a source of meat, its low massive body having the same relationship to the contours of a normal dog as our own Angus steer has to the basic configuration of wild cattle," he writes. "The presence of this highly specialized breed of dog in Chorrera before 500 B.C. suggests a long prior history of attention to the food potential of this oldest of domesticated animals, and argues that the breed first appeared in Ecuador and from there spread to northern Peru and West Mexico."[8] This is of course a lot to conclude from just one dog effigy, but Lathrap is not alone in proposing early cultural contact between Ecuador and western Mexico.[9] Of course, Tlatilco, nearer to Colima in distance, might well have introduced the notion of burying dogs "in effigy" to western Mexico.

Almost as old as the Chorrera bottle is the curled-up spotted dog effigy jar recovered from the Jequetepeque Valley near the town of Tembladera on the north coast of Peru, dating to 700–400 B.C. This dog's tail is considerably longer than that of the Chorrera dog, but otherwise the two animals look very similar. This effigy is the first of the "sleeping dogs" that also show up at Colima, Monte Alban, Teotihuacán, and Kaminaljuhu.[10]

In addition to the plethora of ceramic dogs produced at Colima starting in about 300 B.C., small "toy" dogs with big ears were fashioned during Monte Alban II (100 B.C.–A.D. 100) in the Oaxaca Valley.[11] At Teotihuacán small, crude clay dogs started to become common in about A.D. 100. At the same time, Caribbean artisans were making a hollow, short-tailed dog with a toothy grin.

The Chorrera (Ecuador) whistling bottle dog effigy at left was created 2,000 years before the "weeping eye" dog pot from the Mississippian period (Georgia), at right. Considering the distance in time and space between them, they are remarkably similar. The underside of the Georgia pot has ten oval spots in rows to signify nipples. This dog was a female. Drawings by Susan Hochgraf. After Lathrap, 1975, and Schnell, Knight, and Schnell, 1981.

On the coast of Peru, the Moche and the Nazca were also creating spotted, spouted, stirruped, and bridged dogs after A.D. 100.[12]

Finely crafted ceramic dogs were made in about A.D. 600 in coastal Veracruz, and some of the animals have prominent vertebrae and ribs, making them look emaciated, a condition shown in some dogs from Colima as well. These skele-

Two effigy vessels. The black-and-white spotted dog (right) with a long tail comes from Tembladera, Peru (600 B.C.), and the thin orange ware dog (left) comes from Teotihuacán (100 A.D.), in central Mexico. Food offerings were probably placed in the central hole. Drawings by Susan Hochgraf. After Lapiner, 1976, and Moctezuma, 1990.

tal dogs may also be linked with death and the underworld. Also from the Veracruz region comes a series of wheeled dog toys, proving that the concept of
the wheel was known, if only used to amuse children. The Toltec, who immediately preceded the Aztec as lords of the Basin of Mexico, imported wheeled
ceramics from the east and highly burnished dog effigy jars from the Pacific
coast around A.D.1100. Dog effigy pots were made in North America during
the Mississippian (after A.D. 1000) and have been recovered sporadically
throughout the Southeast at sites dating to this period.[13] These dog effigy bot-
tles have the same small round bodies that we have seen throughout the Americas, starting 2,000 years earlier in Ecuador.

For thousands of years Native Americans molded images from clay to represent the dogs they lived with every day. Some results may seem more realis-
tic, but somehow the essential dog was preserved in the ceramic one. There are
striking similarities in the pose and expressiveness of the dogs across time and
space and between cultures. This convergence has several possible interpreta-
tions. It is reasonable to assume that dogs looked and acted in similar ways
across pottery-making America and that therefore their depictions should also
be similar. On the other hand, it is also true that dog pots were among the high-
status goods actively traded between neighboring
groups. Thus, the receivers might emulate the givers
in creating a "proper" dog pot. Specific pot forms
were frequently dispersed from their point of origin.[14] And an argument can also be made for the
movement of the dogs themselves, as seems clearly
to be the case for the hairless dog.[15]

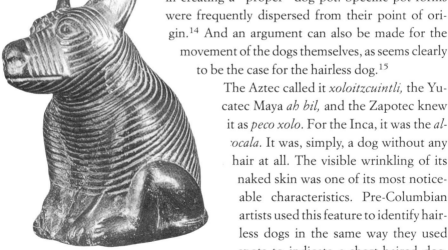

The Aztec called it *xoloitzcuintli,* the Yucatec Maya *ah bil,* and the Zapotec knew
it as *peco xolo*. For the Inca, it was the *al-*
·ocala. It was, simply, a dog without any
hair at all. The visible wrinkling of its
naked skin was one of its most noticeable characteristics. Pre-Columbian
artists used this feature to identify hairless dogs in the same way they used
spots to indicate a short-haired dog.
And thanks to the representation of
wrinkled dogs in clay effigy pots we can
trace the history of these animals
through time.

A seated hairless dog effigy in the reduction-fired
blackware typical of Chimú pottery. From the north
coast of Peru. A.D. 1200. Photograph courtesy of
Banco de Crédito del Perú, Lima.

The earliest "wrinkled" dog effigies are from Colima, whose artisans produced both smooth-skinned and wrinkled dogs. Some Maya dog effigies have wrinkles on their bodies, and when Aztec dogs show facial creases it probably indicates hairlessness. At some point after A.D. 500 this nude dog arrived in Peru; it is portrayed at first rarely among the Moche and then commonly among the potters of Chimú, Chancay, and Lambayeque. The most plausible explanation for the appearance of a "new" dog on the coast of Peru is that it was introduced as part of a longstanding exchange system between western Mexico and South America.[16]

Even though Fray Sahagún describes pouring an unguent on dogs to make them lose their hair (epigraph), hairlessness in dogs is more likely the result of genetic mutation. These dogs must have been viewed as valuable, for the mutation for hairlessness was maintained in Mexico's dog population as well as in pockets in South America.[17] The mutant gene for hairlessness also causes abnormal dentition, so that a dog with such a gene had a high probability of lacking a full set of teeth. Mandibles with missing teeth preserved in the archaeological record should serve as a means of distinguishing bald from haired animals. However, Elizabeth Wing has examined a number of buried dogs from the western Mexico post-Classic site Marismas Nacionles and has detected no abnormal dentition, which would be expected in dogs with a genetically based hairless condition. In addition, most Colima effigy dogs are portrayed with a mouth full of teeth.[18] Dog remains from Peru do not seem to have congenitally missing teeth either.[19] We must wait for archaeological confirmation to add to the evidence for hairlessness that "wrinkled" dog pots, accounts of chroniclers, and remnant populations supply.

Hairless dogs are known from the Greater Antilles, Paraguay, and Argentina, and are actively being bred in Peru and Mexico.[20] In recent years these dogs have been involved in an array of traditional cures. Their most universal use has been, and continues to be, as a living hot-water bottle; their warm skin against that of a human can take the chill off the coldest Andean night. In addition, it is thought that if a dog is placed directly on an afflicted part of the body it can help draw out and ease the pain. Among the other claims made for cures from hairless dogs, both dead and alive, are cauterization of wounds, healing of broken legs, and the curing of eye inflammations, paralysis, toothaches, gangrene, colic, and urine retention.[21] These folk remedies undoubtedly are part of the reason for the continuing appeal of hairless dogs in Mexico and Peru.

Sometimes dogs and people are placed together in a way that clearly shows an affectionate relationship between them, particularly when women were

A pug-nosed hairless dog effigy jar from the central coast of Peru shows the crowded teeth that result when a dog's mandible is so reduced. This terra cotta ceramic from Chancay is more crudely made than most pottery dating to this era from the north coast of Peru. A.D. 1200. Photograph courtesy of Banco de Crédito del Perú, Lima.

shown with dogs. The most poignant such scene, and also the most ancient, is that of a Tlatilco woman who holds a small wide-eyed dog on her lap as she receives its kiss. A Colima woman dressed only in turban and earrings holds a puppy over her shoulders as she would a baby. A Veracruz matron with an elaborate headdress holds a small spotted dog on her lap the way she might hold her human child. A well-dressed Maya matron cradles a small dog in her left arm. As mentioned previously, it is probable that among the Maya it was the women who raised the dogs. Here, in these works of art, are further reaffirmations of the antiquity of this female-canid bond.

Most of the dog effigies that we have seen so far celebrate dogs for their own sake. At least it is difficult to attribute further symbolic meaning to them based on our present knowledge. They do not appear to be players on the cosmological stage, nor do they in any obvious way "stand" for some other entity or concept. As we move into areas where dog representations seem to be primarily symbolic, we need help to understand the nature of the metaphor. The form of the dog and the meaning it conveys now take on more abstract and more complex dimensions.

Calendar Dogs and Codex Dogs

According to Mayanist Eric Thompson, only one Maya vase scene shows a naturalistic, real-life dog. This codex-style scene shows a man being carried in a litter and holding a fan, a symbol of the merchant class.[22] Behind the litter is a heavily laden porter and two other individuals carrying ceremonial staves or paddles, all of which suggest that a trading trip is being illustrated. Underneath the litter, and central to the scene, is a dog with a dark patch on its back. The prominence of the dog coupled with its uniqueness in Maya painted pottery indicates that dogs were connected to merchants, symbolically and literally.

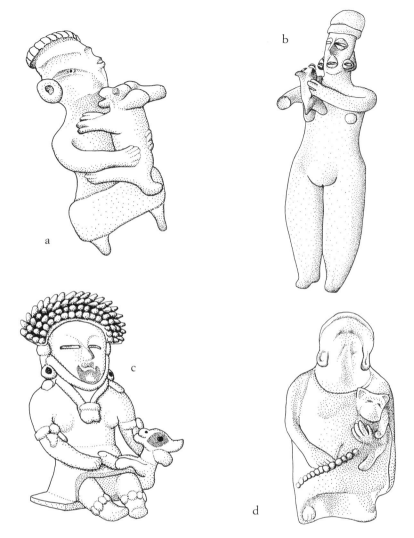

These four ceramic figures of women holding dogs in their laps or arms illustrate that the female-canine bond has deep roots in Mesoamerica. The figures are from: a. Thatilco (1200 B.C.); b. Colima, Tuxcacuesco-Ortices phase (225 B.C.); c. Veracruz (A.D. 600); and d. Altar de Sacrificios (A.D. 700). The small size of the animals suggests that these women may be holding puppies. Drawings by Susan Hochgraf. After Piña Chan, 1955, Reynolds, 1993, Goldstein, 1988, and Willey, 1972.

A dog walks underneath a litter-born man fanning himself. The dog bears one large dark patch on its back, often a Maya sign for death. The dog may be on its way to be sacrificed to Ek Chuah, the god of merchants. Rollout drawing of late Classic Maya Ratinlixul vase.

Early Yucatan chronicler Bishop Diego de Landa reports that, among the Lacandón Maya, dogs "spotted with the color of cacao" (chocolate) were sacrificed to *Ek Chuah,* the god of merchants, as well as the god of cacao.[23] Merchants thus may have been actively involved in locating and trading dogs with the right coloration for use in Maya festivals. It also is possible that the Mesoamerican merchant classes were responsible for introducing the previously unknown hairless dog into the Maya area.[24]

In 1974 a series of brightly colored murals, including one depicting Ek Chuah, the god of merchants, was discovered at Cacaxtla, a ninth-century Maya stronghold in the Puebla-Tlaxcalaba area of central Mexico. Ek Chuah is dressed in jaguar garb, and beside him rests a pack loaded with quetzal feathers, copal incense, and rubber. His headdress rests on the bundle. Although he is clearly a Maya deity he has been given a non-Maya name, 4-Dog.[25] We know 4-Dog is his name because of the four circles below the head of a dog just above his outstretched arm and the central Mexican tradition of naming an individual for a day of the ritual 260-day calendar. Usually a person's name-day was the same as his or her birthday. However, in the case of Maya God L, for whom any name-day could be selected, a name appropriate for merchants, 4-Dog, was chosen. Again, merchants and dogs seem to be linked.

Throughout pre-Conquest Mesoamerica, people placed great importance on recording the passage of time. To accomplish this they had two calendars based on a 260-day ritual cycle and a 365-day solar cycle. The 260-day ritual calendar consisted of twenty name-days and thirteen day-numbers. The 365-day solar calendar contained eighteen months of twenty days each and five nameless days. When these two calenders were joined it took fifty-two years to complete the entire cycle and return to the beginning. This was the Calendar Round. Keeping precise and long-term track of time had been at the core of Mesoamerican thought for 1,500 years before the arrival of Europeans. One of the ways they documented these cycles was in a folded, painted picture book known as a codex. Some of these precious documents presented entirely visual myths in which gods and goddess presided over their portion of the calendar. In others, the lives of nobles were recorded, festivals were described, and conquests and extracted tribute were listed.

Mesoamericans believed wholeheartedly in portents and omens. For all of life's activities there were good days and bad days, and much codex space was devoted to divining auspicious times for events to take place, particularly with regard to the agricultural cycle. The dog served as the tenth name-day in both the Maya and Aztec calendrical systems, although whether this was lucky or unlucky varied from region to region. For the Aztec it was a lucky name-day (see epigraph), while for most Maya-speaking peoples it was bad sign.[26] According to the fourth book of the Florentine Codex, bad day signs far outnumbered good day signs, but one of the rare and particularly good day signs was One Dog. This was the sign of Xiuhtecuhtli, the god of fire. On this day a great festival was held in his honor, and great riches would come to anyone born on One Dog. "And also it was said that on One Dog the owners and breeders of dogs rubbed ochre on all the dogs' heads."[27]

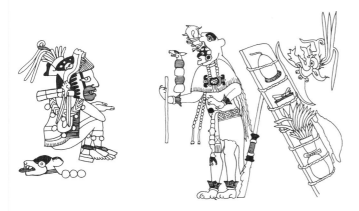

The Maya god of merchants, Ek Chuah, as 4-Dog (right), in this mural from ninth-century center of Cacaxtla, seems to be named in the Mixtec tradition as seen in the Codex Nuttall where the warrior 3-Dog (left) wears a dog headdress to reinforce his identity with the animal for whom he is named. Redrawn by Susan Hochgraf. After Nuttall, 1975, and Coe, 1994.

In addition to lending its image to part of the 260-day ritual calendar, the dog shows up in these painted books in a number of situations. In the following paragraphs I share some of my favorite dog imagery from the pages of the Mesoamerican codices. The examples were chosen to illustrate how the ancients ordered their temporal, spatial, and mythical world, as well as to add to our growing list of canine conceptualizations.

The Codex Nuttall,[28] an early colonial manuscript, is primarily a historical document recording births, marriages, victories, and other important events of the lives of flesh-and-blood Mixtec nobility, the successors to the Zapotec in the Oaxaca Valley.[29] In the Codex Nuttall, Mixtec painters made good use of day and number signs to identify the individuals being depicted. A seated male figure, 3-Dog, wears a dog headdress; by embedding his name in his head gear, this Mixtec warrior is reinforcing his name-day. Curiously, 3-Dog's feathered dog headdress appears to be similar to that on the embroidered Paracas figure from distant Peru. An analysis of known Mixtec names reveals that name-days are not randomly distributed. Certain names seemed to have been preferred and others avoided. Men were frequently called 2-Dog, which was also the name of one of the Mixtec gods, but it was an uncommon name among women.[30]

Full-bodied but dying dogs are illustrated several times as participants in heart sacrifice ceremonies. In one scene both a man and a dog are having their hearts removed, and in another, a turkey joins company with the dog. The only other use of a dog image in the Nuttall Codex is a scene in which a dog-shaped incense burner is being held by a priest. For the Mixtec, it seems, dogs were important in ritual life, warriors sometimes wore dog headdresses, and the name-day "dog" had positive male attributes.

Although probably dating to the early colonial period, the Aztec Codex Borbonicus is painted in a pure native style and is unaccompanied by text. The first part of this picture book is the *tonalamatl,* the "book of days," and the last section presents the annual festival cycles. The tonalamatl is a divinatory almanac, each page of which illus-

Blood spurts from the chest of a dog whose heart has been removed as an offering being made by the prince 5-Flower and his wife, 3-Flint, to two priests named 10-Grass and 10-Rain. A turkey has also been sacrificed. Redrawn by Susan Hochgraf. After Nuttall, 1975.

trates the gods, goddess, and objects associated with a particular thirteen-day period of the ritual 260-day calendar. This book of days contains some highly symbolic canine imagery that reveals the complexity of Aztec thought and the ways that dogs have been integrated into it. The sixteenth period is presided over by the canine god, Xolotl, and the dead sun god. The Nahuatl word *xolo,* meaning slave or attendant, forms the basis for the name of this god as well as for xoloitzcuintli, the hairless dog. Perhaps because of this connection, a slave collar is centrally placed just under the sky band in this illustration. Dogs are iconographically linked in a number of ways to the Dead Sun, who is being consumed by the Earth Monster. For the Aztec this would not have been an auspicious time.

In Aztec art the Earth Monster was female, but femininity at its most dangerous. This female entity was always trying to devour the sun. Female Aztec goddesses were generally pretty scary.[31] Take, for example, Xochiquetzal (flower quetzal-feather), who personified the youthful aspect of that great and terrifying womb, the Earth Monster. The alluring Xochiquetzal was the goddess of love and female sexual power and mistress of the nineteenth period of the tonalamatl. She served as the patroness of weavers[32] and presided over pregnancy and childbirth but was also associated with licentiousness.[33] In the Codex Borbonicus she is shown sitting on a spotted dog. The heavily burdened dog joins Xochiquetzal in its role as eater of carrion and human excrement and indiscriminate copulater.[34] A snake exits from between the goddess's legs and a centipede crawls from beneath the stool. Here we see, graphically, that female sexuality is linked to other bodily functions, defecation (the dog), menstruation (the snake), and urination (the centipede). This connection is even more explicit in another tonalamatl, from the Telleriano-Remensis Codex, in which the dog extrudes from Xochiquetzal's feathered rear end. This is a perception of dogs that we have seen before and will discuss in detail later.

In the second part of the Codex Borbonicus, one of the most important of all Aztec festivals, the New Fire Ceremony, is visually portrayed. This *toxiuh-molpilli* ("the binding of our years") rite was held every fifty-two years when the Calendar Round had finished its cycle. At the start of the festival, all fires, whether in homes or in temples, were extinguished, and every floor was swept clean. Next, special deity impersonators moved in slow procession to light the new fire in a sacred spot. All other fires were then lit with sparks from this sacred fire. If this ceremony was not performed properly, the Aztec believed that their world—the World of the Fifth Sun—would end. Dogs, according to the Legend of the Five Suns, were associated with this rite from the beginning.

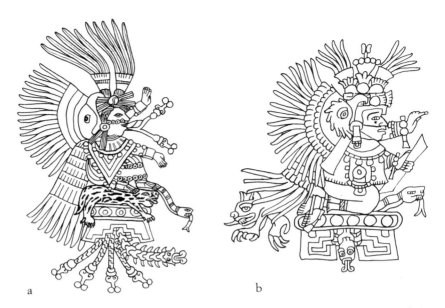

Views of Xochiquetzal, the goddess of sexual love, in two Aztec tonalamatl *(book of days). In each she wears the head of a quetzal bird and large flowers to connote her name (flower quetzal-feather). The lower part of her face is painted red. Dogs, centipedes, and snakes are her companion animals. She is associated with flowers, feasting, pleasure, and other morally questionable aspects of Aztec life.* a. Codex Borbonicus, 19, *and* b. Codex Telleriano-Remensis, 22V. *Redrawn by Susan Hochgraf.*

The very first fire was started by the only couple left after the flood at the end of the fourth sun; they were then turned into dogs. When the skies were created at the beginning of the fifth sun, the "dogs sent up smoke" and the New Fire Ceremony was established.[35]

In the implementation of the New Fire Ceremony as shown in Codex Borbonicus 34, four impersonators are dressed as dead warriors, the younger brothers of the fire god, Xiuhtecuhtli. Each dead warrior carries, along with his bundles of long sticks, a blue dog. The dead warriors represent the four cardinal directions; Xiuhtecuhtli himself is in the center of the conflagration. The blue dog joins the dead warrior and the god of fire to start time's cycle again and keep the fifth sun of the Aztec in the sky.[36] In another tonalamatl, in the Aubin Collection, the god of fire has as his companion the blue dog while carrying on discussions with the god of the planet Venus. Here the blue dog's association with fire continues but the dog also serves as a day sign. Remember that Xiuhtecuhtli's day sign is 1-Dog.

The Florentine Codex, as I have mentioned, is the master work of Fray

Bernardino de Sahagún. It contains his interviews with people from all levels of Aztec society with illustrations by native artists and texts in Nahuatl and Spanish. This is an English translation of how dogs were described to Sahagún by Aztec people in Nahuatl: "Some [are] shaggy, woolly. . . . The muzzles are large, with large teeth [and] with small, pointed teeth. The ears are pointed, concave, hairy, shaggy. The head is round, bowl-shaped. It has claws, long claws. It is domesticated, a house-dweller, a favorite companion, a constant companion, which follows running. It is happy, amusing; a tail-wagger, a barker, which lays its ears back, it wags its tail. . . . Its food is maize, raw meat, cooked meat. It eats all: the flesh of the dead, the spoiled; it eats the revolting, the stinking, the rotting."[37]

Even though the Aztec recognized the companionable nature of the dog, they seemed unable to overlook its eating habits. In a manner that seems to be universal, when the Aztec compared an individual to a dog it was never intended to be a compliment to the person or to the animal. This point is driven home in Book 10 of the Florentine Codex, in which we learn about the people who made up Aztec society—their occupations and their family life. In typical Nahuatl moralizing style, as each virtuous maiden, well-spoken noble, and accomplished stonecutter is described, so is his or her opposite character put forth. Thus we also have the dishonored maiden, the greedy noble, and the builder of leaning walls. However, there are only two types of people whose characters are described as doglike: "The Harlot" and "The Possessed One." Neither of these types has a good side, as these passages make quite clear. "[The harlot is] oblivious of what all know her to be; a petty old woman, a free yielder of herself, a whore from a brothel, a deflowered one, a lascivious old woman; of itching buttocks—an old woman of itching buttocks; an aged woman, a flabby old woman, a filthy one; a filthy old dog who brings herself to ruin like a dog."[38] The possessed one "destroys people, he burns wooden figures of them; he bleeds himself over others, destroys them by deception, depresses their hearts. He turns himself into a dog, a bird, a screech owl, an owl, a horned owl."[39] The "filthy old dog" of the Florentine Codex is also an amusing, happy tail-wagger of all colors and shapes. It is the animal cooked with turkey but hidden underneath it when served, and the dog guide in the underworld.

The Codex Mendoza, a colonial Aztec painted book, is concerned with worldly affairs. Its first part parades before us each Aztec conquest and presents itemized lists of the tribute extracted from all the defeated pueblos. In this codex one sees the full ability of the Aztec to convey information through picture writing. To record the conquered lands they combined several conventional images to express the place name phonetically. The Codex Mendoza contains 612 such name glyphs. Although two identical dogs were used as part of place names, they represent different sounds. One place was called *Yzcuin-tepe* ("On the hill of the dog"), the combined Nahuatl word for "dog" *itzcuin(tli)*, "hill" *tepe(tli)*, and "on" *c*. Another glyph shows the same spotted dog under a tree. The place name is *Chichiquavtla*, or "where there are many *chichiquauhtla* trees." Here the informal Nahua name for dog, *chichi*, is used to refer to the spotted animal.[40]

In Maya codices dogs play phonetic roles similar to their roles in the Codex Mendoza. The Maya, however, had a true writing system and the ability to convey information grammatically as well as phonetically and through images. Although not all Maya hieroglyphics have been deciphered, what is known reveals a subtlety and richness lacking in the pictographic systems of the Aztec and the Mixtec. The Maya also made greater use of dog-related syllables and symbols.

The Maya hieroglyphic that stands for "dog" consists of two phonetic signs, the first of which is *tzu*, which resembles (a dog's?) ribs and a back bone. *Tzu* is attached to the second syllable *l(u)* to form the word *tzul*. In Yucatec Maya *tzul* means both dog and backbone. After the Conquest, the more common word for dog among the Yucatec was *pek* for the short-haired dog and *ah bil* for the hairless dog. The Tzeltal Maya referred to the dog as *tz'i*, closer to central Mexican words for the animal. The word *pek* has several secondary meanings, including bad weather, water tank, chills and fever, and certain skin diseases, and may be a post-Conquest word and cognate for "pig."[41]

In addition, the tenth day sign of the Maya calender was *Oc* (dog). The glyph for Oc appears as a varyingly abstract head of a dog, represented as a dog with two black spots by its ear or just by black dots and a suggested ear. These sore ears are similar in origin to the ragged ears on Xolotl and on other dogs of central Mexico. Sore and ripped ears on dogs in lowland Mexico such as those depicted in Maya and Aztec art are probably the result of Chiclero's ulcer (*Leishmaniasis*), a disease caused by a biting fly.[42] Chiclero's ulcer must have had a substantial impact on Mesoamerican dog populations to show up as often as it does in the mangled ears of dog effigies. Western Mexican effigies as well as those from North and South America show no such deformities.

The sixth month of the Maya 365-day calendar is *Xul*, often depicted by a dog's head with a "tail" of the sun. This interpretation is strengthened by the Xul sign's likeness to a wrinkled Xolotl and the fact that the words *xol* and *sul* mean both dog and Xolotl in various Mesoamerican languages. Thus the Xul animal may be the ritual dog that led the sun to the underworld. The fourteenth

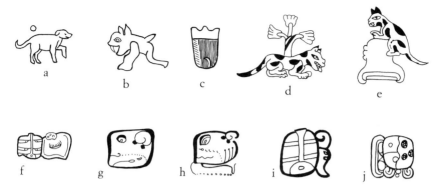

Dogs as glyphs in Mesoamerican writing systems. In top row are Aztec glyphs for Ce itzcuintli, "One Dog," the day sign: a. from the Florentine Codex, b. from the Codex Aubin, c. from the Codex Fejéráry-Mayer; d. Chichiquauhtla, *"where there are many Chichiquahtla trees" (place name), Codex Mendoza; e.* Yzcuitntepec *"on the hill of the dog" (place name), Codex Mendoza. Maya glyphs: f.* tzul, *dog; g.* Oc, *tenth day of 260-day ritual calendar; h.* Xul, *sixth month of the 365-day solar calendar; i.* Kankin, *fourth month of 365-day solar calendar; j.* way, *animal soul companion. Drawings by Susan Hochgraf.*

month of the 365-day calendar, *Kankin,* is sometimes represented as the ribs of a dog in a similar manner to that of the dog glyph. At other times Kankin is represented by a glyph with a doglike head or with a circle with crosshatching meant to stand for black and also the spot of a dog.[43]

The Dresden Codex, one of four Maya picture books that survive, is a series of ritual-astronomical almanacs in which the dog appears in a number of guises. Most often it is shown holding a torch. This is the dog of fire and lightning. In one section a spotted dog with its tongue protruding hangs from a bar that is the glyph for sky. In its left forelimb it holds a flaming torch while over its head is the *kan* glyph and the headdress of the maize god. Both the glyph and the headdress stand for an abundance of maize. This kan dog is an augury that brings the best of tidings. In another Maya codex, the Madrid, dogs are also connected with maize. In one scene a dog sits beside Chac, the rain god, as he plants corn, and in another a dog is perched on a stool with tortillas on his back.[44] Bishop Landa mentions that old women danced holding ceramic dogs with bread on their backs during a festival that he witnessed (see epigraph).

Not all Dresden dogs predict a good harvest. Elsewhere we see a bound upside-down dog being kneeled upon by Chac. In the next scene Chac is holding the tail of the still tied-up dog and throwing it onto a stone pyramid for sacrifice. This dog is the tzul dog of bad weather.[45] As in this case, Maya dog im-

Dogs of the Madrid (a–b) and Dresden (c–f) codices: a. dog beside Chac, the god of rain, who plants maize; b. dog with maize bread on its back sitting on a stool; c. fire dog with abundance of maize sign hanging from a sky band; d. dog with "speech scroll" as Husband of Moon Goddess; e. dog with "speech scroll" in sexual union with female vulture; f. tied and upside-down dog under a kneeling Chac. Redrawn by Susan Hochgraf. After Villacorta and Villacorta, 1930.

agery sometimes is used in connection with the north, a direction from which an ill wind blows.

Another section of the Dresden Codex presents a series of highly repetitive prognostications featuring the moon goddess and protagonists with whom she is interacting. In one of these encounters she sits eyeball to eyeball with a spotted dog with a speech scroll coming from its mouth, sores on its ears, and prominent vertebrae. The dog and the goddess are the same size, wear identical necklaces, and sit in a position meant to represent coitus. The accompanying hieroglyphics state that on one *Manik* (the seventh day) Little Chel (the moon goddess) is the Wife of Dog, its omen.[46] In another scene a large spotted cropped-eared dog with an erect penis is talking to a female king vulture with a human body as she sits on a mat. The mat may symbolize marriage. This couple is also wearing matching beads. A celestial conjunction is the most probable event being evoked by the union of these two scavengers and eaters of filth.

Two of the fire dogs are white except around the eyes, and all the other dogs from the Dresden Codex are uniformly spotted. The kan dog of maize, the tzul dog of bad weather, and the dogs of fire and lightning have unblemished ears while the dogs conjoining with the moon goddess and the female vulture have sores or disfigured ears. The connection of sexual activity with disease, and particularly with syphilis, is being evoked here with the sore ears of these dogs. The exposed backbone of the moon goddess dog signals death. Death is part of these couplings: women and dogs equal sex and death.

Women, Men, and Dogs: More on the Triangle

For the Aztec, sexuality was controlled by the liver in the lower part of the body. This area belonged to the female sphere and to such bodily functions as digestion and excretion. The lower body also corresponded to the rotten, smelly spheres of death and the underworld. This was the realm of Xochiquetzal and dogs, as we saw in the Codex Borbonicus. These dual concepts of above and below fit equally with the cardinal directions, the south being above, following the course of the sun and warmth, and north being below and associated with cold and the underworld. Dogs, as promiscuous and as eaters of excrement, are logically associated with the lower part of the body and with females. They are also linked with the north and the underworld. In the Maya codices we have seen these same canine associations with the north, the underworld, and the carnal. The Maya calendric canine sign *Oc* was linked with adultery, and a person born under that sign was thought to be prone to sexual excess.[47] In the Dresden Codex male dogs were involved in sexual union with the moon goddess and a female king vulture.

The dog and vulture were paired in another medium from the Weeden Island McKeithern Site I (A.D. 500), in northern Florida, on a pot with a pair of dogs facing two vultures, one of which has been made into a spout. Discovered in a cache with seventeen other vessels, the dog and vulture pot had a prefired "kill" hole indicating that it had been made for ceremonial purposes. In Florida, as in the Yucatan, dogs and vultures were paired because of their habit

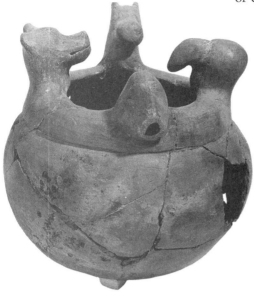

Dogs paired with vultures on a pottery vessel from the Weeden Island McKeithen Site I, Florida. 14 cm at lip. Photograph courtesy of Jerald T. Milanich.

of eating carrion. They may have also been regarded by this early Florida society as symbols of impropriety and incest and therefore inedible.[48]

Fertility and sexual excess were themes sometimes expressed using dog subjects. Reproductive activity in canines may have been an easier subject to deal with than human sexuality. As if to make that point precisely, potters from Colima created a female dog with human legs provocatively spread, as well as copulating animals.[49] In addition, bitches who are about to give birth or who have just given birth can be seen in numerous ceramic pieces. A squat dog pot recovered from a grave at Cemochechobee, a Mississippian ceremonial center in Georgia, had ten oval spots painted on its belly indicating that the dog was pregnant or lactating.[50] Lying upon a beautifully crafted stirrup pot, a hairless dog from the Chimú contentedly nurses four puppies.

Male dogs with prominent genitalia were often depicted as well. In central Mexico the Toltec produced a somber stone sculpture of a hairless hound. This dog has very small ears relative to the size of his face, and a pronounced sagittal ridge running the length of his skull. He is well equipped genitally. On the north coast of Peru, the Nazca landscape line dog drawing has a penis as long as its legs. It seems clear that the Nazca dog was meant to invoke fertility. In addition, the dog also appears to have nipples just behind its front legs. Perhaps the people of the Nazca though that a dog with both male and female sexual organs would increase their chances for successful harvests.

At Teotihuacán, warfare was a reality of political life, and it was the coyote rather than the dog who symbolized military might. Warriors dressed in costumes that evoked jaguars, eagles, or coyotes to bring to themselves some of the fierceness of these predators. In addition, human heart sacrifice was illustrated for the first time in Mesoamerica, and the coyote was clearly associated with this ritual. In the White Patio at Atetelco, one of Teotihuacán's residential palaces, a mural covers an entire wall in vivid shades of red. Along its base are four large coyotes wearing feathered headdresses. Speech scrolls are coming from their mouths. Above these quadrupeds are biped coyotes in full military regalia flanked by coyote heads. The mural is filled with coyote warrior/sacrifice imagery. On an adjoining wall are more coyotes, this time with hearts dripping with blood just below their gaping mouths.[51] The nobles living in this palace clearly identified their ethnic group with this powerful talking coyote.

Two other murals from Teotihuacán are silent but awesome testimony to the importance of this animal being. In one painting two coyotes are ripping the heart from a deer, a metaphorical depiction of human heart sacrifice by the victorious coyote warriors. This powerful image is unique in Teotihuacán art, which is frequently characterized by standardized motifs and repetitious design elements. Another striking painting shows a coyote with an elaborate headdress holding a large sacrificial knife while an equally impressive speech scroll emerges from his open mouth. The scroll is decorated with waterlily pads and buds. Speech and oration must have been the key method of communication in a society that did not record its history in written form. Thus, this coyote figure must be making a monumental pronouncement that citizens of the city would already be familiar with through the oral tradition of the society. In conjunction with the netted jaguar, the plumed puma, and

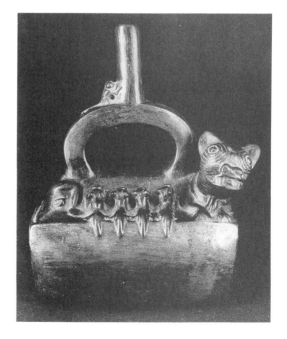

A hairless bitch wearing a collar nurses her puppies on this square-based stirrup bottle from Chimú, Peru. Note an additional pup clings to the junction of the arch and spout. Placing such a figure at this location is typical of Chimú pottery. A.D. 1200. Courtesy of the Banco de Crédito del Perú, Lima.

the feathered serpent, the coyote of the heart sacrifice embodied one of the core beliefs of Teotihuacános.[52] Unlike elsewhere in Mesoamerica, cults and worship did not revolve around individuals striving to record their conquests through monuments, written texts, or the keeping of time. History did not seem to be central to Teotihuacán's view of itself. Rather, the place itself, with its sacred caves and mountains, symbolized the corporate existence of this great city. In such a place animal beings seemed to control the natural order and were imbued with the wisdom by which the society organized itself.

Dogs were viewed very differently from coyotes in the Teotihuacán universe. A dog mural from the residential compound of Tetitla has no speech scroll or headdress.[53] Dogs were most commonly represented on a small scale, as in the

small sleeping dog pots in thin orange ware imported from the Putun Maya area. These and other dog effigies were crafted without adornment and in naturalistic poses. A total of 1,068 animal figurines and motifs were found among the artifacts collected from excavations at two of the elite residential compounds, Yayahuala and Tetitla. The most common animals depicted were dogs, with 402 examples.[54] Some dog heads show wrinkling, suggesting that they might have been hairless, while others have rounded or floppy ears. The small size of the figurines and their expressive puppylike faces make one wonder if they were children's toys or diminutive models of pet dogs. The dog was a docile domestic creature, whereas the coyote was a warrior. These canids stood at the two poles of human existence: hearth, home, and companionship on the one hand, and the outward projection of blood sacrifice and warfare on the other.

A stone sculpture of a seated male dog with ridged skull, cropped ears, and wrinkled face. The wrinkles may indicate a hairless condition, and the ears suggest Chiclero's ulcer. The prominent sagittal ridge is puzzling, but it might be present to reinforce this dog's other male attributes. Toltec, A.D. 1200. 17 cm. Courtesy of the Yale University Art Gallery, Stephen Carlton Clark, B.A. 1903, Fund.

Seven hundred years after the demise of the great city of Teotihuacán, when the Aztec came into power, the coyote warrior cult was still a powerful presence in the Basin of Mexico. The coyote warrior suit is illustrated six times in the Codex Mendoza and appears in other Aztec documents as well. The headdress of the Mendoza costume consisted of a frame fashioned like a coyote head and covered with yellow parrot feathers. It also had a crest of quetzal feathers. Other early documents show that these costumes were also made from blue, white, red, black, and violet feathers.[55] The Aztec used their ability to extract tribute from areas where birds with brilliantly colored feathers lived and were able to obtain

Mural of a coyote wearing a feather headdress with a speech scroll coming from its mouth. Directly below its mouth is a heart dripping with blood. At the Atelelco compound, Teotihuacán, coyotes patrol the bottom level of a room filled with repeating warrior and geometric motifs. All the murals were painted in contrasting shades of red. Photograph courtesy of Michael D. Coe.

the most glorious regalia of any warrior. But the tradition from which the Aztec drew their coyote garb started at Teotihuacán.

South America's Dogs of the Ancestor Spirits and Companion Dogs

In South America, the fox or zorro (*Dusicyon*) performed much the same role as the coyote in the Basin of Mexico. It was sometimes referred to as *perro de los machulas* (dog of the ancestor spirits) and was considered the younger brother of the puma. In Andean communities it is thought that a fox's howling predicts the success or failure of the growing season. If howling was heard in October and November, plenty of rain and a good harvest would follow. It was bad luck for a fox to howl in March.[56] As mentioned earlier, during Vegas times in Ecuador (6500–5000 B.C.) twenty-seven foxes provided teeth for a single human grave, signaling an early start to the symbolic importance of this animal in South American folklore.[57]

In the time of the Inca, young unmarried men were assigned the duty of guarding the crops that were some distance from the village. The Inca chronicler Guaman Poma illustrated these men with fox skins on their backs attempting to scare away crop-raiding birds and foxes. In addition to its ability to predict the outcome of the harvest, the fox was considered a thief and a trickster.[58] On the other hand, this astute animal also symbolized the ability to over-

Pre-Columbian men often chose to "put on the dog" for warfare and ritual: a. Eastern Woodland shaman wearing wolf skin and teeth; b. Nazca shaman wearing fox skin headdress; c. Inca youth wearing fox skin to protect crops; d. Teotihuacán coyote warrior; e. Aztec warrior wearing yellow feather coyote suit; f. Colima "warrior" with dog on helmet; g. Maya man wearing dog headdress; h. Moche fox warrior. Drawing by Susan Hochgraf.

come obstacles.[59] Foxes were well integrated into the mythic fabric of Andean worldviews, and their role was quite distinct from that played by domestic dogs. The contrasting iconography devoted to these animals is evident in two of the most provocative ceramic styles to develop in the Americas.

After 100 A.D. several artistically and technically accomplished regional pottery styles developed on the coast of Peru.[60] The most distinctive of these styles were those of the Nazca potters on Peru's south coast and the Moche artisans on the north coast. The double-spout-and-bridge and the stirrup bottle were among the most characteristic ceramic forms developed in South America. The Nazca typically produced the double-spout-and-bridge bottle while the Moche made the stirrup bottle with a single spout. Both cultures developed complex iconography with mythical beings, as well as depicted naturalistic animals and plants from their environment. In addition, the Nazca and the Moche, like the Teotihuacáno, produced unadorned dogs but imbued wild canids with mythical powers.

The Nazca people flourished on the south coast of Peru from A.D. 100 to 600. Cahuachi, a large ceremonial complex, served as the central pilgrimage site for the lineage groups living in the surrounding area.[61] Overlooking Cahuachi was an arid plateau on which the Nazca people created monumental "geoglyphs," or ground drawings. These Nazca "lines" can be thought of as sacred walkways and images used to implore the gods for rain, the designs being visible to deities residing in the nearby mountains. The lines were created by removing the dark-

The Moche stirrup bottle (left) of a spotted dog and the Nazca double spout and bridge bottle (right) of a dog playing with a stick illustrate both the differences in the ceramic styles of the two cultures and the similarity of the naturalistic way they represented their dogs. Drawing by Susan Hochgraf. After Alva and Donnan, 1993; Tello, 1931.

colored stones that littered the plateau and then sweeping the area clean to reveal the white soil beneath. Most of the designs consist of straight lines, geometric forms, and spirals, but some are figures of animals. The animals depicted have water associations, such as the shark and the killer whale, and the spider, a creature whose appearance above ground is a portent of rain.[62] The same motifs are found on Nazca pots. The purpose of the dog, in conjunction with the other lines, was to facilitate the Nazca people's continual quest for rain.

Pilgrimages to sacred places have a long tradition in the Andes. The person making a pilgrimage becomes the ritual representative of his community, and thus the individual enhances his own prestige by undertaking such a journey. In an unusual modeled scene, a Nazca potter created a group of people making such a pilgrimage. According to Julius Tello, an early Peruvian archaeologist, this is a family, dressed in their very best clothes, on their way to a ceremonial center and bringing with them offerings or tribute.[63] The father plays a panpipe while the mother walks behind him carrying another pipe. Two parrots are on her shoulders. The daughter brings up the rear, carrying a double-spouted bottle and another parrot. The two sons head the procession, and four spotted dogs flank the parents. A fifth dog, a puppy, is held by the patriarch. The dogs and parrots may have been gifts intended for the priests or items to exchange with other pilgrims. Or perhaps these five dogs were to be sacrificed

A modeled Nazca scene in which five spotted dogs and three pet parrots accompany three men and two women, perhaps a family, on a pilgrimage. All are dressed in their best clothes and carry items of value to offer to priests or to exchange with other pilgrims. The dogs and parrots may be offerings as well. After Tello, 1931.

and eaten at journey's end. Whatever the case, this scene indicates that dogs were important participants in the pilgrimage.

As the Nazca line dog suggests, dogs may have been key elements in ceremonies to create rain. The Inca reportedly tied up dogs to make them howl so that it would rain. A story from Mexico is also about dogs and rainmaking. Shortly after the Conquest, a Spaniard named Diego Muñoz Camargo witnessed a scene that may have been similar to the one created by the Nazca potter. He says that during a time of drought the local people, after fasting and doing penance, went in a procession carrying a large number of hairless dogs (*xoloitzcuintli*) in a litter to a temple named for the dogs, *Xoloteupan*. After arriving at the temple the people sacrificed the dogs by removing their hearts. As soon as the dogs died there was lightning, thunder, and great quantities of rain. The sacrificed dogs were later eaten.[64] At Nazca artists have shown another procession of dogs in a place where water was always the focus of attention. Perhaps, in the parched southern area where the Nazca lived, dogs were also sacrificed to ease droughts.

Foxes, on the other hand, had a different function in Nazca iconography. When portrayed in a naturalistic fashion their whiskers are always prominently featured. Whiskers were the essential part of their being that was "borrowed" by the Nazca to create mythical composite deities. These complex forms include feline, falcon, and fox motifs intertwined with human elements, particularly heads with protruding tongues. One ceramic piece portrays a man, probably a shaman, with a fox skin on his head. The fox's protruding tongue, white whiskers, and the whites of his eyes are mirrored on the mask that the individual wears. The man's body is enshrouded by a garment decorated with twisted elements consisting of many human "trophy heads" with their tongues hanging from their mouths. Such powerful and twisted imagery was reserved for foxes and other wild beings, not the Nazca spotted dogs.

The Moche style of fine-line drawing on ceramic pieces is matched only by the master painters of the Maya vase. Foxlike figures are frequently illustrated in these complex Moche scenes, usually in warrior apparel. These figures represent either human warriors dressed in fox regalia or mythical foxes symbolizing those warrior clans that were associated with foxes. Whatever the case, the fox holds a place quite a distinct from that of the dog in Moche art. Fox warriors are fully equipped with clubs, throwing sticks, darts, and shields.[65]

The dog, always unadorned, performs its role as companion at the main ritual events depicted on Moche ceramics. In a ritual that Christopher Donnan calls the Sacrifice Ceremony the Warrior Priest receives a goblet filled with the

A black and white spotted dog is companion to the Moche Warrior Priest in these two scenes. On the top the Warrior Priest prepares to drink from a cup of the blood of captives. Below he rides in his litter, surrounded by his animal warriors. In both scenes his dog is at his side. Drawing by Donna McClelland from photographs by Christopher Donnan (top), and after Kutscher, 1954 (bottom).

blood of vanquished foes from the owl deity. Between this pair and directly beneath the goblet is a small spotted dog. A priestess with braided snake hair and a priest with a headdress with serrated streamers observe the ritual. In the lower register captives are having their throats slit to add to the bloody drink. A seal sits in the Warrior Priest's snaked-headed litter. In Sipán Tomb 1, the main body had beside him ritual paraphernalia very similar to that of the central figures in this scene. Donnan and others are convinced that the Sacrifice Ceremony was actually performed by a real Warrior Priest, one of whom was buried at Sipán.[66] For this story, however, what is most significant is that the Moche Warrior Priest had a dog by his side in life as well as in death.

In another Moche vase scene the Warrior Priest is riding in the rayed litter. He is blowing a fox trumpet and is surrounded by humanized animal warriors armed for combat. Animal beings of all sorts have joined the march. Flying fish, hummingbird, and iguana warriors march beside hawk and owl fighters. The three fox warriors can be recognized by their bicolored tails. Two black dogs and one black dog with white spots are in the procession, though they remain on all fours and without weaponry. In the litter, the white dog with black spots sits beside the Warrior Priest. From its privileged perch, the dog peeks out, its face revealing pleasure at getting such a ride. Wherever the Warrior Priest goes, his dog is right beside him.

Discussions with a contemporary *curandero* (shamanic folk healer), Eduardo Calderón, have provided some hints to the possible meaning of some of the iconography depicted in Moche art. He explains that Peruvians on the north coast value the dog because of its swiftness and its ability to track lost items and runaway people. Dogs can also see spirits. Eduardo says that two types of dogs possess these supernatural qualities: the *alcosunca* (the spotted short-haired dog) and the *alcocala* (the hairless dog).[67] In other words, the native dogs of Peru are the only ones with these special abilities. These dogs were the dogs of the Moche.

The Eastern Woodlands Dog: Pipes and Pots

Dogs and other canids were associated with war in North America. Preparation for battle included ritual consumption of dog meat, particularly in the northeast. Dog soldiers were considered the bravest of all the military societies on the Plains in the nineteenth century. In artistic renditions of North America, however, dogs show up predominately in the form of small round effigy pots or in connection with a more peaceful ritual, smoking tobacco in pipes. Animals portrayed on North American pipes tended to be naturalistic in form although they were representing spirit emissaries. These animal spirits had the ability to bestow power to those who sought them out. The smoking of tobacco in ceremonial pipes functioned as a prayer, an invocation to the spirit world for guidance and aid.[68] Dogs were among the animals portrayed on pipes.

An early example of a dog effigy pipe comes from the Woodland period Copena mound in

A tubular dog-effigy pipe carved from steatite. Animals portrayed on these "great pipes" were those who acted as spiritual guides and protectors. From Copena Mound, Alabama. Middle Woodland Period, A.D. 200–660. Photograph © 1996 The Detroit Institute of Arts, © Dirk Bakker.

*Large stone effigy pipe with an animal clinging to the square-
rimmed bowl. The finely incised lines ringing the bowl were
probably made with metal tools. From Burr's Hill, a
seventeenth-century Wampanoag burial ground, Warren,
Rhode Island. Courtesy of the National Museum of the
American Indian, Smithsonian Institution.*

Alabama. This dog, whose body forms the body of the pipe, has small pointed ears and a stub-like tail. The pipe is ground stone steatite and fifteen centimeters long. A second dog effigy pipe, from the Mississippian period, is ceramic rather than of stone and depicts a short-legged, curly-tailed animal.[69] Much smaller than the Woodland pipe, it is only four centimeters in length.

This dog and some Mississippian effigy pots show remarkably curly tails, a feature not characteristic of Mesoamerican or South American canids. Curly tails are, of course, typical of arctic dogs. Both of the buried dogs from the Mississippian Etowah site had their tails curled over their backs, suggesting that they had some affinities to northern dogs.[70] Curly tails may have been a predominantly North American trait.

A stone pipe from New England has a long-tailed animal clinging to its cup. This pipe was excavated from Burr's Hill mound in Warren, Rhode Island. Burr's Hill is a seventeenth-century contact period Wampanoag site whose artifacts include objects made of iron and other trade goods in addition to ceramics and lithics. A site report published in 1980 identifies this animal as a wolf or mountain lion.[71] The open mouth and floppy ears suggest a panting dog, whereas the long tail has a more feline than canine look to it. Although the identification of the type of animal being portrayed is often not possible or subject to conflicting opinions, the quadruped on this Wampanoag pipe looks most like a dog to me.

Transformations and Composite Creatures

Perhaps the most difficult art to grasp is that illustrating transformational and composite figures. These representations depict events in which people ceremonially transform themselves into animals or deities. People performed these rites for a number of reasons: to increase their power in warfare, for success in hunting, for rain and a good harvest, and for healing the sick. One way this transformation could be achieved was to wear the skin of the animal spirit being called forth. In North America medicine men and shamans wore wolf skins and bearskins and danced as long as it took to get the results they were looking for.

Pre-Conquest evidence of this well-known historic phenomenon was unearthed at the Late Woodland Adena site at Wright's Mound in Kentucky. A spatula-shaped cut wolf maxilla was discovered partially within the mouth cavity of a man's skull. This worked maxilla was part of the wolf mask worn by this individual in life as well as death. The man's incisor teeth were missing and the alveoli were resorbed, showing that the tooth loss occurred well before death. The transformation of this individual into his wolf alter-ego took place when the wolf's skin was placed on his head and the wolf's teeth placed in his mouth.[72]

We have already seen records of animal masks and headdresses associated with warriors and with shamans, but these were not the only people for whom such transmissions were deemed appropriate. We know that some transformations occurred best in the context of dancing, and that dancing was an essential part of public rituals for many American peoples. No group, however, left behind the visual record of the supreme significance of dancing as did the Maya. During the act of dancing, humans underwent mystical alterations into supernatural beings by means of a visionary trance. The Maya transformed into their *wayob,* their animal soul companions, their animal co-essences. Not only do we see that humans merged with their wayob because they dance and because of their appearance, but also because the literate Maya had a glyph for *way.* This small sign lets us know that people are transforming or have transformed into their soul companions.[73]

One way, *sak ox oc,* or White-Three-Dog, is of particular interest. The dancer on the vase, painted by the Altar de Sacrificios artist, is wearing a large canine headdress and, according to his glyph, dancing his *way* as White-Three-Dog.[74] White is a color associated with nobility, suggesting royal rank for this dancer. Dancing thus attired, the Maya reached out to their co-essences and transcended reality and its boundaries. In another scene, set in a palace, the dancing has proceeded so far that the dog has lost all human features except bipedality. But it is clearly dancing and holds a spider monkey on its back while other monkeys frolic nearby.[75] And, for the final stage of this transforming process, on a vase with many mythic underworld creatures are three ragged-eared dogs with the *way* sign and the White-Three-Dog sign telling us where this *way* resides. All its human qualities have been lost in this land of spirits.[76]

As supernaturals, dogs transcended earthly species and moved into another realm along with other powerful *ways.* The most powerful of all beings and all

A Maya lord dancing as his way *White-Three-Dog in a detail from a late Classic Maya vase by the Altar de Sacrificios master painter. To invoke his spirit companion he wears a dog headdress with spotted ears, furry pants, and spotted cuffs. At his waist is a sacrificial knife, and he carries a serpent-shaped staff. As Maya lords danced, trancelike, they reached the places where otherworldly creatures lived. Drawing by Susan Hochgraf. After Freidel, Schele, and Parker, 1993.*

ways was the jaguar. And when dog and jaguar merge in the Maya underworld, the most bizarre of creatures is formed: the jaguar-dog. We have already seen a long-eared underworld dog with jaguar spots (see page 28).[77] In another series of pots this merging has gone further still. More monstrous than the others, these jaguar-dogs show the wrinkled faces of hairless dogs as well as a canine's ragged ears. They wear fringed sacrificial shawls and hold an eyeball, a long bone, and a hand in a bowl. Their bodies have jaguar spots, as do many underworld animals, and their tails are featherlike. The glyphs refer to the tail as a "fire tail," suggesting that it is smoking or on fire.[78] The Maya jaguar-dog has a combination of features that joined a host of concepts into a single creation. This creature is the embodiment of death, fire, disease, and sacrifice. This is the most abstract yet most inclusive metaphorical dog that was ever produced in the Americas.

Peter Roe has put forth the argument that dogs, on the predator-poor Caribbean Islands, functioned as mythic substitutions for jaguars of a distantly remembered past.[79] The Maya vase painters produced the otherworldly jaguar-dogs. The Achuar of the Peruvian Amazon did not have dogs before the Conquest, and when European bred animals arrived among them, the Achuar classified them with the jaguar. *Yawa* means both jaguar and dog in the language of the Achuar.[80]

The Teotihuacáno, on the other hand, saw nothing catlike about dogs but, in contrast to Maya and Caribbean peoples, had a real-life canid predator, the coyote, living among them.[81] The coyotelike South American fox was the canine predator of choice for Andean potters. The wolf and the coyote had those predatory instincts on which so much North American imagery is built. In fact, in all areas of the Americas, dogs have been traditionally viewed as quite separate animals from "wild dogs," although their interrelatedness was understood. Instead, otters, because of their propensity for playfulness, were some-

The jaguar-dog is one of an underworld triad that includes a toad, also with jaguar spots, and a spider monkey with deer ears. Both the dog and the toad carry sacrificial bowls containing body parts. The inscription tells us that these creatures are wayob, *animal spirit companions. Late Classic Maya vase. Rollout photograph K1181, © Justin Kerr, 1980.*

times considered to be closer to dogs and domesticity than were "wild dogs." The Tzeltal Maya called otters *ha'al tz'i* (water dog). In the Guianas people refer to the otter as the "fishing dog."[82] In North America, in the Ojibwa worldview, "the otter is the domestic animal of the spirit of the water; what the dog is to man, so the otter is to the spirits."[83] And in Mesoamerica, the Aztec had a mythical otter-dog called Ahuitzotl. The eighth Aztec emperor, who built a series of aqueducts around Tenochtitlan, had this water monster as his name glyph. In glyph as well as in stone sculpture, Ahuitzotl was depicted with a dog's head and body and an otter's tail.

In art as well as in life, the dog's image was an ambiguous one. Dogs were universally regarded as "unclean" in their habits.[84] At the same time, they were seen as domestic, friendly, and nonthreatening. For Native Americans, both notions were easily combined in the same animal. In their dualistic universe, nothing was true unless its opposite was also true. Good and bad, life and death, and fire and water often existed in the same entity. The "meaning" of artistic dogs, like the "meaning" of life, is constructed from the worldview of the people doing the creating.

To make any "sense" out of pre-Columbian art requires an understanding of the pre-Columbian conception of the world. I have not made an attempt to explain the "meaning" behind the larger artistic expressions of diverse cultures, however. Rather, I have been searching for insight about the perceptions of selected groups of peoples about dogs. What metaphors seemed appropriate to them and why? What linguistic clues are there to enrich this slim grasp of pre-Hispanic human-dog relationships? Dogs with different physical traits were usually placed in separate linguistic categories. Wild and domestic canids were further distinguished with isolating and usually contrary symbolic qualities. Sometimes the "dogs" were placed in distinct and often polar groupings, yet at other times jaguars and otters were totally merged with domestic dogs. And, all the time, human-animal composite beings seem to have unlimited possibilities in the iconography of the Americas.

Endnote

Some mention of crossing boundaries seems appropriate here. Dogs and dog images have moved across all manner of cultural boundaries and physical barriers. Hairless dogs have been transported from Mexico to Peru. Mute dogs have traveled with Arawak speakers from the Orinoco River to the Greater Antilles. Both of these trips involved long water journeys. Dog imagery, employed to bind the days and months into the cycle of time, was used throughout Mesoamerica. Dogs have also served to connect this world with the next, the sky with the earth, and culture with nature. Dogs have followed people in a way not possible for wild animals. Their place beside humans is theirs alone. This has set them apart.

Epilogue: After the Conquest

Then, their [Spanish] dogs are enormous, with ears hanging down and close to the head, with long tongues hanging out; they have eyes which shoot out fire, throw out sparks; their eyes are yellow, a deep yellow. Their bellies are proud, distended like a ribbed framework. They are very stout and strong; they are not peaceful, they go panting, they go with their tongues hanging out. They are marked the color of tigers, with many colored spots.—Fray Bernardino de Sahagún, 1547–1575, *General History of the Things of New Spain: Florentine Codex, Book XII*

And when the expeditionary force [of Francisco de Orellana, the first European to penetrate the Amazon] had, having gone that far, saw the junction and realized that there was no relief for them in the way of food, . . . they became greatly discouraged, because for days the whole expeditionary force had eaten nothing but palm shoots and some fruit stones which they found on the ground [and] which had fallen from the trees, together with all the various kinds of noxious beast which they were able to find, because they had eaten in this wild country more than one thousand dogs and more than one hundred horses, without any other kind of food whatsoever. —Gonzalo Pizarro, Letter to the King of Spain (1542)

It has already been stated that in the New World the Spaniards have a number of wild and ferocious dogs which they have trained especially to kill the people and tear them to bits. It is not difficult to discover who are the real Christians and who are not when one learns that, to feed these dogs, they ensure that whenever they travel they always have a ready supply of natives, chained and herded like so many calves on the hoof. These they kill and butcher as the need arises. Indeed, they run a kind of human abattoir, or flesh market, where a dog-owner can casually ask, not for a quarter of pork or mutton, but for "a quarter of one of those likely lads over there for my dog."—Bartolomé de las Casas, *A Short Account of the Destruction of the Indies* (1542)

Diego de Landa, writing from the Yucatan Peninsula in 1566, and fellow Franciscans Bernardino de Sahagún and Ramón Pané and such Jesuits as Father Marc Lescarbot, Gabriel Sagard, and Bernabe Cobo are sixteenth- and seventeenth-century clerics whose works have contributed greatly to our understanding of pre-Columbian America. In spite of Landa's mission to destroy indigenous ways of life and traditions in favor of Spanish Catholicism, his *Relación de las cosas de Yucatán* remains the primary source on Maya culture at the time of the Conquest.

Revealing more than a pinch of ethnocentric pride, Landa reported that the "Indians have not lost but have gained much with the coming of the Spaniards, even in smaller matters. . . . There are many fine cows, boars, sheep, ewes, goats, and *such of our dogs as suit their needs, and which have come to be regarded as beneficial in the Indies.*"[1] I have emphasized the last part of Landa's statement as a jumping-off place for some concluding remarks about the Native American dog. In the rosy glow of hindsight, Landa's casual remark contains a fair amount of truth and some dreadful irony as well.[2] The European dog breeds were, in time, to prove beneficial to native peoples. Indeed, well-trained hunters were eagerly sought after, especially by those who did not possess dogs before the arrival of Westerners. The larger, stronger European dogs proved invaluable in the arctic and subarctic for pulling sleds and toboggans. At first, however, these new dogs were anything but beneficial.

The Spanish conquistadors brought with them to America large mastiffs and greyhounds that had been trained for war and killing people. These animals were unlike any dogs Native Americans had ever seen. When the Aztec ruler heard from his lieutenants what the approaching Spanish were like he was filled with alarm. When the nature of the Spanish dogs was described to him, he was terrified (see epigraph).

In the Caribbean the Spanish used their dogs as food tasters, to hunt for game, guard their settlements, and track recalcitrant Indians. It was in battle, however, that Spanish dogs reached their full potential. As early as 1495, at the battle of Vega Real, Hispaniola, Christopher Columbus' pack of twenty dogs was reported to have killed large numbers of people in very short order. Within a few years, public markets sold human body parts for training Spanish dogs to develop a taste for people, and these dogs were pitted against Native Americans for sport.[3]

Elsewhere in America the pattern, with local variations, was repeated. Fear of the huge and ferocious "demon dogs" caused many to surrender without a fight. These dogs seemed to be immortal and supernatural in their ability to distinguish between hostile and friendly groups and to track and rip apart the former. Rodrigo Rangel, traveling with DeSoto in Florida, recounts that, sent in pursuit of an "Indian fleeing from Christians the next day, a noble greyhound from Ireland plunged after him into the multitude of Indians that were on a densely wooded hill. It rushed to the clamor and entered among all the Indians; and although it passed by many, not one did it seize but the one who had fled, who was among the multitude, and it held him by the fleshy part of the arm in such a manner that the Indian was thrown down and apprehended."[4]

Once Native Americans got over the shock of learning the hard way about such animals, they were eager to get their hands on this new "technology." European dogs made what appears to have been a seamless transition into American societies and have adapted as effortlessly into lowland tropical forest life as they did to arctic cold. Once again, it is the superb adaptability of this animal to humans that is so striking.

The dog population in many groups increased after the Conquest. This certainly holds true for the Amazon, where dogs were absent before the arrival of European dogs. The numbers of dogs among arctic and subarctic groups, and in certain Plains

The Spanish conquistador Balboa sets the dogs on some Antiguans to punish them for "immoral" behavior. Engraving by Theodore de Bry in Americae Pars IV. *Frankfort, 1594. Courtesy of Beinecke Rare Book and Manuscript Library.*

tribes, also increased. On the other hand, European dogs rapidly interbred with native dogs and have, for the most part, succeeded in completely replacing them. Native peoples incorporated the new "foreign" dogs into their societies and put them to good use if they could. For many the distinctions between the breeds blurred, and only memories of the dogs from "ancient times" remained. Even so, some of the old breeds have left their genes recognizably behind. Hairless dogs can still be found in parts of Peru, Argentina, and Mexico. Today's Alaskan malamute is characterized by the stocky body and wolflike appearance of the Inuit dogs of the past. The small, lightly built, narrow-faced, yellow-haired dog of southern Mexico has an appearance that suggests a longtime relationship with Maya people. "Four-eyed" dogs can still be found among the Apache and the Sioux. Traces of Glover Allen's seventeen types of American dogs exist even though untangling the new dogs from the old is no simple matter. Sometimes, words help.

Yawa means both jaguar and dog in the language of the Achuar. For the Tupian people, *iawara* means dog and *iawarate* means jaguar.[5] Dogs, coming to both of these Amazonian peoples after the Conquest, were classified with jaguars. On the North American Plains it was wild horses, escapees from Spanish settlements to the south, that were newcomers requiring names. At first these new animals were thought of as "mysterious" dogs and used on the travois, not ridden. Horses received dog names. The Cree simply called horses and dogs the same thing: *atim.* A white dog or horse was *wapastimw.* For the Sioux, a horse was *šunkawakan,* sacred dog.[6] In the Amazon, dogs were regarded as predators and aligned with cats and, on the Great Plains, dogs were work animals and closest in function to horses.

In some parts of America, dogs and horses were associated with Europeans, so European names were adopted. Some California groups borrowed the Russian word for dog, which became *cuku* for the Miwok and *suku* for the Wintu. In northern California dogs seemed to have been absent before the Conquest, but when they arrived they were said to have come from the north. This may explain the Russian derivation for the Wintu and Miwok word for dog. The Arawak dog is called *péero,* from the Spanish *perro.* In other places, European dogs were given separate names to distinguish them from indigenous breeds. In the Greater Antilles, *aon* was the native breed, *satos* the mixed or European dog. The Tlingit called their indigenous breed *katle* and long-eared European dogs *sawá.* The dogs of the Choctaw were *ipaf* or *ofi,* but English dogs were *na holipafi.* Many native peoples adopted the Spanish word for horse. The Hopi horse is *kawaayo,* their reworking of the Spanish *caballo.* The Hopi word for dog, *pohko,* also means automobile. Useful indicators of the history of dogs among a particular group frequently are the terms that those people used to refer to their animals. The linguistic connections that people make can also reveal their perceptions of dogs in general, as well as their feelings for their own dogs.[7] As it turns out, the connections that Native Americans have made between themselves and their dogs are in some ways very familiar yet in other ways very foreign to "Western" thought.

How do the roles that dogs play in our own highly stratified and complex society differ from those played by American dogs of the past 12,000 years? Some of the differences are obvious. The affluence of our society has successfully "trickled down" to our pets, which are pampered in ways inconceivable to earlier Americans. Indeed, in many households the dog seems to have trained the human to anticipate its every need. Even so, the concept of ownership is deeply imbedded in our feelings for dogs. They are "our" dogs; we are their masters. To own an exotic breed of dog enhances our status in the same way that our other possessions do. We announce our rank. We may or may not treat our dogs well, but we never consider them beings that should be "set free." We have the

This large aboriginal dog, the first casuality of the Conquest of North America, was buried in a Timucua Village on St. Simons Island, Georgia. A small musket ball in its leg is the first archaeological evidence of the arrival of Europeans in North America. The Spanish slaver Pedro de Quejo, who landed on the island in 1525 in an attempt to establish a colony, is the most likely suspect in the killing (Milanich, 1996). Photograph courtesy of Jerald T. Milanich.

"right" to select any physical characteristic we choose as we control their reproductive activities. We may do this because we own them. We may love our dogs and feel our love is returned, but people of whom we think very poorly are "bitches" or "sons of bitches," depending on their gender.

What about in earlier times? Then, survival was a great challenge for human and animal alike, and dogs had to earn their keep or feed themselves. As a result, there were far fewer and many hungrier dogs in the past. And yet dogs seem to have evoked from humans some of the same responses they do today. In common with "modern" times is the ambiguity of the dog's position, its delicate straddling of the opposing spheres of nature and culture. In earlier times people projected human traits onto their dogs, used dogs as child substitutes and as recipients of redirected hostility. These "feelings" about dogs cross cultural boundaries and can be found in small egalitarian societies as well as in the hyperstratified, globally connected communities in which most people live today. An unusual-looking or exceptionally talented dog conferred status on its owner in the past just as it does today. Some dogs were owned while others were feral. Mistreating one's own dog was perfectly acceptable, mistreating someone else's dog was not. Killing another person's dog was a grave offense. So it is today. It is, however, the contrasting points of view about dogs that are the keys to understanding how beliefs underlie and define all relationships, including this most enduring one.

"The Sioux Dog Dance" (appendix 2), written by the poet Red Hawk in 1991, and *White Dog Dream,* painted by Seneca artist Peter Jemison in 1985, both exemplify how contemporary Native Americans strive to perpetuate their cultural identity through artistic expression. These modern works also illustrate some part of the unbridgeable gap between America's first people and its newcomers. These are symbols that have no translation. In Red Hawk's poem, Washington's elite arrive on the reservation to see how well their policy of making Indians more like themselves is working. The Sioux choose to honor their guests with a special dance in which dogs are sliced "from tongue to tail" and their severed ears placed in front of the viewing stand. The women faint and the men retch at this bloody sight. The message of the dance was lost on the visitors who saw in this "uncivilized" behavior something far more barbaric than what had transpired at Wounded Knee.[8]

Peter Jemison's painting recalls the White Dog Sacrifice of the Iroquois, a New Year's sacred ritual of thanksgiving. As this rite began, a pure white dog was strangled and then decorated, with white wampum in early times and later with colored ribbons, and hung on a post for five days. At the conclusion of the ceremony the dog was burned and offered to the Great Spirit as a symbol of fidelity. Although the idea of using a dog to symbolize faithfulness is something most could understand, burnt offerings featuring "faithful Fido" might strike many as a betrayal of the dog's trust. An Iroquois, I suspect, would consider such a dog to have received a great honor in its sacrifice.

To eat an animal "contrary" to the wolf, as the Cheyenne did when eating a puppy, is an idea that has no meaning to us. We would not quake to see our dog chewing on the bones of moose or bear because we do not see the offended animal spirits. We do not think horses and dogs or dogs and jaguars are logical pairs. Our lives do not depend on our dogs. We do not count on them to haul our housing from one spot to the next or to pull a seal out onto the ice. Dog meat is not the only meat available to us in hard times. Today dogs do not compete with us for food, nor do they relieve us of unwanted carcasses. They do not tree bears for us or keep wolves at bay. They do not live with us in a difficult, dangerous place filled with spirits and demons, nor do they wander with us across the stars and keep us safe after death. Dogs are no longer part of a rich and complex metaphorical world such as that of the Classic Maya; gone are the jaguar-dogs, the tzul dogs of bad weather, the dogs of lightning and thunder, and the dancing White-Three-Dog. Xolotl, the canine god of the Aztec, Opiyel-Guaobiran, the Taíno watch dog of the dead, and Huallallo, the dog-eating deity of the Huancas, no longer roam in the Americas. Today, dogs are, for the most part, the well-fed pets of well-fed people.

Amid all manner of human social arrangements and subsistence strategies, dogs have managed to hold their own. Archaeological evidence of carefully buried dogs attests to the fact that dogs have, from the first, enjoyed considerable status among some of America's earliest settlers. Ethnographic reports show that eating dogs was often accompanied by great ritual and ceremony and that dog meat was considered a spiritual food. In reality and in myth the "helpful dog" was part of everyday life while also operating in the land of the dead. The history of dogs in the Americas is, ultimately, a success story. Even though American aboriginal dogs have all but disappeared, their legacy remains. It remains in myths and stories, in art, in burial remains, and in the genes of their relatives. Like the people with whom they lived, they form part of the history of the Americas.

Appendix 1 Words for Dogs and Related Concepts in Selected Native American Languages

Ethnic Group	Language Family	Word	Translation	Source
Intuit dialects (Arctic)	Eskimo-Aleut	*qipmiq, qimmiq, qiŋmiq*	dog	Webster and Zibell, 1976
		amaRug	wolf	
Natchez (Southeast)	Isolated Language	*wáshkup*	dog	Van Tuyl, 1979
		waskkōp	young dog	
		wáshkup shī´ ´l	horse ("large dog")	
		hádawa	wolf	
Choctaw (Southeast)	Muskogean	*ipaf, ofi*	dog	Byington, 1915
		na holipafi	English dog	
		ofi tek	female dog, slut	
		ofi tohbi I hina	Milky Way	
		nashoba	wolf	
		isuba	horse	
Cherokee (Southeast)	Iroquoian	*gi:li´*	dog	Floyd Lounsbury, personal communication
		Gi:li´-utsûñ´ stăn ûñ´ yĭ	Milky Way (where the dog ran)	
		wahya	wolf	
		sa:gwili	horse	
Oneida Iroquois (New York state)	Iroquoian	*é:lhal*	dog	Floyd Lounsbury, personal communication
		kitshene	dog, pet, slave, captive	
		othyūni	wolf	
		lodigwáho'	wolf clan	
		gohsades	horse (one whose back is ridden)	

(continued)

Ethnic Group	Language Family	Word	Translation	Source
Huron (Eastern Great Lakes)	Iroquoian	*gagnenon*	dog	Tooker, 1964
		gagnenon youry	there is a dog cooked!	
		gagnenon andahatey	the path of the dogs (celestial)	
		anarisqua	wolf	
Micmac (Eastern Canada)	Algonquian	*e'lmutc*	dog	Wallis and Wallis, 1955
		e'lmutcitc	pup	
		Elmutc Ulugwetc	"Dog howling"—dog turned to rock by culture hero Kulóskap	
Cree (Eastern subarctic)	Algonquian	*atim*	dog, horse	Hewson, 1993
		acimosis	puppy	
		wapastimw	white dog, white horse	
		mahihkan	wolf	
Ojibwa (Southern subarctic)	Algonquian	*animosh*	dog	Hewson, 1993
		animoshish	dog (derogatory)	
		aabita-animosh	half-dog being	
		ma'iingan	wolf	
		awakaan	horse, domestic animal	
Cheyenne (Great Plains)	Algonquian	*oeškēso*	dog	Leman, 1980
		hótame	dog (old term)	
		ka?éè-hótame	short-faced dog	
		o?kohōme	coyote	
		ho'néheo'o	wolf	
		mo?éhèno?ha	horse	
Blackfoot (Great Plains)	Algonquian	*imitá*	dog	Uhlenbeck and Gulik, 1934
		imitáikoăn	puppy	
		Imitáiks	member of Dog Society	
		imitáunistsi	dog travois	
		mako, ako	wolf	
		ponokâmita	"Big Dog" (horse)	
Chipewyan (Central subarctic)	Athapaskan	*łį*	dog	Li and Scallon, 1976
		łį-yaze	young dog	
		nụniyε	wolf	
		łįtcạyạ'	Dogrib Indian	
Hare (Western subarctic)	Athapaskan	*tłį, łį*	dog	Rice, 1989
		tłįl'ulé	dog harness	
		tłịcho	horse	
		beleséle	coyote	
		bele	wolf	
Winnebago (Midwest)	Siouan	*cuŋgerī ja*	dog	Radin, 1990
		cûŋgewaksiga	hunting dog	
		cûŋkycaŋk'a	wolf	

Ethnic Group	Language Family	Word	Translation	Source
Oglala Sioux (Great Plains)	Siouan	*šunka*	dog	Powers and Powers, 1986
		šunkamanitu tanka	wolf ("large wild dog")	
		šunkawakan	horse ("sacred dog")	
Tlingit (Pacific Northwest)	Isolated Language	*katle*	dog	Emmons, 1991
		sawá·	long-eared dog; European dog	
		ha·da·katle	coyote (dog of the interior)	
		goutch	wolf	
Miwok (California)	Penutian	*cuku*	dog (from Russian)	Callaghan, 1987
		'ole'cu	coyote	
		kawaju	horse (from Spanish)	
Paiute (Great Basin)	Uto-Aztecan	*sari*	dog	Sapir, 1931
		sari tiqats	dog-eater or Arapahoe	
		cinaŋwavi	coyote	
		qavd'	horse	
Hopi (Northern Arizona)	Uto-Aztecan	*pohko*	dog, pet, car	Seaman, 1985
		ivoko	my dog	
		iisaw	coyote	
		kawaayo	horse (from Spanish)	
		kweewu	wolf	
Aztec (Basin of Mexico)	Uto-Aztecan	*itzcuintli, chichi*	dog	Sahagún, 1950–1982; Berdan and Anawalt, 1992
		thalchichi	small squat dog	
		Chichimeca	Dog People	
		xolo	slave, attendant	
		xoloitzcuintli	attendant or slave dog, hairless dog	
		Xolotl	canine god of twins and monsters	
		coyotl	coyote	
Yucatec Maya (Yucatan Peninsula)	Mayan	*tzul*	dog, backbone	Alvarez, 1980; Coe, 1992
		ah-bil	hairless dog	
		pek	dog, watertower, fever	
		alak-bil pek	servant dog of the house	
		ah ceh pek	hunting dog	
		tzimin	tapir, horse	
		tzula	seal ("water dog")	
Tzeltal Maya (Southern Mexico)	Mayan	*tz'i'*	dog	Hunn, 1977
		batz'il tz'i'	true dog (Indian dog)	
		kaslan tz'i'	Ladino dog (long haired)	
		pinto tz'i'	spotted (from Spanish *pintojo*) dog	
		ha'al tz'i'	otter ("rain dog")	
		'ok'il	coyote	

(continued)

Ethnic Group	Language Family	Word	Translation	Source
Guaymi (Isthmus of Panama)	Chibchan	*nukrö'*	dog	Alphonse, 1956
		nu	dog, armadillo	
		nuké, nu	to come, came	
		nuke, kudolo	fox	
		madó	horse	
Inca Peru (Andes)	Quechuan	*allqo, alko, alco*	dog, an undignified person	Weiss, 1970;
		alcocala, muro-muro	spotted dog	Sharon and
		alcosunca, alcoyana	hairless dog	Donnan, 1974;
		allqochay	to insult, to despise	Bingham, 1922
		Alcomicoc	a dog-eater	
		Guana Alcomico	Huanca Indian ("guanoco who eats dogs")	
		sunnca, chono	long-haired dog	
		pichi	puppy	
		atoq	fox	
		kaballu	horse (from Spanish)	
		Huallallo	dog-eating deity of the Huancas	
Achuar (Western Amazon)	Jivaroan	*yawa*	dog or spotted jaguar	Descola, 1994
		tanku yawa	domesticated dog	
		suach jawa	black jaguar	
		patukam yawa	bush dog	
		tanku pama	cow ("domestic tapir")	
Tupi (Central Amazon)	Tupian	*iawara*	dog	Lévi-Strauss, 1973
		iawarate	jaguar	
		iawacaca	otter	
		iawapopé	fox	
Guiana Arawaks (Northeastern Amazon)	Arawakan	*péero, pero*	dog (from Spanish)	Drummond, 1977
		lepéeronkan	his little dog	
		pero-kuru-kuyaha	dog spirit people	
Maipure (Venezuela)	Arawakan	*auri*	mute dog	Taylor, 1977
Waiwai (East Amazon)	Arawakan	*shapali*	dog	Fock, 1963
		råkåchi	bush dog	
		kamara	jaguar	
Island Caribs (Lesser Antilles)	Arawakan	*â'oli, âori, ánli, áµli*	dog	Taylor, 1977
		auri	mute dog	
		kabayu'	horse (from Spanish)	
Taino (Greater Antilles)	Arawakan	*aon*	mute dog	Roe, 1993
		satos	mixed-breed dog	
		Opiyel-Guaobiran	Watch Dog of the Dead	

(continued)

Ethnic Group	Language Family	Word	Translation	Source
Yahgan (Tierra del Fuego)	Isolated Language	*yöšöl-aiamalim* *twīiū-a* *iūak-amātū* *iūm-a* *iūat-ēnaka*	dogs, hunters with dogs to catch with dogs to pick up as a dog would to bite as a dog would to catch as a dog would	Bridges, 1933

Appendix 2 The Sioux Dog Dance: shunk ah weh

By Red Hawk

They came from Washington by special train
generals, senators, their wives and mistresses
to see how the reservation had civilized the Sioux

The Sioux made a new dance for the occasion.

The day was so hot flies died in the dust
and the women in lace, men in starched collars
suffered the moment their train ride ended

but they were in the fort's reviewing stand talking
when the big drum started on the parade ground.
They were pleased by the wooden cross they spied

in the center of the field; then the 2 leaders came,
the Medicine man and his woman, dancing naked;
holding up 2 howling dogs by their hind legs tied;

by their hind legs they hung them from the cross;
all talking ceased at once and there was just
the drumming and the flies buzzing in the dust.

From her hair she pulled a knife and in one sweep
sliced the first dog from tail to tongue,
then passed the knife; he did the same.

Published with permission from Red Hawk and the Cleveland State Poetry Center.

Women on the stand fainted dead away,
senators retched as the bowels tumbled out.
The generals froze in their chairs, wide-eyed.

She pulled and sliced the organs into strips;
he took one in his teeth,
swung his head from side to side.

and there was in that hot place
the slap slap slap
the 7 naked drummers on the big drum drumming
and the black flies buzzing as they died.

2 lines of naked dancers spun onto the field,
one by one approached the leaders,
with their teeth received the strips, replied

to the drum by howling, crouching, leaping,
slapped the strips around their heads
until they all had taken and the blood had dried

upon their faces. Then they ate them
one by one, the leaders going last

and on the stand there was no place to hide,

no one made the slightest move to leave
as the dancers circled and sat down:
2 old women step-danced then, cried

in a high scream   aieee ip
and cut the ears from the hanging dogs;
they step-danced in their slow and ancient pride

to the base of the review stand,
laid the 4 ears neatly in the dust,
bowed and laid the 2 long knives beside.
The drums went silent, the dancers sighed
and the black flies buzzed there as they died.

Appendix 3 Additional Reading on the Early History of Dogs

Benecke, N. 1987. Studies on Early Dog Remains from Northern Europe. *Journal of Archaeological Science* 14:31–49.

Bökönyi, S. 1975. Vlasac: An Early Site of Dog Domestication. *Archaeozoological Studies,* ed. A. T. Clason, 167–168. Amsterdam: North-Holland.

Budiansky, S. 1992. *The Covenant of the Wild: Why Animals Chose Domestication.* New York: William Morrow.

Chang, K. C. 1977. *The Archaeology of Ancient China.* New Haven: Yale University Press.

Clutton-Brock, J. 1981. *Domesticated Animals from Early Times.* Austin: University of Texas Press; British Museum (Natural History).

Clutton-Brock, J., and N. Noe-Nygaard. 1990. New Osteological and C-Isotope Evidence on Mesolithic Dogs: Companions to Hunters and Fishers at Starr Carr, Steamer Carr, and Kongemose. *Journal of Archaeological Science* 17:642–653.

Coppinger, R., J. Glendinning, E. Torop, C. Matthay, M. Sutherland, and C. Smith. 1987. Degree of Behavioral Neoteny Differentiates Canid Polymorphs. *Ethology* 75:89–108.

Davis, S. J. M., and F. Villa. 1978. Evidence for the Domestication of the Dog 12,000 Years Ago in the Nautufian of Israel. *Nature* 276:608–610.

Dayan, T. 1994. Early Domestic Dogs in the Near East. *Journal of Archaeological Science* 21:633–640.

Green, M. 1992. *Animals in Celtic Life and Myth.* London: Routledge.

Harcourt, R. A. 1974. The Dog in Prehistoric and Early Historic Britain. *Journal of Archaeological Sciences* 1:151–175.

Larsson, L. 1989. Big Dog and Poor Man: Mortuary Practices in Mesolithic Societies in Southern Sweden. In *Approaches to Swedish Prehistory,* ed. T. B. Larsson and H. Lundmark, 221–223. B. A. R. Oxford.

Livingstone, A. 1988. The Isin "Dog House" Revisited. *Journal of Cuneiform Studies* 40:54–60.

Luomala, K. 1960. The Native Dog in the Polynesian System of Values. In *Essays in Honor of Paul Radin,* ed. S. Diamond, 190–240. New York: Columbia University Press.

Méniel, P. 1992. *Les Sacrifices d'Animaux chez les Gaulois.* Paris: Errance Editions.

Serpell, J., ed. 1995. *The Domestic Dog: Its Evolution, Behavior, and Interactions with People.* Cambridge: Cambridge University Press.

Shigehara, N. 1994. Morphological Changes in Japanese Ancient Dogs. *Archaeozoologia* 6:79–94.

Tchernov, E., and L. Horwitz. 1991. Body Size Diminution Under Domestication: Unconscious Selection in Primeval Domesticates. *Journal of Anthropological Archaeology* 10:54–75.

Titcomb, M. 1969. Dog and Man in the Ancient Pacific with Special Attention to Hawaii. *Bernice P. Bishop Special Publication 59.* Honolulu.

Turnbull, P. F., and C. A. Reed. 1974. The Fauna from the Terminal Pleistocene of Palegawra Cave. *Fieldiana Anthropology* 63:81–164.

Wapnish, P., and B. Hesse. 1993. Pampered Pooches or Plain Pariahs? The Ashkelon Dog Burials. *Biblical Archaeologist* 56:55–80.

Zeuner, F. E. 1963. *A History of Domesticated Animals.* London: Hutchinson.

Notes

Chapter 1: The Creation of the American Dog

1. Columbus was not the first seafarer to reach the Americas. Certainly Vikings and possibly Polynesians reached American shores before Columbus. In addition, Inuit people have always moved freely between Asia and North America.
2. Alexander Pope, "*Essay on Man,*" in Abrams, 1979:2246.
3. Moehlman, 1992.
4. Churcher, 1959.
5. Anderson, 1984.
6. Langguth, 1975; Sheldon, 1992.
7. Descola, 1994.
8. Sheldon, 1992.
9. Ibid.
10. Roy, Geffen, Smith, Ostrander, and Wayne, 1994.
11. Charles Remington, Yale University, personal communication.
12. Templeton, 1989; Morey, 1992; Wayne, 1993.
13. Templeton (1989) explains these issues in detail and with clarity.
14. Ibid.
15. Clutton-Brock, 1988.
16. Fox, 1978.
17. Zimen, 1975.
18. Wayne, 1993:220.
19. Ibid.
20. Wayne, 1986:247.
21. Clutton-Brock, 1995.
22. Peterson and Page, 1988.
23. Reed, 1960; Olsen, 1985; Clutton-Brock, 1984.

24. Luomala, 1960; Hamilton, 1972.

25. Roth, 1924:551.

26. Serpell, 1983:62.

27. Corbett, 1995.

28. Ibid.

29. Gould, 1980:243.

30. Hamilton, 1972.

31. Ibid.

32. Brisbin, 1992.

33. Nowak and Paradiso, 1983.

34. Darwin, 1952:250.

35. Clutton-Brock, 1977.

36. Berta, 1987.

37. Clutton-Brock, 1995.

38. In addition, the sagittal crest, the keel along the midline of the cranium, is more rounded and less posteriorly projecting in dogs. The tympanic bulla, the round structure directly behind and below the ear hole, is smaller and more compressed. The palate of the dog is elongated and extends beyond the level of the third molar. One key feature that seems to be diagnostic for dogs is the "turned-back" apex of the coronoid process of the mandible, those portions that top the vertical portions at the posterior ends of the bone. For further characteristics see Benecke, 1987, and Lawrence and Reed, 1983.

39. Olsen, 1985:22; Walker and Frison, 1982.

40. Other fossils, with unmistakable dog morphology, have uncertain dates. Dog mandibles from La Brea, California, Old Crow, Yukon, and a Florida sinkhole were all reported to be associated with Pleistocene deposits. Each, however, is probably intrusive from higher, more recent levels, and must be discounted. See Olsen, 1985 for a detailed discussion.

41. Morey and Wiant, 1992.

42. Ibid.

43. Paul Martin (1984) is one of the strongest advocates for human involvement in the extinction of large mammals in North America. For other points of view see other articles in Martin and Klein's edited volume *Quaternary Extinctions: A Prehistoric Revolution,* 1984.

44. Aveleyra Arroyo de Anda and Maldonado-Koerdell, 1953; Hannus, 1990.

45. Hannus, 1990.

46. McCartney, 1990.

47. Wheat, 1972.

48. Walker and Frison, 1982.

49. Audubon, 1960.

50. The following researchers have studied camelid remains in highland Peruvian caves and have argued that the age distribution of animals under human control would include much higher numbers of infants and still-born individuals than would that of hunted animals: Lavallee, Julien, Wheeler, and Karlin 1985; Pires-Ferreira, Pires-Ferreira, and Kaulicke, 1976; Wing, 1986.
51. Clutton-Brock, 1988; Cardich, 1978; Politis and Salemme, 1990.
52. Caviglia, Yacobaccio, and Borrero, 1986.
53. Langguth, 1975.
54. Brightman, 1993:135.
55. Seger, 1934:153.
56. Dorsey, 1905.
57. Wilson, 1924:199.
58. Howard, 1965.
59. Voegelin, 1936.
60. Speck, 1925.
61. Leland, 1884:39.
62. Fock, 1963.
63. Leach, 1961.
64. Curtain and Hewitt, 1910–1911:236.
65. Powers, 1976.
66. Underhill, 1965.
67. Dyk, 1959.
68. White, 1991.
69. Bierhorst, 1985.
70. Between 1789 and 1793, Sir Alexander Mackenzie, a young Scot in service of the North West Company, attempted to reach the Pacific coast from a starting point on Lake Atabasca, Canada. His journals provide one of the first descriptions of the Chipewyan, Slavey, Yellowknife, and Dogrib of northwestern Canada (Lamb, 1970:151).
71. Hearne, 1971.
72. Bloomfield and Nichols, 1991.
73. According to Lévi-Strauss (1995) versions of the dog husband myth exist throughout northwestern North America, where dogs are regarded as quasi-human.
74. Lévi-Strauss, 1979.
75. Sapir and Swadesh, 1939.
76. Dorsey and Kroeber, 1903.
77. Grinnell, 1962.
78. Campbell, 1989b.
79. See Drummond, 1977 for a structuralist viewpoint of the meaning of this myth and the use of the color white for the dog.

80. Sections 111 and 112 from *The Huarochirí Manuscript* (Salomon and Urioste, 1991:70).

81. Bierhorst, 1992:144.

82. Keber, 1992.

83. Ibid.

84. See Tedlock, 1985, for the definitive edition of the *Popol Vuh*.

85. Tedlock, 1985.

86. Ibid., pp. 84–85.

87. Jeffrey Quilter points out that the Moche of Peru had a similar myth, which he calls the "Revolt of the Objects," in which shields, capes, clubs, and helmets attack their masters. In the Moche myth as shown in several line drawings on pots, the dog stands firmly with humans against the attacking objects. The Zuni of North America also have a similar myth in which "our possessions will turn into beasts and devour us whole" (1990, 60).

88. Throughout Mesoamerica and into the American southwest and the Caribbean, the ball game, played on a special court with a solid rubber ball, was an important event. The loser might lose his life as well as the game.

89. Tedlock, 1985:152.

90. A dog of the same body size as a wolf has a brain 20 percent smaller. See also Fox, 1978.

91. Floyd Lounsbury, Yale University, personal communication.

Chapter 2: Hunting, Hauling, and Herding Dogs

1. Allen, 1920.

2. Ibid., p. 442.

3. Mary-Rousseliere, 1984.

4. Arima, 1984; Dumas, 1984.

5. Birket-Smith, 1929.

6. Spencer, 1959.

7. Ibid.

8. Rogers and Smith, 1981.

9. The only mention of the Hare Indian dog comes from John Richardson, who in 1829 wrote from first-hand experience a description of a small, well-furred spotted dog. See Allen, 1920:491.

10. Savishinsky, 1974a, 1974b.

11. Savishinsky, 1974b.

12. Drucker, 1951:109.

13. Emmons, 1991.

14. de Laguna, 1960:131.

15. Barbeau, 1953.

16. Murdock, 1936. See Kroeber, 1941, for a list of other Pacific Northwest groups noted for performing dog-eating ceremonies.
17. Drucker, 1941.
18. See 1991 poem by Native America poet Red Hawk (appendix 2) for another example of dog eating ritual, this time among the Sioux. Dog-eating rituals also are described in chap. 3.
19. Miller, 1978; LaPena, 1978; Kroeber, 1941.
20. Aginsky, 1941:456.
21. Driver, 1939.
22. Gayton, 1946:183.
23. The Maidu and the Wiyot Indians have similar stories, and dogs were associated with fire throughout Mesoamerica. See chap. 5.
24. Kroeber, 1941.
25. Powers, 1976.
26. Wallace, 1978.
27. Stewart, 1941.
28. Kroeber, 1941:11.
29. Howard, 1965.
30. Reeves, 1990.
31. Steward, 1948; Warren DeBoer, Queens College, N.Y., has told me that he does not know of any evidence of the dog in the pre-Conquest faunal remains from the Amazon proper, further indication that dogs had not penetrated very far into the South American rainforest.
32. Steward, 1948.
33. Roth, 1924.
34. Gilmore, 1947.
35. See Wayne, 1993. Although the karyotype of the pampas fox is not reported in this paper, all tested South American canids had diploid chromosome numbers of 74 or 76, and all *Canis* species had 78.
36. Roth, 1924.
37. Farabee, 1918.
38. Roe, in press.
39. Fock, 1963.
40. Crocker, 1985.
41. Varner and Varner, 1983.
42. Yost and Kelley, 1983:206.
43. Descola, 1994.
44. Ibid.
45. Ibid., p. 234.
46. Allen, 1920:477.
47. Fitz-Roy, 1839, 2:136.

48. Reeves, 1990.

49. Cooper, 1946a.

50. Cooper, 1946c.

51. Lothrop, 1928.

52. Fitz-Roy, 1839, 2:184.

53. Bird, 1946; Cooper, 1946b.

54. Allen, 1920.

55. Bridges, 1949.

56. Bridges, 1933. The Reverend T. Bridges was superintendent of the South American Missionary society in Tierra del Fuego from 1870 to 1887. As the Rev. Bridges explains, members of the ethnic group usually called the Yahgan call themselves "Yamana," a term he adopts for this compendium. His dictionary contains 32,000 words and inflections.

57. Clutton-Brock, 1988; Politis and Salemme, 1990.

58. Lothrop, 1928.

59. Pohl and Feldman, 1982; Donnan, 1982.

60. Grant, Baird, and Pringle, 1968; Wellmann, 1979.

61. Steward, 1941; Shimkin, 1986.

62. Francis, Loendorf, and Dorn, 1993.

63. Teit, 1930; Ray, 1940.

64. Steedman, 1930.

65. Wallis and Wallis, 1955:115.

66. Descola, 1994:232.

67. Roe, in press; Farabee, 1918.

68. Roe, in press.

69. Speck, 1925.

70. Whitehead, 1991:17.

71. Giddings, 1967.

72. Seidelman and Turner, 1994.

73. Brightman, 1993.

74. Ibid.

75. Lévi-Strauss, 1979.

76. Ibid.

77. Roe, 1955.

78. Burpee 1927:317–318. La Vérendryes, traveling with his sons from 1738 to 1743, was the last great French explorer of North America.

79. Franklin, 1824:118.

80. Driver and Massey, 1957; Birket-Smith, 1929.

81. Hearne, 1971:322.

82. Ibid.

83. Colton, 1970.

84. Bolton, 1916:227.

85. Schroeder and Matson, 1965:56.

86. Roe, 1955.

87. Walker and Frison, 1982.

88. Young and Goldman, 1944:181.

89. Henderson, 1994.

90. Ibid.

91. Roe, 1955; Ewers, 1955.

92. Ewers, 1955.

93. Henderson, 1994.

94. Perhaps the most richly detailed account of the way that working dogs were developed and used by Plains people comes from Gilbert Wilson's 1924 article "The Hidatsa Horse and Dog Culture."

95. Wilson, 1924:204.

96. Ewers, 1955.

97. Wing, 1986.

98. Jesse, 1886.

99. Bingham, 1922.

100. Thomas, 1973.

101. Underhill, 1944. The artist Paul Kane did a small number of sketches and paintings of the Salish wool dogs. Harper, 1971, illustrates some of these studies as well as listing the others. These are the only known drawings or photographs of this breed of dog.

102. Vancouver, 1801:136.

103. Howay, 1918:91.

104. Winship, 1896:553.

105. Descola, 1994.

Chapter 3: The Edible Dog

1. Magana, 1986; Trigger, 1985; Weiss, 1970.

2. Green, 1992; Meniél, 1992.

3. See Simoons, 1994, for a more detailed discussion of dog-eating in the Old World.

4. Luomala, 1960.

5. Personal communication, Harold Conklin, Yale University.

6. Afable, 1995.

7. Tambiah, 1969:455.

8. McBrearty and Moniz, 1991.

9. Churchill, 1993.

10. Harlan, 1992.

11. Fritz, 1994.
12. Lyon, 1970.
13. Fritz, 1994, claims that no securely dated cultigens from Mesoamerica date earlier than 3000 B.C., though claims for older dates have been made by others (see, for example, MacNeish, Peterson, and Neely, 1972).
14. Flannery, 1967.
15. Sanders, Parsons, and Santley, 1979
16. Starbuck, 1975.
17. Wing, 1978.
18. Ibid., p. 39.
19. Rice, Rice, and Deevey, 1985.
20. Dillon, 1988.
21. S. D. Coe, 1994.
22. Pohl and Feldman, 1982.
23. Mary Pohl (1991), in "Women, Animal Rearing, and Social Status: The Case of the Formative Period Maya of Central America," and Elizabeth Wing (1978) in "Use of Dogs for Food: An Adaptation to the Coastal Environment" both make the case for domesticated and husbanded animals being much more important to lowland subsistence than had been previously supposed.
24. Pohl, 1991.
25. John Gerry (1993) points out that if dogs were consuming human fecal material containing maize, a strong positive carbon isotope reading would also result. He also notes that deer and peccary did not have access to maize and were primarily browsers.
26. Hammond, 1991.
27. Miksicek, Wing, and Scudder, 1991.
28. Clutton-Brock and Hammond, 1994.
29. Carr, 1985.
30. Pohl, 1991; Olsen, 1978.
31. Pohl, 1985.
32. Pohl, 1991
33. Olsen, 1972.
34. Hamblin, 1984.
35. White and Schwarcz (1989), using carbon and nitrogen isotope frequencies on human bones from the Lowland Maya site of Lamanai, could detect no change in the balance of protein sources over a 2,000-year period. Because of the locality's proximity to the sea and this technique's lack of precision, no conclusions about terrestrial versus aquatic resources can be more than preliminary.
36. Nimis, 1982.
37. Pohl and Feldman, 1982.
38. Tozzer, 1941; Roys, 1976.

39. Recall the discussion in Chapter 1 about groups that considered themselves descended from dogs. These include the Huichol from northern Mexico. David Gorden White in *Myths of the Dog-Man* (1991) discusses the widespread Old World tradition of Dog People, those hybrids who live outside civilized society. These outcasts dwelled in areas where chaos reigned. For the civilized Toltec, the nomadic peoples to their north were just such "barbarians," as the Dog Jung were to the Chinese. What is striking is that in China and in Mexico, dogs and people were linked to signify these outcasts. The Chichimec then fit in with a worldwide tradition.

40. Pasztory, 1983.

41. Sanders, Parsons, and Santley, 1979.

42. Cortés, 1843:112–113.

43. diaz del Castillo, 1968:216.

44. See Chapter 5 for a discussion of day signs.

45. Sahagún, 1950–1982, book 4/5:19–20.

46. Ibid., 10:48.

47. Coe, 1994.

48. Thomas, 1993.

49. diaz del Castillo, 1968:213.

50. Ibid., p. 237.

51. Bruhns, 1994.

52. Byrd, 1976.

53. Burger, 1992.

54. Pozorski, 1979; Miller and Burger, n.d.; Wing, 1986.

55. Shimada and Shimada, 1981.

56. Von Hagen, 1959:317. I find no other reference for *chono* as a Quechua word for dog, but note that the Chono Indians had long-haired dogs whose fur they apparently used in weaving short mantles (see Chapter 2). Perhaps this name for dogs comes from these Indians to the south of Cuzco.

57. "Black" refers to the Peruvian hairless dog with its dark pigmented skin rather than a dog with a black coat. See Chapter 5 for more on the hairless dog.

58. Rowe, 1946.

59. Weiss, 1970. This article has a wealth of information regarding hairless Peruvian and Mexican dogs.

60. Gheerbrant, 1961.

61. Guaman Poma de Ayala, 1978:72.

62. Earle et al., 1980.

63. von Hagen, 1959.

64. Gheerbrant, 1961.

65. Sandefur, 1988.

66. Cognates for the Taino word for dog—*aon*—occur in several Arawak languages.

See Appendix 1 for a partial list. *Auri* is the word for dog among the Adzaneni, Maipure, and Piapoco peoples of the Orinoco River drainage region. These words for dog are not derived from any European language and are further evidence of the existence of an indigenous breed of dog in northern South America that was imported into the Caribbean islands.

67. Acosta, 1604:272.
68. Fewkes, 1907:50.
69. Sauer, 1966.
70. Figueredo, 1978.
71. Rouse, 1992; Roe, 1995; Steward, 1948.
72. Walker, 1985; Wing, 1990.
73. Wing, 1991a.
74. Wing, 1991b.
75. Wing, 1978; Pohl, 1991.
76. Shimada and Shimada, 1981; Byrd, 1976; Sandefur, 1988.
77. Clayton, Knight, and Moore, 1993:77.
78. Ibid., p. 281.
79. Ibid., p. 77.
80. Ibid., p. 87.
81. Milner, 1990.
82. Parmalee, 1957.
83. Milner, 1984.
84. See Chapter 5 for a discussion of the distribution of the hairless dog.
85. Weiss, 1970; Cordy-Collins, 1994.
86. Milanich and Hudson, 1993.
87. Willey, 1941; Rouse, 1951; Griffin and Smith, 1954; Milanich, 1994; Wheeler and McGee, 1994.
88. Houck, 1951.
89. Griffin and Smith, 1954.
90. Wing, 1965.
91. Webb, 1959.
92. Hudson, 1976.
93. Ibid.
94. Le Page du Pratz, 1975:368.
95. Ibid., pp. 350, 257.
96. Thwaites, 1898, *Jesuit Relations* 7:223.
97. Sagard, 1939:226.
98. Thwaites, 1898, *Jesuit Relations* 13:31.
99. Ibid., 19:115.
100. Kraft, 1986:143.
101. Harrington, 1921.

102. Fenton, 1978:316.
103. Morgan, 1962:217.
104. Michelson, 1925:39.
105. Ibid.
106. Radin, 1990.
107. Ibid., p. 405.
108. Gifford, 1939.
109. Leach, 1961.
110. Gifford, 1939. The Hopi now live on the tops of four mesas surrounded on all sides by the much more numerous Navaho.
111. Bourke, 1884:253.
112. Simmons, 1942.
113. Russell, 1908.
114. Bourke, 1984.
115. Lang and Harris, 1984; Kelley, 1975.
116. Olsen, 1990.
117. Although some have identified these dogs merely as "canines" due to the abstract nature of Mimbres art, the white "collar" around the neck and the upturned tail as well as the scenes in which these animals appear suggest that no wild canine was intended. For more examples of these Mimbres dogs see Brody, 1977, Brody, Scott, and LeBlanc, 1983, and Anyon and LeBlanc, 1984.
118. Berlandier, 1969:119.
119. Thurman, 1988.
120. The Comanche, Paiute, and Shoshone all spoke languages of the Uto-Aztecan family, and their words for dog are similar: *sati'i* (Comanche), *sari* (Paiute), *satii* (Shoshone). While most Plains groups ate dogs, the Arapaho seem to have had the dog-eater name to themselves in the nineteenth century.
121. Wilson, 1924:230.
122. Ibid.
123. Catlin, 1841.
124. Powers and Powers, 1986:16.
125. Denig, 1931:489.
126. See Chapter 4 for further comments on the star Sirius and its mythological linkage with canids.
127. Schlesier, 1987.
128. Murie, 1989.
129. Bozell, 1988.
130. O'Shea and Ludwickson, 1992.
131. Lehmer and Jones, 1968.
132. Ewers, 1955:167.
133. Thurman, 1988.

134. Thurman (1988) makes a case for southern Athapaskan dog-eaters, but the identity of this group is not entirely clear. Navaho and Apache claim not to have eaten dog.

Chapter 4: Dogs in the Land of the Dead

1. See White, 1991, for more on mythology of dogs in the Old World.
2. This Milky Way Canoe carries the Maize God (First Father) to the place of creation in the Night Sky. See Freidel, Schele, and Parker, 1993, for a full discussion of this scene and Maya celestial imagery.
3. Heidenreich, 1978.
4. Kraft, 1986.
5. Greenlee, 1945.
6. Benson, 1991.
7. Rights, 1947.
8. Voegelin, 1936.
9. Roe, 1993.
10. Arriaga, 1968.
11. Skinner, 1921.
12. Arrom, 1975:99.
13. Roe, 1993; Olivier, 1992.
14. Von Winning, 1974:43.
15. Conzemius, 1932.
16. Nordenskiöld, 1938.
17. Starr, 1900.
18. Underhill, 1965.
19. Thwaites, 1898, *Jesuit Relations,* 3:127.
20. LaPena, 1978.
21. Cooper, 1946a.
22. Swanton, 1908:430–431.
23. Emmons, 1991.
24. Henry, 1921:107.
25. See Coe, 1982, and Grube and Nahm, 1994, for further discussion of the creatures illustrated on this vase.
26. Markman and Markman, 1992.
27. Soustelle, 1962.
28. See Seler, 1990, for more about this blue dog, which also appears in several places in the Codex Borbonicus in connection with dead warriors and in the Codex Aubin with the Turquoise Lord, the God of Fire.
29. Lopez Lujan, 1994; Soustelle, 1962.
30. Murie, 1948; Tuck, 1970.

31. Morey, 1992.
32. McMillan, 1970.
33. Lewis and Lewis, 1961.
34. Ibid.
35. Ritchie, 1980.
36. For example, see Haag, 1948.
37. Ritchie, 1945.
38. Ritchie, 1980.
39. Schwartz, 1967.
40. Webb, 1946.
41. Webb, 1950b.
42. Webb, 1950a.
43. Webb and DeJarnette, 1942.
44. Kerber, Leveille, and Greenspan, 1989.
45. Lopez and Wisniewski, 1956.
46. Guernsey and Kidder, 1921.
47. Allen, 1920.
48. Amsden, 1949.
49. Moore, 1897:127.
50. Caldwell, 1952.
51. Milner, 1984.
52. Parmalee, 1957, 1975.
53. Welch, 1991.
54. Parmalee, 1956; Webb and DeJarnette, 1942.
55. See, for example, William Webb's reports of 1946, 1950a, and 1950b, and Webb and DeJarnette's of 1942.
56. Smith, 1975.
57. Tafolla, 1983.
58. Ibid.
59. Furst, 1973.
60. Elizabeth Wing generously allowed me to cite from her unpublished study of the vertebrate remains from Marismas Nacionales. This study could not have done without the financial support of the University of New York at Buffalo, the Center for Latin American Studies at the University of Florida, and a Grant-in-Aid from Sigma Xi and the cooperation of all those involved with the Marismas project.
61. Sempowski and Spence, 1994.
62. Moctezuma, 1990.
63. Kidder, Jennings, and Shook, 1946.
64. Ibid.
65. Lothrop, 1937.
66. Linares, 1977.

67. Wafer, 1903:112.

68. Lothrop, 1937.

69. Cook and Ranere, 1989.

70. Wafer, 1903:160.

71. Wing, 1988a.

72. Lathrap, Marcos, and Zeidler, 1977.

73. Marcos, 1988.

74. Benfer, 1984.

75. Engel, 1960.

76. Reitz, 1988.

77. Tello and Xesspe, 1979.

78. Willey and Corbett, 1954.

79. Ibid.

80. Larco Hoyle, 1946.

81. Strong and Evans, 1952.

82. Gheerbrant, 1961:36.

83. Carrion Cachot de Girard, 1959.

84. Weiss, 1970.

85. Kirkpatrick, 1992; Alva and Donnan, 1993.

86. Ibid.

87. Sharon and Donnan, 1974.

88. Donnan and McClelland, 1979.

89. Wing, 1989.

90. Lavallee, 1977; Lavallee et al., 1985; Wing, 1986.

91. Rowe, 1946.

92. Ibid., p. 304.

93. Wing, 1988b.

94. Eaton, 1916.

95. Because of the mixed nature of the sample it was impossible to tell what was originally placed in the seven caves containing dog remains (Schwartz, n.d.).

96. Wilson, 1924.

Chapter 5: Molded, Carved, and Painted Dogs

1. Lothrop, 1937, illustrates this begging dog as well as others recovered from Coclé graves.

2. Harcourt, 1962, has a photograph of the entire frieze plus stretches of the small figures. Only one of these figures appears to be holding a dog.

3. Blanton et al., 1993.

4. Pasztory, 1983.

5. See Willey, 1972, for the complete catalogue and illustrations of these artifacts.

6. For a full view and discussion of this scene see Freidel, Schele, and Parker, 1993, chap. 6.

7. For more on Tlatilco figurines see Piña Chan, 1955, or Coe, 1965. Among the earliest presumed dog figures worldwide are those found at Jarmo, on the edge of the Zargos Mountains in Iran, dating to between 7000 and 6500 B.C. Clay animal figurines with upturned tails recovered at the site are thought to be dogs by Lawrence and Reed, 1983. The tail position characteristic of wolves and other wild animals is straight out or pointing downward. A dog, on the other hand, holds its tail up, ready to wag it in greeting. The authors believe that the position and length of the tail signals that a dog is being represented even in an otherwise generic-appearing quadruped. In addition, skull fragments of large, massively built dogs were found at the site. Reed and Lawrence (1983) describe these dog remains.

8. Lathrap, 1975:23.

9. Anawalt, 1992; Cordy-Collins, 1994.

10. Sempowski and Spence, 1994; Gallagher, 1983; Kidder, Jennings, and Shook, 1946.

11. Caso, Bernal, and Acosta, 1967.

12. Donnan, 1976; Roe, 1993.

13. The following sources give a fairly complete list and some photographs of Mississippian "dog" pots: Webb and DeJarnette, 1942; Phillips, Ford, and Griffin, 1951; Schnell, Knight, and Schnell, 1981; Chapman, 1985; Dye and Wharey, 1989.

14. Donald Lathrap (1973) and Mary Helms (1991) both discuss the importance of long-distance trade in pre-Hispanic America.

15. Although the Chinese developed a hairless breed, the Chinese crested, there is no evidence that it is related in any way to Mexican or Peruvian hairless dogs. Some breeders, however, believe otherwise.

16. Weiss, 1970; Cordy-Collins, 1994.

17. A dog with one copy of the mutant gene would be hairless, but with two copies of the gene an animal would not live. The mating of two hairless dogs would produce, on average, two puppies who were hairless but carrying both types of genes, one haired puppy carrying only the gene for hair, and no puppies with two hairless genes. Thus, by eliminating the puppy with hair, the trait for baldness could easily be maintained in a population by breeding hairless animals.

18. Wing, 1984.

19. Weiss, 1970.

20. Wing, 1984; Delia P. Mathews, Yale University, personal communication.

21. Weiss, 1970.

22. Thompson, 1970.
23. Tozzer, 1941:164.
24. Thompson, 1970.
25. Coe, 1994.
26. Thompson, 1960.
27. Sahagún, 1950–1982, part 4:87.
28. See Nuttall, 1975, for recent facsimile edition of the Codex Nuttall.
29. See Marcus, 1992, for an in-depth look at the Mixtec writing system compared with other systems in Mesoamerica.
30. Whallon, 1992.
31. Pasztory, 1983; Mary Miller, Yale University, personal communication.
32. In Aztec society, weaving was done by female noblewomen.
33. Sullivan, 1982.
34. Ibid.
35. Bierhorst, 1992:145.
36. Remember from Chapter 4 that the blue dog also appears in the Codex Magliabechiano mummy bundle. The blue color may be a reference to the blue-turquoise shade sometimes seen in fires.
37. Sahagún, 1950–1982, book 11, p. 16.
38. Sahagún, 1950–1982, book 10, p. 55.
39. Ibid., p. 32.
40. Berdan and Anawalt, 1992.
41. Coe (1992) discusses the deciphering of the Maya hieroglyphic for dog as *tzul* by Russian scholar Yuri Knorosov in 1952. The word *pek,* when referring to a dog, may be a cognate for pig. If so, the word would have been introduced after the Conquest, probably because dogs, like pigs, were used as food animals. David Kelley, personal communication.
42. Thompson, 1961.
43. Thompson, 1960.
44. Taube, 1989.
45. Thompson, 1972; Seler, 1990.
46. Hofling, 1988.
47. Austin (1990) explains in depth the concepts of binary polarities that were at the core of ancient Mesoamerican belief systems as well as the complexities of their mythological structures.
48. Milanich et. al., 1984; Milanich, 1994.
49. See Furst (1973) for illustration of a dog-woman from Colima.
50. Schnell, Knight, and Schnell, 1981.
51. Miller, 1973; Berrin, 1988.
52. Berrin, 1988.

53. See Moctezuma (1990) for illustration of dog mural.

54. Séjourné, 1966.

55. Seler, 1990.

56. Urton, 1985.

57. Wing, 1988a.

58. Urton, 1985.

59. Sharon and Donnan, 1974.

60. Christopher Donnan's *Ceramics of Ancient Peru* (1992) is a well-illustrated introduction to the better-known pottery styles of pre-Hispanic Peru.

61. Silverman, 1993.

62. See Aveni, 1990, for a thorough discussion of the Nazca line drawings.

63. Tello, 1931.

64. Muñoz Camargo, 1972 (1892).

65. Donnan, 1976; Alva and Donnan, 1993.

66. Alva and Donnan, 1993.

67. Sharon and Donnan, 1974.

68. Brose, Brown, and Penney, 1985.

69. Webb and DeJarnette, 1942.

70. Van der Schalie and Parmalee, 1960.

71. Gibson, 1980.

72. Webb and Baby, 1957.

73. Freidel, Schele, and Parker, 1993.

74. Ibid.

75. Robiscek and Hales, 1981:132.

76. Ibid.

77. Another example of this long-eared dog can be seen in Robiscek and Hales, 1981:34, where such a dog lies on its back, one foot crossing the other, front paw in the air, laughing.

78. Grube and Nahm, 1994.

79. Roe (1995) suggests that Caribbean people who migrated from northern South America had "deep" memories of a fearsome jungle predator that they maintained in their myths and stories, and they imbued dogs with some feline characteristics in their art. Dogs were "stand-ins" for jaguars.

80. Descola, 1994.

81. Neither the coyote nor the wolf inhabited Maya territory, although the secretive gray fox did. See Sheldon, 1992.

82. Lévi-Strauss, 1973:193.

83. Ibid., p. 202.

84. See Simoons, 1994, and Tambiah, 1969, for the Old World perspective and the Florentine Codex and works of Lévi-Strauss for the New World.

Epilogue: After the Conquest

Epigraph: Medina, 1988:248–249. Medina reports that Orellana took almost 2,000 dogs with him on his expedition into the Amazon Basin. Orellana thought that they would be useful for hunting and "dogging" Indians but the Spaniards were forced to eat the dogs when hunger overcame them.

1. Tozzer, 1941:111. Emphasis added.
2. See Crosby, 1972, for an account of the impact of Old World animals in the New World.
3. Varner and Varner, 1983, using original sources, shows how highly regarded the Spanish dogs were by their owners. In fact, these animals were held in much greater esteem than the human beings they were trained to kill.
4. Clayton, Knight, and Moore, 1993:262–263.
5. Lévi-Strauss, 1973.
6. Roe, 1955; Powers and Powers, 1986.
7. Appendix 1 gives a fuller listing of the linguistic terms for dogs and related concepts discussed in this book.
8. Wounded Knee, site of a massacre of Native American men, women, and children and the final in a series of betrayals by the U.S. government, was the location of the last armed conflict between Plains Indians and the Army. Dee Brown (1970) chronicles the conflicts leading to this termination of armed Indian resistance.

References

Abrams, M. H., ed. 1979. *The Norton Anthology of English Literature*. New York: Norton.

Acosta, J. de. 1604. *The Natural and Moral History of the Indies*. English translation by Edward Grimston. London: Hakluyt Society.

Afable, P. 1995. The Peoples of Eduardo Masferé's Photographs. *Discovery* 25:10–19.

Aginsky, B. W. 1941. Culture Element Distributions: XIV. Central Sierra. *University of California Anthropological Records* 4:393–468.

Allen, G. M. 1920. Dogs of American Aborigines. *Bulletin of the Museum of Comparative Zoology, Harvard University* 63:431–517.

Alphonse, E. S. 1956. Guaymi Grammar and Dictionary. Bureau of American Ethnology Bulletin 162, Smithsonian Institution. Washington, D.C.: Government Printing Office.

Alva, W., and C. Donnan. 1993. *Royal Tombs of Sípan*. Los Angeles: Fowler Museum of Cultural History.

Alvarez, C. 1980. *Diccionario Etnolingüístico del Idioma Maya Yucateco Colonial*. Mexico City: Universidad Autónoma de México (Institute of Philological Investigations, Center of Maya Studies).

Amsden, C. A. 1949. *Prehistoric Southwesterners from Basketmaker to Pueblo*. Los Angeles: Southwest Museum.

Anawalt, P. R. 1992. Ancient Cultural Contacts Between Ecuador, West Mexico, and the American Southwest: Clothing Similarities. *Latin American Antiquity* 3:114–129.

Anderson, E. 1984. Who's Who in the Pleistocene: A Mammalian Bestiary. In *Quaternary Extinctions: A Prehistoric Revolution,* ed. P. S. Martin and R. Klein, 40–89. Tucson: University of Arizona Press.

Anyon, R., and S. A. LeBlanc. 1984. *The Galaz Ruin: A Prehistoric Mimbres Village in Southwestern New Mexico*. Albuquerque: Maxwell Museum of Anthropology and University of New Mexico Press.

Arima, E. 1984. Caribou Eskimo. *Handbook of North American Indians,* vol. 5, ed. D. Dumas, 397–414. Washington, D.C.: Smithsonian Institution.

Arriaga, Pablo Joseph de. 1968. *The Extirpation of Idolatry in Peru.* Lexington: University of Kentucky Press.

Arrom, J. J. 1975. *Mitología y Artes Prehispánicas de las Antillas.* Mexico City: Siglo Veintiuno.

Audubon, M. R. 1960. *Audubon and His Journals.* New York: Dover.

Austin, A. L. 1990. *The Myths of the Opossum: Pathways of Mesoamerican Mythology.* Albuquerque: University of New Mexico Press.

Aveleyra Arroyo de Anda, L., and M. Maldonado-Koerdell. 1953. Association of Artifacts with Mammoths in the Valley of Mexico. *American Antiquity* 4:332–340.

Aveni, A., ed. 1990. *The Lines of Nazca.* Philadelphia: American Philosophical Society.

Barbeau, M. 1953. Haida Myths Illustrated in Argillite Carvings. Anthropological Series, Bulletin 127. Ottawa: National Museums of Canada.

Benecke, N. 1987. Studies on Early Dog Remains from Northern Europe. *Journal of Archaeological Science* 14:31–49.

Benfer, R. A. 1984. Challenges and Rewards of Sedentism: The Preceramic Village of Paloma, Peru. In *Paleopathology at the Origins of Agriculture,* ed. M. Cohen and G. Armelogas, 531–558. New York: Academic Press.

Benson, E. P. 1991. The Chthonic Canine. *Latin American Indians Literatures Journal* 7:95–107.

Berdan, F. F., and P. R. Anawalt. 1992. *The Codex Mendoza.* Berkeley: University of California Press.

Berjonneau, G., E. Deletaille, and J. L. Sonnery. 1985. *Rediscovered Masterpeices of Mesoamerica: Mexico-Guatemala-Honduras.* Boulogne, France: Arts Editions.

Berlandier, J. L. 1969. *The Indians of Texas in 1830,* ed. J. C. Ewers. Washington, D.C.: Smithsonian Institution Press.

Berrin, K., ed. 1988. *Feathered Serpents and Flowering Trees.* San Francisco: Fine Arts Museums of San Francisco.

Berta, A. 1987. Origins, Diversification, and Zoogeography of the South American Canidae. In *Studies in Neotropical Mammalogy: Essays in Honor of Philip Hershkovitz,* ed. B. D. Patterson and R. M. Timms, 455–471.

Bierhorst, J. 1985. *The Mythology of North America.* New York: William Morrow.

————. 1992. *History and Mythology of the Aztecs: The Codex Chimalpopoca.* Tucson: University of Arizona Press.

Bingham, H. 1922. *Inca Land.* Cambridge, Mass.: Riverside Press.

Bird, J. 1946. The Alacaluf. *Handbook of South American Indians,* vol. 1, ed. J. Steward, 55–79. Bureau of American Ethnology Bulletin 143, Smithsonian Institution. Washington, D.C.: Government Printing Office.

Birket-Smith, K. 1929. *The Caribou Eskimo: Material and Social Life and Their Cultural Position.* Copenhagen: Gyldenalske Boghandel Nordisk Forlag.

Blanton, R., S. Kowalewski, G. Feiman, and L. Finsten. 1993. *Ancient Mesoamerica: A Comparison of Change in Three Regions*. Cambridge: Cambridge University Press.

Bloomfield, L., and J. D. Nichols, eds. 1991. *The Dog's Children: Anishinaabe Texts Told by Angeline Williams*. Publications of the Algonquian Text Society. Winnipeg: University of Manitoba Press.

Bolton, H. E. 1916. *Spanish Exploration of the Southwest, 1542–1706*. New York: Scribners.

Bourke, J. G. 1884. *The Snake Dance of the Moquis of Arizona*. New York: Charles Scribner's Sons.

Bozell, J. R. 1988. Changes in the Role of the Dog in Protohistoric Pawnee Culture. *Plains Anthropologist* 33:95–111.

Bridges, E. L. 1949. *The Uttermost Part of the Earth*. New York: Dutton.

Bridges, T. 1933. *Yamana-English: A Dictionary of the Speech of Tierra del Fuego*, ed. T. Hestermann and L. Gusinde. Mödling, Austria: Missionsdruckerei St. Gabriel.

Brightman, R. A. 1993. *Grateful Prey: Rock Cree Human-Animal Relationships*. Berkeley: University of California Press.

Brisbin, I. L. 1992. Carolina Dog. *Wolves and Related Canids* (Fall):41–44.

Brody, J. J. 1977. *Mimbres Painted Pottery*. Sante Fe: School of American Research, and Albuquerque: University of New Mexico Press.

Brody, J. J., C. J. Scott, and S. L. LeBlanc. 1983. *Mimbres Pottery: Ancient Art of the American Southwest*. New York: Hudson Hill.

Brose, D. E., J. A. Brown, and D. W. Penney. 1985. *Ancient Art of the American Woodland Indians*. New York: Harry Abrams.

Brown, D. 1970. *Bury My Heart at Wounded Knee: An Indian History of the American West*. New York: Henry Holt.

Bruhns, K. O. 1994. *Ancient South America*. Cambridge: Cambridge University Press.

Burger, R. L. 1992. *Chavin and the Origins of Andean Civilization*. London: Thames and Hudson.

Burpee, L. J., ed. 1927. *Journals and Letters of Pierre Gaultier de Varennes de la Verendrye and His Sons*. Toronto: Champlain Society.

Byington, C. 1915. A Dictionary of the Choctaw Language. Bureau of American Ethnology Bulletin 46, Smithsonian Institution. Washington, D.C.: Government Printing Office.

Byrd, K. A. 1976. Changing Animal Utilization Patterns and Their Implications: Southwest Ecuador, 6500 B.C.–A.D. 1400. Ph.D. diss., University of Florida.

Callaghan, C. A. 1987. Northern Sierra Miwok Dictionary. *University of California Publications in Linguistics,* vol. 110. Berkeley: University of California Press.

Caldwell, J. R. 1952. The Archaeology of Eastern Georgia and South Carolina. In *Archeology of Eastern United States,* ed. J. Griffin, 312–321. Chicago: University of Chicago Press.

Campbell, J. 1989a. *Historical Atlas of World Mythology*. Vol. 2: *The Way of the Seeded*

Earth, part 2: *Mythologies of the Primitive Planters: The Northern Americas*. New York: Perennial Library, Harper and Row.

————. 1989b. *Historical Atlas of World Mythology*. Vol. 2: *The Way of the Seeded Earth*, part 3: *Mythologies of the Primitive Planters: The Middle and Southern Americas*. New York: Perennial Library: Harper and Row.

Cardich, A. 1978. Recent Excavation at Lauricocha, Central Andes, and Los Toldos, Patagonia. In *Early Man in America from a Circum-Pacific Perspective*, ed. A. L. Bryan, 296–300. Department of Anthropology, University of Alberta, Occasional Papers, no. 1. Edmonton.

Carr, H. S. 1985. Subsistence and Ceremony: Faunal Utilization in a Late Preclassic Community at Cerros, Belize. In *Prehistoric Lowland Maya Environment and Subsistence Economy*, ed. M. Pohl, 115–132. Cambridge, Mass.: Peabody Museum of Archaeology and Ethnology.

Carrion Cachot, R. 1959. *La Religión en el Antiguo Peru Norte y Centro de la Costa, Período Post-Clásico*. Lima.

Caso, A., I. Bernal, and J. Acosta. 1967. *La Cerámica de Monte Alban*. Mexico City: National Institute of Anthropology.

Catlin, G. 1841. *Letters and Notes of the Manners, Customs, and Condition of the North American Indians*. London: Tosswill and Meyers.

Caviglia, S. E., H. Yacobaccio, and L. Borrero. 1986. Las Buitreras: Convivencia del Hombre con Fauna Extinta en Patagonia Meridional. In *New Evidence for the Pleistocene Peopling of the Americas*, ed. A. Bryan, 295–315. Orono, Maine: Center for the Study of Early Man.

Chapman, J. 1985. Tellico Archaeology: 12,000 Years of Native American History. *Publications in Anthropology*, no. 40. Tennessee Valley Authority.

Churcher, C. S. 1959. Fossil *Canis* from the Tar Pits of La Brea, Peru. *Science* 130:564–565.

Churchill, S. E. 1993. Weapon Technology, Prey Size Selection, and Hunting Methods in Modern Hunter-Gatherers: Implications for Hunting in the Paleolithic and Mesolithic. In *Hunting and Animal Exploitation in the Later Paleolithic and Mesolithic of Eurasia*, ed. G. L. Peterkin, H. M. Bricker, and P. Mellars, 11–24. *Archeological Papers of the American Anthropological Association*, no. 4.

Clayton, L. A., V. J. Knight, and E. C. Moore, eds. 1993. *The DeSoto Chronicles: The Expedition of Hernando de Soto to North America in 1539–1543*. Tuscaloosa: University of Alabama Press.

Clutton-Brock, J. 1977. Man-Made Dogs. *Science* 197:1340–1342.

————. 1984. Dog. In *Evolution of Domestic Animals*, ed. I. L. Manson, 198–211. London: Longman.

————. 1988. The Carnivore Remains Excavated at Fell's Cave in 1970. In *Travels and Archaeology in South Chile*, ed. J. Hyslop, 188–196. Iowa City: University of Iowa Press.

———. 1995. Origins of the Dog: Domestication and Early History. In *The Domestic Dog*, ed. J. Serpell, 8–20. Cambridge: Cambridge University Press.

Clutton-Brock, J., and N. Hammond. 1994. Hot Dogs: Comestible Canids in Preclassic Maya Culture at Cuello, Belize. *Journal of Archaeological Science* 21:819–826.

Coe, M. D. 1965. *The Jaguar's Children: Pre-Classic Central Mexico*. Greenwich, Conn.: New York Graphic Society.

———. 1982. *Old God and Young Heroes: The Pearlman Collection of Maya Ceramics*. Jerusalem: Israel Museum.

———. 1988. Ideology of the Maya Tomb. In *Maya Iconography*, ed. E. P. Benson and G. G. Griffin, 222–235. Princeton: Princeton University Press.

———. 1992. *Breaking the Maya Code*. London: Thames and Hudson.

———. 1994. *Mexico*. London: Thames and Hudson.

Coe, S. D. 1994. *America's First Cuisines*. Austin: University of Texas Press.

Codex Borbonicus. 1899. Commentary by M. E.-T. Hamy. Paris: E. Leroux.

Codex Magliabechiano. 1970. *Codex Magliabechiano CL. XLLL. 3 B.R. 232 Biblioteca Nazionale Centrale di Firenze*. Commentary by J. DeDurand-Forest. Graz: ADEVA.

Codex Vaticanus A. 1900. *Il manoscritto messicano Vaticano 3738, detto il Códice Rios*. Commentary by F. Ehrle. Rome: Danesi.

Colton, H. S. 1970. The Aboriginal Southwestern Indian Dog. *American Antiquity* 35:153–159.

Conzemius, E. 1932. Ethnographic Survey of the Miskito and Sumu Indians of Honduras and Nicaragua. Bureau of American Ethnography Bulletin 106, Smithsonian Institution. Washington, D.C.: Government Printing Office.

Cook, R. G., and A. J. Ranere. 1989. Hunting in Pre-Columbian Panama: A Diachronic Perspective. In *Foraging and Farming*, ed. D. Harris, 295–307. Boston: Unwin Hyman.

Cooper, J. 1946a. Patagonian and Pampean Hunters. *Handbook of South American Indians*, vol. 1, ed. J. Steward, 127–168. Bureau of American Ethnology Bulletin 143, Smithsonian Institution. Washington, D.C.: Government Printing Office.

———. 1946b. The Yahgan. *Handbook of South American Indians*, vol. 1, ed. J. Steward, 81–106. Bureau of American Ethnology Bulletin 143, Smithsonian Institution. Washington, D.C.: Government Printing Office.

———. 1946c. The Chonos. *Handbook of South American Indians*, vol. 1, ed. J. Steward, 47–53. Bureau of American Ethnology Bulletin 143, Smithsonian Institution. Washington, D.C.: Government Printing Office.

Corbett, L. 1995. *The Dingo in Australia and Asia*. Sydney: University of New South Wales Press.

Cordy-Collins, A. 1994. An Unshaggy Dog Story. *Natural History* 103:34–41.

Cortés, Hernando. 1843. *Dispatches of Hernando Cortés*. New York: Wiley and Putnam.

Crocker, J. C. 1985. My Brother the Parrot. In *Animal Myths and Metaphors in South America*, ed. G. Urton, 13–47. Salt Lake City: University of Utah Press.

Crosby, A. W. 1972. *The Columbian Exchange: Biological and Cultural Consequences of 1492.* Westport, Conn.: Greenwood.

Curtin, J., and J. N. B. Hewitt. 1910–11. Seneca Fiction, Legends, and Myths. *Thirty-Second Annual Report of the Bureau of American Ethnology.* Washington, D.C.: Government Printing Office.

Darwin, C. 1871. *The Descent of Man and Selection in Relation to Sex.* London: Murray.

———. 1952. *Journal of Researches into the Geology and Natural History of the Various Countries Visited by* H. M. S. Beagle. Facsimile of the first edition (1839). New York: Hafner.

de Laguna, F. 1960. *The Story of a Tlingit Community: A Problem in the Relationship Between Archeological, Ethnological, and Historical Methods.* Bureau of American Ethnology Bulletin 172, Smithsonian Institution. Washington, D.C.: Government Printing Office.

Denig, E. T. 1931. *Indian Tribes of the Upper Missouri.* 46th Annual Report of the Bureau of American Ethnology. Washington, D.C.: Government Printing Office.

Descola, P. 1994. *In the Society of Nature: A Native Ecology in Amazonia.* Cambridge: Cambridge University Press.

diaz del Castillo, Bernal. 1968. *The Discovery and Conquest of Mexico, 1517–1521.* Trans. A. P. Maudslay. New York: Noonday Press.

Dillon, B. D. 1988. Meatless Maya? Ethnoarchaeological Implications for Ancient Subsistence. *New World Archaeology* 7:59–70.

Donnan, C. B. 1976. *Moche Art and Iconography.* Los Angeles: University of California, UCLA Latin American Center Publications.

———. 1982. La Caza del Venado en el Arte Mochica. *Revista del Museo Nacional* 46:235–251. Lima.

———. 1992. *Ceramics of Ancient Peru.* Los Angeles: Fowler Museum of Cultural History, University of California.

Donnan, C. B., and D. McClelland. 1979. *The Burial Theme in Moche Iconography.* Studies in Pre-Columbian Art and Archaeology, no. 23. Washington, D.C.: Dumbarton Oaks.

Dorsey, G. 1905. *The Cheyenne.* Part 1: Ceremonial Organization. Field Columbian Museum Pub. 5, Anthro. Ser., 1. Chicago.

Dorsey, G., and A. L. Kroeber. 1903. *Traditions of the Arapaho.* Field Columbian Museum Pub. 81, Anthro. Ser., 5. Chicago.

Driver, H. E. 1939. Culture Element Distributions: X. Northwest California. *University of California Anthropological Records* 1:306–397.

Driver, H. E., and W. C. Massey. 1957. *Comparative Studies of the North American Indians.* Philadelphia: American Philosophical Society.

Drucker, P. 1941. Kwakiutl Dancing Societies. *University of California Publications in Anthropological Records* 2:201–230.

————. 1951. *The Northern and Central Nootkan Tribes.* Bureau of American Ethnology Bulletin 144, Smithsonian Institution. Washington, D.C.: Government Printing Office.

Drummond, L. 1977. Structure and Process in the Interpretation of South American Myth: The Arawak Dog Spirit People. *American Anthropologist* 79:842–868.

Dumas, D. 1984. Copper Eskimo. *Handbook of North American Indians,* vol. 5., ed. D. Dumas, 397–414. Washington, D.C.: Smithsonian Institution.

Duran, D. 1971. *Book of the Gods and Rites and the Ancient Calendar.* Trans. F. Horcasitas and D. Heyden. Norman: University of Oklahoma Press.

Dye, D. H., and C. Wharey. 1989. Exhibition catalog. In *The Southern Ceremonial Complex: Artifacts and Analysis,* ed. P. Galloway, 321–379. Lincoln: University of Nebraska Press.

Dyk, A. 1959. *Mixteco Texts,* ed. B. Elson. Norman: Publication of the Summer Institute of Linguistics of the University of Oklahoma.

Earle, T., T. D'Altroy, C. LeBlanc, C. Hastorf, and T. LeVine. 1980. Changing Patterns in the Upper Mantaro Valley, Peru. *Journal of World Archaeology* 4:1–14.

Eaton, G. F. 1916. *The Collection of Osteological Material from Machu Picchu.* New Haven: Connecticut Academy of Arts and Sciences. Memoirs of the Connecticut Academy of Arts and Sciences, Vol. 5.

Emmons, G. T. 1991. *The Tlingit Indians,* ed. F. De Laguna. Seattle: University of Washington Press.

Engel, F. 1960. Un Group Humain datant de 5000 ans a Paracas, Pérou. *Journal de la Société des Américanistes,* n.s., 49:1–37.

Ewers, J. C. 1955. *The Horse in Blackfoot Culture.* Bureau of American Ethnology Bulletin 159, Smithsonian Institution. Washington, D.C.: Government Printing Office.

Farabee, W. C. 1918. *The Central Arawaks.* University Museum Anthropological Publications, no. 9. Philadelphia: University Museum.

Fenton, W. 1978. Northern Iroquoian Culture Patterns. *Handbook of North American Indians,* vol. 15, ed. B. Trigger, 296–321. Washington, D.C.: Smithsonian Institution.

Fewkes, J. W. 1907. The Aborigines of Porto Rico and Neighboring Islands. *25th Annual Report of the Bureau of American Ethnology.* Washington, D.C.: Government Printing Office.

Figueredo, A. E. 1978. Prehistoric Ethnozoology of the Virgin Islands, 39–45. In *Seventh Congress of the International Association for Caribbean Archeology, Caracas.*

Fitz-Roy, R. 1839. *Narrative of the Surveying Voyages of His Majesty's Ships Adventure and Beagle, Between the Years 1826 and 1836, Describing Their Examination of the Southern Shores of South America.* 3 vols. London: Henry Colburn, Great Marlborough Street.

Flannery, K. V. 1967. Vertebrate Fauna and Hunting Patterns. In *The Prehistory of the Tehuacan Valley,* vol. 1, ed. D. S. Byers, 132–177. Austin: University of Texas Press.

Fock, N. 1963. *Waiwai: Religion and Society of an Amazonian Tribe.* Nationalmuseets Skrifter: Etnograpfisk Rakke, VIII. Copenhagen: National Museum.

Fox, M. W., ed. 1975. *The Wild Canids: Their Systematics, Behavioral Ecology and Evolution.* New York: Van Nostrand Reinhold.

Fox, M. W. 1978. *The Dog: Its Domestication and Behavior.* New York: Garland STPM Press.

Francis, J., L. L. Loendorf, and R. L. Dorn. 1993. AMS Radiocarbon Dating and Radio Carbon Dating of Rock Art in the Bighorn Basin of Wyoming and Montana. *American Antiquity* 58:711–737.

Franklin, J. 1824. *The Journey to the Polar Sea.* New York.

Freidel, D., L. Schele, and J. Parker. 1993. *Maya Cosmos: Three Thousand Years on the Shaman's Path.* New York: William Morrow.

Fritz, G. J. 1994. Are the First Americans Getting Younger? *Current Anthropology* 35:305–309.

Furst, P. T. 1973. West Mexican Art: Secular or Sacred? In *The Iconography of Middle American Sculpture,* ed. I. Bernal, 98–118. New York: Metropolitan Museum of Art.

Gallagher, J. 1983. *Companions of the Dead: Ceramic Tomb Sculpture from Ancient West Mexico.* Los Angeles: UCLA Museum of Cultural History.

Gayton, A. H. 1946. Yokuts and Western Mono Ethnography. *University of California Anthropological Records* 10:10–230.

Gerry, J. 1993. Diet and Status Among the Classic Maya: An Isotopic Perspective. Ph.D. diss., Harvard University.

Gheerbrant, A. 1961. *The Incas: The Royal Commentaries of the Inca Garcilasco de la Vega, 1539–1616.* New York: Orion.

Gibson, S. G. 1980. *Burr's Hill: A Seventeenth-Century Wampanoag Burial Ground.* Providence: Haffenreffer Museum of Anthropology, Brown University.

Giddings, J. L. 1967. *Ancient Men of the Arctic.* New York: Alfred A. Knopf.

Gifford, E. W. 1939. Culture Element Distributions: XII. Apache-Pueblo. *University of California Anthropological Records* 4:1–207.

Gilmore, R. M. 1947. Fauna and Ethnozoology of South America. *Handbook of South American Indians,* ed. J. H. Steward, 345–464. Bureau of American Ethnology Bulletin 143, Smithsonian Institution. Washington, D.C.: Government Printing Office.

Goldstein, M. 1988. *Ceremonial Sculpture of Ancient Veracruz.* Long Island, N.Y.: Hillwood Art Gallery, Long Island University.

Gould, R. A. 1980. *Living Archaeology.* Cambridge: Cambridge University Press.

Grant, C., J. W. Baird, and J. K. Pringle. 1968. *Rock Drawings of the Coso Range.* Maturango Museum, publication 4. China Lake, California.

Greenlee, R. F. 1945. Folk Tales of the Florida Seminoles. *Journal of American Folklore* 58:138–139.

Green, M. 1992. *Animals in Celtic Life and Myth.* London: Routledge.

Griffin, J. W., and H. G. Smith. 1954. The Cotton Site: An Archaeological Site of Early

Ceramic Times in Volusia County, Florida. *Florida State University Studies: Anthropology* 16:27–51.

Grinnell, G. B. 1962. *The Cheyenne Indians: Their History and Ways of Life.* New York: Cooper Square.

Grube, N., and W. Nahm. 1994. A Census of Xibalba: A Complete Inventory of *Way* Characters on Maya Ceramics. In *The Maya Vase Book,* vol. 4, ed. J. Kerr, 686–712. New York: Kerr Associates.

Guaman Poma de Ayala, F. 1936. *Nueva Corónica y Buen Gobierno (Codex péruvien illustré).* Paris: Institut d'Ethnologie.

———. 1978. *Letter to a King: A Peruvian Chief's Account of Life Under the Incas and Under Spanish Rule,* ed. C. Dilke. New York: Dutton.

Guernsey, S. J., and A. V. Kidder. 1921. *Basket-Maker Caves of Northeastern Arizona.* Papers of the Peabody Museum of Archaeology and Ethnology, Harvard University. Vol. 8. Cambridge, Mass.

Gyles, John. 1869. *Memoirs of Odd Adventures, Strange Deliverances, etc. in the Captivity of John Gyles, Esq.* Cincinnati: Spiller and Gates.

Haag, W. G. 1948. An Osteometric Analysis of Some Aboriginal Dogs. *University of Kentucky Reports in Anthropology* 7:1–264.

Hamblin, N. L. 1984. *Animal Use By the Cozumel Maya.* Tucson: University of Arizona Press.

Hamilton, A. 1972. Aboriginal Man's Best Friend? *Man* 8:287–295.

Hamilton Smith, C. 1843. *Dogs.* Part 1. In *Naturalist Library,* vol. 4, ed. W. Jardine. Edinburgh: Lizars.

Hammond, N., ed. 1991. *Cuello: An Early Maya Community in Belize.* Cambridge: Cambridge University Press.

Hannus, A. 1990. Mammoth Hunting in the New World. In *Hunters of the Recent Past,* ed. L. B. Davis and B. Reeves, 47–67. London: Unwin Hyman.

Harlan, J. 1992. *Crops and Man.* Madison: American Society of Agronomy.

Harcourt, R. 1962. *Textiles of Ancient Peru and Their Techniques.* Seattle: University of Washington Press.

Harrington, M. R. 1921. Religion and Ceremonies of the Lenape. *Indian Notes and Monographs,* ed. F. W. Hodge. New York: Museum of the American Indian Heye Foundation.

———. 1922. Cherokee and Earlier Remains on Upper Tennessee River. In *Indian Notes and Monographs,* ed. F. W. Hodge. New York: Museum of the American Indian Heye Foundation.

Harper, J. R. 1971. *Paul Kane's Frontier.* Austin: University of Texas Press.

Hearne, S. 1971. *A Journey from Prince of Wales's Fort in Hudson's Bay to the Northern Ocean.* Rutland, Vt.: Charles E. Tuttle.

Heidenreich, C. E. 1978. Huron. *Handbook of North American Indians,* vol. 15, ed. B. Trigger, 368–388. Washington, D.C.: Smithsonian Institution.

Helms, M. 1991. Esoteric Knowledge, Geographical Distance, and the Elaboration of Leadership Status. In *Profiles in Cultural Evolution,* ed. A. Rambo and K. Gillogly, *University of Michigan Anthropological Papers* 85:330–350.

Henderson, N. 1994. Replicating Dog Travois Travel on the Northern Plains. *Plains Anthropologist* 39:145–159.

Henry, A. 1921. *Travels and Adventures in Canada and the Indian Territory Between the Years 1760–1776,* ed. M. Quaife. Chicago: Lakeside Press.

Hewson, J. 1993. *A Computer Generated Dictionary of Proto-Algonquian.* Hull, Quebec: Canadian Museum of Civilization.

Hofling, C. A. 1988. Venus and the Miscellaneous Almanacs in the Dresden Codex. *Journal of Mayan Linguistics* 6:79–102.

Houck, M. 1951. *Animal Remains from South Indian Field.* Yale University Publications in Anthropology, no. 45, appendix pp. 51–60.

Howard, J. H. 1965. The Ponca Tribe. Bureau of American Ethnology Bulletin 190, Smithsonian Institution. Washington, D.C.: Government Printing Office.

Howay, F. W. 1918. The Dog's Hair Blankets of the Coast Salish. *Washington Historical Quarterly* 10:83–92.

Hudson, C. M. 1976. *The Southeast Indians.* Knoxville: University of Tennessee Press.

Hunn, E. S. 1977. *Tzeltal Folk Zoology.* New York: Academic Press.

Jesse, G. 1886. *Researches into the History of the British Dog.* London: Hardwicke.

Keber, E. Q. 1992. Xolotl: Dogs, Death, and Deities in Aztec Myth. *Latin American Indian Literatures Journal* 8:229–239.

Kelley, J. E. 1975. Zooarchaeological Analysis at Antelope House: Behavioral Inferences from Distributional Data. *The Kiva.* Arizona Archaeological and Historical Society, 41:81–85. Tucson.

Kerber, J. E., A. Leveille, and R. Greenspan. 1989. An Unusual Dog Burial Feature at the Lambert Farm Site, Warwick, Rhode Island: Preliminary Observations. *Archaeology of Eastern North America* 17:165–174.

Kidder, A. V., G. Jennings, and E. Shook. 1946. *Excavations at Kaminaljuyu, Guatemala.* Carnegie Institute of Washington Publication No. 561. Washington, D.C.

Kipling, R. 1982. *Just So Stories.* Garden City, N.Y.: Doubleday.

Kirkpatrick, S. D. 1992. *Lords of Sípan.* New York: William Morrow.

Kraft, H. C. 1986. *The Lenape.* Newark: New Jersey Historical Society.

Kroeber, A. L. 1941. Culture Element Distributions: XV. Salt, Dogs, Tobacco. *University of California Anthropological Records* 6:1–20.

Kutscher, G. 1954. *Nordperuanische Keramik: Figürlich Verzierte Gefässe der Früh-Chimu.* Berlin: Verlag Gebr. Mann.

Lamb, W. K., ed. 1970. *The Journals and Letters of Sir Alexander Mackenzie.* Cambridge: Cambridge University Press.

Lang, R. W., and A. H. Harris. 1984. *The Faunal Remains from Arroyo Hondo Pueblo,*

New Mexico. Santa Fe: School of American Research Press. Arroyo Hondo Archaeological Series, no. 5.

Langguth, A. 1975. Ecology and Evolution in the South American Canids. In *The Wild Canids: Their Systematics, Behavioral Ecology and Evolution,* ed. M. W. Fox, 179–191. New York: Van Nostrand Reinhold.

LaPena, F. R. 1978. Wintu. *Handbook of North American Indians,* vol. 8, ed. R. F. Heizer, 324–340. Washington, D.C.: Smithsonian Institution.

Lapiner, A. 1976. *Pre-Columbian Art of South America.* New York: Harry N. Abrams.

Larco Hoyle, R. 1946. A Cultural Sequence for the North Coast of Peru. *Handbook of South American Indians,* vol. 2, ed. J. Steward, 145–175. Bureau of American Ethnography Bulletin 143, Smithsonian Institution. Washington, D.C.: Government Printing Office.

Las Casas, Bartolomé de. 1992. *A Short Account of the Destruction of the Indies.* London: Penguin Classics.

Lathrap, D. 1973. The Antiquity and Importance of Long-Distance Trade in the Moist Tropics of Pre-Columbian South America. *World Archaeology* 5:170–186.

———. 1975. *Ancient Ecuador: Culture, Clay and Creativity, 3000–300 B.C.* Chicago: Field Museum of Natural History.

Lathrap, D., J. Marcos, and J. Zeidler. 1977. Real Alto: An Ancient Ceremonial Center. *Archaeology* 30:2–13.

Lavallee, D. 1977. Telarmachay: Campamento de Pastores en la Puna de Junin del Periodo Formativo. *Revista del Museo Nacional* 43:61–105.

Lavallee, D., M. Julien, J. Wheeler, and C. Karlin. 1985. *Chasseurs et Pasteurs Prehistoriques Des Andes*—I. Paris: Institut Français d'Etudes Andines.

Lawrence, B., and C. Reed. 1983. The Dogs from Jarmo. In *Prehistoric Archaeology Along the Zargos Flanks,* ed. L. Braidwood, R. Braidwood, B. Howe, C. Reed, and P. Watson, 485–489. Chicago: Oriental Institute, University of Chicago.

Leach, M. 1961. *God Had a Dog.* New Brunswick, N.J.: Rutgers University Press.

Lehmer, D. J., and D. Y. Jones. 1968. *Arikara Archeology: The Bad River Phase.* Publications in Salvage Archeology, no. 8. Lincoln, Neb.

Leland, C. G. 1884. *The Algonquian Legends of New England.* London: Sampson Law, Marston, Searle and Rivington.

Leman, W. 1980. *A Reference Grammar of the Cheyenne Language.* Occasional Publications in Anthropology, Linguistics Series, no. 5. Museum of Anthropology, University of Northern Colorado.

Le Page du Pratz, A. 1975. *The History of Louisiana.* Baton Rouge: Louisiana State University Press.

Lescarbot, M. 1907–1915. *The History of New France [1618].* 3 vols. Trans. W. L. Grant. Toronto: Champlain Society.

Lévi-Strauss, C. 1973. *From Honey to Ashes.* New York: Harper and Row.

———. 1979. *The Way of the Masks.* Seattle: University of Washington Press.

————. 1995. *The Story of the Lynx*. Chicago: University of Chicago Press.

Lewis, T. M., and M. Kneberg. 1946. *Hiwassee Island: An Archaeological Account of Four Tennessee Indian Peoples*. Knoxville: University of Tennessee Press.

Lewis, T. M., and M. K. Lewis. 1961. *Eva: An Archaic Site*. Knoxville: University of Tennessee Press.

Li, F. K., and R. Scallon. 1976. *Chipewyan Texts*. Nanking, Taipei: Institute of History and Philology, Academia Sinica.

Linares, O. F. 1977. *Ecology and the Arts of Panama: On the Development of Social Rank and Symbolism in the Central Provinces*. Studies in Pre-Columbian Art and Archaeology, no. 17. Washington, D.C.: Dumbarton Oaks.

Lopez, J., and S. Wisniewski. 1956. Discovery of a Possible Ceremonial Dog Burial in the City of Greater New York. *Archeological Society of Connecticut Bulletin* 29:14–19.

Lopez Lujan, L. 1994. *The Offerings of the Templo Mayor of Tenochtitlan*. Trans. B. Ortez de Montellano and T. Ortez de Montellano. Niwot, Colo.: University of Colorado Press.

Lothrop, S. K. 1928. The Indians of Tierra del Fuego. *Contributions to Museum of the American Indian,* vol. 10. New York: Heye Foundation.

————. 1937. *Coclé: An Archaeological Study of Central Panama*. Part 1. Memoirs of the Peabody Museum of Archaeology and Ethnology. Harvard University.

Luomala, K. 1960. The Native Dog in the Polynesian System of Values. In *Essays in Honor of Paul Radin,* ed. S. Diamond, 190–240. New York: Columbia University Press.

Lyon, P. J. 1970. Differential Bone Destruction: An Ethnographic Example. *American Antiquity* 35:213–215.

McBrearty, S., and M. Moniz. 1991. Prostitutes or Providers? Hunting, Tool Use, and Sex Roles in Earliest *Homo. Archaeology of Gender: Proceedings of the Twenty-Second Annual Conference of the Archaeological Association of the University of Calgary,* 71–83. Calgary, Alberta: University of Calgary.

McCartney, P. H. 1990. Alternative Hunting Strategies in Plains Paleoindian Adaptations. In *Hunters of the Recent Past,* ed. L. B. Davis and B. O. K. Reeves, 111–121. London: Unwin Hyman.

McMillan, R. B. 1970. Early Canid Burial from the Western Ozark Highland. *Science* 167:1246–1247.

MacNeish, R. S., F. A. Peterson, and J. A. Neely. 1972. The Archaeological Reconnaissance. *The Prehistory of the Tehuacan Valley,* vol. 1, ed. D. S. Byers, 132–177. Austin: University of Texas Press.

Magana, E. 1986. Paisajes, Hombres y Animales Imaginarios de Algunas ribus Ge del Brasil Central. In *Myth and the Imaginary in the New World,* ed. E. Magana and P. Mason. Smithfield: Foris Publications.

Marcos, J. G. 1988. *Real Alto: La Historia de un Centro Ceremonial Valdivia*. Quito: Corporaci en Editora Nacional.

Marcus, J. 1992. *Mesoamerican Writing Systems: Propaganda, Myth, and History in Four Ancient Civilizations*. Princeton: Princeton University Press.

Markman, R. H., and P. T. Markman. 1992. *The Flayed God*. San Francisco: Harper.

Martin, P. S. 1984. Prehistoric Overkill: The Global Model. In *Quaternary Extinctions: A Prehistoric Revolution,* ed. P. S. Martin and R. Klein, 354–403. Tucson: University of Arizona Press.

Mary-Rousseliere, G. 1984. Iglulik. *Handbook of North American Indians,* vol. 5, ed. D. Dumas, 397–414. Washington, D.C.: Smithsonian Institution.

Medina, J. T. 1988. *The Discovery of the Amazon*. Trans. B. T. Lee. New York: Dover.

Meniél, P. 1992. *Les Sacrifices d'Animaux chez les Gaulois*. Paris: Editions France.

Michelson, T. 1925. The Mythical Origin of the White Buffalo Dance of the Fox Indians, 12–48. *Fortieth Annual Report of the Bureau of American Ethnology*. Washington, D.C.: Government Printing Office.

Miksicek, C. H., E. Wing, and S. Scudder. 1991. The Ecology and Economy of Cuello. In *Cuello: An Early Maya Community in Belize,* ed. N. Hammond, 70–97. Cambridge: Cambridge University Press.

Milanich, J. T. 1994. *Archaeology of Precolumbian Florida*. Gainesville: University Presses of Florida.

———. 1996. A Host of Would-Be Conquerors. *Archaeology* 49:68–69.

Milanich, J. T., and C. Hudson. 1993. *Hernando De Soto and the Indians of Florida*. Gainesville: University Presses of Florida.

Milanich, J. T., et al. 1984. *McKeithen Weeden Island: The Culture of Northern Florida, A.D. 200–900*. Orlando: Academic Press.

Miller, A. G. 1973. *The Mural Paintings of Teotihuacán*. Washington, D.C.: Dumbarton Oaks.

Miller, G. R., and R. L. Burger. 1995. Our Father the Cayman, Our Dinner the Llama: Animal Utilization at Chavin de Huantar, Peru. *American Antiquity* 60:421–458.

Miller, M., and K. Taube. 1993. *The Gods and Symbols of Ancient Mexico and the Maya*. London: Thames and Hudson.

Milner, G. R. 1984. Social and Temporal Implications of Variation Among American Bottom Mississippian Cemeteries. *American Antiquity* 49:468–488.

———. 1990. The Late Prehistoric Cahokia Cultural System of the Mississippi River Valley: Foundations, Florescence, and Fragmentation. *Journal of World Prehistory* 4:1–41.

Moctezuma, E. M. 1990. *Teotihuacan: The City of Gods*. New York: Rizzoli.

Moehlman, P. 1992. Introduction. In *Wild Dogs: The Natural History of the Nondomestic Canidae,* J. Sheldon, 1–3. San Diego: Academic Press.

Moore, C. B. 1897. Certain Aboriginal Mounds of the Georgia Coast. *Journal of the Academy of Natural Sciences of Philadelphia* 11.

Morey, D. F. 1992. Size, Shape, and Development in the Evolution of the Domestic Dog. *Journal of Archaeological Science* 19:181–204.

Morey, D. F., and M. Wiant. 1992. Early Holocene Domestic Dog Burials from the North American Midwest. *Current Anthropology* 33:224–229.

Morgan, L. H. 1962. *League of the Ho-De-No-Sau-nee, Iroquois.* New York: Corinth.

Muñoz Camargo, Diego. 1972 (1892). *Historia de Tlaxcala por Diego Muñoz Camargo,* ed. A. Chavero. Facsimile 1892 edition. Guadalajara: Biblioteca de Facsimiles Mexicanos 6.

Murdock, J. P. 1936. *Rank and Potlatch Among the Haida.* Yale University Publications in Anthropology, no. 8.

Murie, J. R. 1989. *Ceremonies of the Pawnee,* ed. D. R. Parks. Lincoln: University of Nebraska Press.

Murie, O. J. 1948. Dog Skulls from Ipiutak. *Anthropological Papers of the American Museum of Natural History* 42:255–264.

Nimis, M. N. 1982. The Contemporary Role of Women in Lowland Maya Livestock Production. In *Maya Subsistence,* ed. K. Flannery, 313–325. New York: Academic Press.

Nordenskiöld, E. 1938. *An Historical and Ethnological Survey of the Cuna Indians.* Comparative Ethnographic Studies 10. Göteborg: Göteborgs Museum, Ethnografiska Avdelningen.

Nowak, R. M., and J. L. Paradiso. 1983. *Walker's Mammals of the World.* 4th ed., vol. 2. Baltimore: Johns Hopkins University Press.

Nuttall, Z. 1975. *The Codex Nuttall.* New York: Dover.

Olivier, J. R. 1992. The Caguana Ceremonial Center: A Cosmic Journey Through Taino Spatial and Iconographic Symbolism. Paper presented at the International Symposium, Association of Indigenous Latin American Literature, San Juan.

Olsen, F. 1974. *On the Trail of the Arawaks.* Norman: University of Oklahoma.

Olsen, J. W. 1990. Vertebrate Faunal Remains from Grasshopper Pueblo, Arizona. *Anthropological Papers of the Museum of Anthropology, University of Michigan,* no. 83.

Olsen, S. J. 1972. Vertebrate Faunal Remains. In *The Artifacts of Altar de Sacrificios,* ed. G. Willey, 243–248. Papers of the Peabody Museum of Archaeology and Ethnology, Vol. 64. Cambridge, Mass.: Harvard University.

———. 1978. Vertebrate Faunal Remains. In *Excavations at Seibel,* ed. G. Willey, 172–176. Papers of the Peabody Museum of Archaeology and Ethnology, Vol. 70. Cambridge, Mass.: Harvard University.

———. 1985. *Origins of the Domestic Dog: The Fossil Record.* Tucson: University of Arizona Press.

O'Shea, J. M., and J. Ludwickson. 1992. *Archaeology and Ethnohistory of the Omaha Indians: The Big Village Site.* Lincoln: University of Nebraska Press.

Parmalee, P. W. 1957. Vertebrate Remains from Cahokia Site, Illinois. *Transactions of the Illinois State Academy of Science* 50:235–242.

———. 1975. A General Summary of the Vertebrate Fauna from Cahokia. *Perspectives in Cahokia Archaeology. Illinois Archaeological Survey Bulletin* 10:137–155.

Pasztory, Esther. 1983. *Aztec Art.* New York: Harry Abrams.

Peterson, R. O., and R. E. Page. 1988. The Rise and Fall of Isle Royale Wolves, 1975–1986. *Journal of Mammalogy* 69:89–99.

Phillips, P., J. A. Ford, and J. B. Griffin. 1951. *Archaeological Survey in the Lower Mississippi Alluvial Valley, 1940–1947.* Papers of the Peabody Museum of Archaeology and Ethnology, Harvard University, no. 25.

Piña Chan, R. 1955. *Las culturas preclásicas de la Cuenca de México.* Mexico City: Center for Economic Culture.

Pires-Ferreira, J., E. Pires-Ferreira, and P. Kaulicke. 1976. Preceramic Animal Utilization in the Central Peruvian Andes. *Science* 194:483–490.

Pohl, M. 1985. The Privileges of Maya Elites: Prehistoric Vertebrate Fauna from Seibel. In *Prehistoric Lowland Maya Environment and Subsistence Economy,* ed. M. Pohl, 133–145. Cambridge, Mass.: Peabody Museum of Archaeology and Ethnology.

———. 1991. Women, Animal Rearing, and Social Status: The Case of the Formative Period Maya of Central America. In *The Archaeology of Gender: Proceedings of the Twenty-Second Annual Conference of the Archaeological Association of the University of Calgary,* pp. 295–312. Calgary: University of Calgary.

Pohl, M., and L. H. Feldman. 1982. The Traditional Role of Women and Animals in Lowland Maya Economy. In *Maya Subsistence,* ed. K. Flannery, 353–367. New York: Academic Press.

Politis, G., and M. C. Salemme. 1990. Pre-Hispanic Mammal Exploitation and Hunting Strategies in the Eastern Pampa Subregion of Argentina. In *Hunters of the Recent Past,* ed. L. B. Davis and B. Reeves, 352–365. London: Unwin Hyman.

Powers, S. 1976. *Tribes of California.* Berkeley: University of California Press.

Powers, W. K., and M. N. Powers. 1986. Putting on the Dog. *Natural History* 95:6–17.

Pozorski, S. G. 1979. Prehistoric Diet and Subsistence of the Moche Valley, Peru. *World Archaeology* 2:163–184.

Quilter, J. 1990. The Moche Revolt of the Objects. *Latin American Antiquity* 1:42–65.

Radin, P. 1990. *The Winnebago Tribe.* Lincoln: University of Nebraska Press.

Ray, F. 1940. Culture Element Distributions: XXII. Plateau. *University of California Anthropological Records* 8:99–262.

Reed, C. 1960. A Review of the Archeological Evidence on Animal Domestication in the Prehistoric Near East. In *Prehistoric Investigations in Iraqi Kurdistan,* ed. R. Braidwood and B. Howe, 119–145. University of Chicago, Oriental Institute, Studies in Ancient Oriental Civilization, no. 31. Chicago: University of Chicago Press.

Reeves, B. 1990. Communal Hunters of the Northern Plains. In *Hunters of the Recent Past,* ed. L. B. Davis and B. Reeves, 168–189. London: Unwin Hyman.

Reitz, E. J. 1988. Preceramic Animal Use on the Central Coast. In *Economic Prehistory of the Central Andes,* ed. E. S. Wing and J. C. Wheeler, 31–73. Oxford: BAR International Series.

Reynolds, R. D. 1993. *The Ancient Art of Colima.* Walnut Creek, Calif.: Squibob Press.

Rice, D. S., P. Rice, and E. S. Deevey. 1985. Paradise Lost: Classic Maya Impact on a Lacustrine Environment. In *Prehistoric Lowland Maya Environment and Subsistence Economy,* ed. M. Pohl, 91–103. Cambridge, Mass.: Peabody Museum of Archaeology and Ethnology.

Rice, K. 1989. *A Grammar of Slave.* Berlin: Mouton de Gruyter.

Richardson, J. 1829. *Fauna Boreali-Americana; or the Zoology of the Northern Parts of British America.* Vol. 1: Quadrupeds. London: J. Murray.

Rights, D. L. 1947. *The American Indian in North Carolina.* Durham, N.C.: Duke University Press.

Ritchie, W. A. 1945. *An Early Site in Cayuga County, New York.* Research Records of the Rochester Museum of Arts and Sciences, no. 7.

———. 1980. *The Archaeology of New York State.* New York: Harbor Hill.

Robiscek, F., and D. Hales. 1981. *The Maya Book of the Dead: The Ceramic Codex.* Charlottesville: University of Virginia Art Museum. Distributed by the University of Oklahoma Press.

Roe, F. G. 1955. *The Indian and the Horse.* Norman: University of Oklahoma Press.

Roe, P. G. 1995. Eternal Companions: Amerindian Dogs from Tierra Firma to the Antilles. *Proceedings of the XV International Congress for Caribbean Archaeology,* 155–172, eds. R. Alegría and M. Rodriguez. San Juan, Puerto Rico.

———. In press. *The Domesticated Jaguar: The Symbolism of South Amerindian Dogs from a Lowland Perspective.* Manuscript.

Rogers, E. S., and J. Smith. 1981. Environment and Culture in the Shield and Mackensie Borderlands. *Handbook of North American Indians,* vol. 6., ed. J. Helm, 130–145. Washington, D.C.: Smithsonian Institution.

Roth, W. E. 1924. *An Introductory Study of the Arts, Crafts, and Customs of the Guiana Indians.* Thirty-Eighth Annual Report of the Bureau of American Ethnology. Washington, D.C.: Government Printing Press.

Rouse, I. 1951. *A Survey Indian River Archaeology, Florida.* Yale University Publications in Anthropology, no. 44.

———. 1992. *The Tainos: Rise and Decline of the People Who Greeted Columbus.* New Haven: Yale University Press.

Rowe, J. H. 1946. Inca Culture at the Time of the Spanish Conquest. *Handbook of South American Indians,* vol. 2, ed. J. Steward, 183–330. Bureau of American Ethnography Bulletin 143, Smithsonian Institution. Washington, D.C.: Government Printing Office.

Roy, M. S., E. Geffen, D. Smith, E. A. Ostrander, and R. K. Wayne. 1994. Patterns of Differation and Hybridization in North American Wolflike Canids, Revealed by Analysis of Microsatellite Loci. *Molecular Biology and Evolution* 11:553–570.

Roys, R. L. 1976. *The Ethno-Botany of the Maya*. Philadelphia: Institute for the Study of Human Issues.

Russell, F. 1908. *The Pima Indians*. Twenty-sixth Annual Report of the Bureau of American Ethnology, 3–389. Washington, D.C.: Government Printing Office.

Sagard, G. 1939. *The Long Journey to the Country of the Hurons,* ed. G. M. Wrong. Toronto: Champlain Society.

Sahagún, Bernardino de. 1950–1982. *General History of the Things of New Spain: Florentine Codex*. Santa Fe, N.M.: School for American Research.

Salomon, F., and G. L. Urioste. 1991. *The Huarochirí Manuscript*. Austin: University of Texas Press.

Sandefur, E. C. 1988. Andean Zooarchaeology: Animal Use and the Inca Conquest of the Upper Mantaro Valley. Ph.D. diss., University of California, Los Angeles. UMI Services.

Sanders, W. T., J. R. Parsons, and R. Santley. 1979. *The Basin of Mexico: Ecological Processes in the Evolution of a Civilization*. New York: Academic Press.

Sapir, E. 1931. *Southern Paiute, a Shoshonean Language*. Proceedings of the American Academy of Arts and Sciences, no. 65. Boston.

Sapir, E., and M. Swadesh. 1939. *Nootka Texts: Tales and Ethnological Narrative*. William Dwight Whitney Linguistic Series. Philadelphia: University of Pennsylvania Press.

Sauer, C. O. 1966. *The Early Spanish Main*. Berkeley: University of California Press.

Savishinsky, J. S. 1974a. *The Trail of the Hare: Life and Stress in a Arctic Community*. New York: Gordon and Breach.

———. 1974b. The Child Is Father to the Dog: Canines and Personality Processes in an Arctic Community. *Human Development* 17:460–466.

Saxon, D., L. Saxton, and S. Enos. 1983. *Dictionary: Papago/Pima-English: English-Papago/Pima*. Tucson: University of Arizona Press.

Schlesier, K. H. 1987. *The Wolves of Heaven: Cheyenne Shamanism, Ceremonies, and Prehistoric Origins*. Norman: University of Oklahoma Press.

Schnell, F. T., V. J. Knight, and G. S. Schnell. 1981. *Cemochechobee: Archaeology of a Mississippian Ceremonial Center on the Chattahoochee River*. Gainesville: University Presses of Florida.

Schroeder, A. H., and D. S. Matson. 1965. *A Colony on the Move, Gaspar Castano de Sosa's Journal*. Santa Fe: School of American Research.

Schwartz, D. W. 1967. *Conceptions of Kentucky Prehistory: A Case Study in the History of Archaeology*. Studies in Anthropology, 6. Lexington: University of Kentucky Press.

Schwartz, M. n.d. A Faunal Analysis of the Camelid Bones from the Caves at Machu Picchu. Unpublished manuscript.

Seaman, P. D. 1985. *Hopi Dictionary*. Northern Arizona University Anthropology Papers, no. 2. Flagstaff: Northern Arizona University.

Seger, J. H. 1934. *Early Days Among the Cheyenne and Arapahoe Indians,* ed. S. Vestal. Norman: University of Oklahoma Press.

Seidelman, H., and J. Turner. 1994. *Inuit Imagination.* New York: Thames and Hudson.

Séjourné, L. 1966. *El lenuaje de las Formas en Teotihuacán.* Mexico.

Seler, E. 1990. *Gesammelte Abhandlungen zur Amerikanischen Sprach- und Altertumskunde,* vols. 1–3. English translation by E. R. Thompson and F. R. Richardson. Culver City, Calif.: Labyrinthos.

Sempowski, M. L., and M. W. Spence. 1994. *Mortuary Practices and Skeletal Remains at Teotihuacán.* Salt Lake City: University of Utah Press.

Serpell, J. A. 1983. The Personality of the Dog and Its Influence on the Pet-Owner Bond. In *New Perspectives on Our Lives with Companion Animals,* ed. A. H. Katcher and A. M. Beck, 57–65. Philadelphia: University of Pennsylvania Press.

Sharon, D., and C. B. Donnan. 1974. Shamanism in Moche Iconography. *Ethnoarchaeology Monograph 4,* ed. C. B. Donnan and C. W. Clewlow, 49–77. Los Angeles: Institute of Archaeology.

Sheldon, J. W. 1992. *Wild Dogs: The Natural History of the Nondomestic Canidae.* San Diego: Academic Press.

Shimada, M., and I. Shimada. 1981. Exploitation y Manejo de los Recursos Naturales en Pampa Grande, Sitio Moche V: Significado del Anallisis Organico. *Revista del Museo Nacional* 45:19–73.

Shimkin, D. B. 1986. Eastern Shoshone. *Handbook of North American Indians,* vol. 11, ed. W. L. D'Azevedo, 308–335. Washington, D.C.: Smithsonian Institution.

Silverman, H. 1993. *Caluachi in the Ancient Nasca World.* Iowa City: Iowa University Press.

Simmons, L., ed. 1942. *Sun Chief: The Autobiography of a Hopi Indian.* New Haven: Yale University Press.

Simoons, F. J. 1994. *Eat Not This Flesh: Food Avoidances from Prehistory to the Present.* Madison: University of Wisconsin Press.

Skinner, M. 1921. Material Culture of the Menomini. In *Indian Notes and Monographs,* ed. F. W. Hodge. New York: Museum of the American Indian Heye Foundation.

Smith, B. D. 1975. Middle Mississippi Exploitation of Animal Populations. *Anthropological Papers Museum of Anthropology, University of Michigan* 57:102–180.

Soustelle, J. 1962. *The Daily Life of the Aztecs on the Eve of the Conquest.* New York: Macmillan.

Speck, F. G. 1925. Dogs of the Labrador Indians. *Natural History* 25:58–64.

Spencer, R. F. 1959. *The North Alaskan Eskimo: A Study in Ecology and Society.* Bureau of American Ethnology Bulletin 171, Smithsonian Institution. Washington, D.C.: Government Printing Office.

Starbuck, D. R. 1975. Man-Animal Relationships in Pre-Columbian Central Mexico. Ph.D. diss., Yale University.

Starr, F. 1900. *Ethnography of Southern Mexico*. Davenport Academy of Sciences, no. 6. Davenport, Iowa.

Steedman, E., ed. 1930. *Ethnobotany of the Thompson Indians of British Columbia*. 45th Annual Report of Bureau of American Ethnology. Washington, D.C.: Government Printing Office.

Steward, J. H. 1941. Culture Element Distributions: XIII. Nevada Shoshoni. *University of California Anthropological Records* 4:209–259.

———. 1948. The Circum-Caribbean Tribes. *Handbook of South American Indians*, vol. 4, pp. 1–41. Bureau of American Ethnology Bulletin 143, Smithsonian Institution. Washington, D.C.: Government Printing Office.

Stewart, J. 1941. Culture Element Distributions: XIV. Northern Paiute. *University of California Anthropological Records* 4:361–446.

Strong, W., and C. Evans. 1952. *Cultural Stratigraphy in the Viru Valley, Northern Peru*. New York: Columbia University Press.

Sullivan, T. D. 1982. Tlazolteotl-Ixcuina: The Great Spinner and Weaver. In *The Art and Iconography of Late Post-Classic Central Mexico*, ed. E. Boone, 7–35. Washington, D.C.: Dumbarton Oaks.

Swanton, J. R. 1908. Social Conditions, Beliefs, and Linguistic Relationships of the Tlingit Indians. *Twenty-Sixth Annual Report of Bureau of American Ethnology*, 391–484. Washington, D.C.

———. 1946. *The Indians of the Southeastern United States*. Bureau of American Ethnology Bulletin 137, Smithsonian Institution. Washington, D.C.: Government Printing Office.

Tafolla, G. A. 1983. *Colima Precolombino*. Mexico City: Jorge Porrua.

Tambiah, S. J. 1969. Animals are Good to Think and Good to Prohibit. *Ethnology* 7:423–459.

Taube, K. A. 1989. The Maize Tamale in Classic Maya Diet, Epigraphy, and Art. *American Antiquity* 54:31–51.

Taylor, D. 1977. *Languages of the West Indies*. Baltimore: Johns Hopkins University Press.

Tedlock, D. 1985. *Popol Vul*. New York: Simon and Schuster.

Teit, J. A. 1930. *The Salishan Tribes of the Western Plateaus*. Forty-Fifth Annual Report of the Bureau of American Ethnology, 3–389. Washington: Government Printing Office.

Tello, J. C. 1931. Un Modelo de Escenograpfia Plástica en el Arte Antiguo Peruano. *Wira Kocha, revista de estudios Antropológicos* 1:87–112. Lima.

Tello, J. C., and T. M. Xesspe. 1979. *Paracas, Segune Parte: Cavernas y Necrópolis*. Lima: Universidad Nacional Myor de San Marcos.

Templeton, A. R. 1989. The Meaning of Species and Speciation: A Genetic Perspective. In *Speciation and Its Consequences*, ed. D. Otte and J. Endler, 3–27. Sunderland, Mass.: Sinaur.

Thomas, H. 1993. *The Conquest of Mexico*. London: Hutchinson.

Thomas, R. B. 1973. *Human Adaptation to a High Andean Energy Flow System.* Occasional Papers in Anthropology, no. 7. University Park: Pennsylvania State University,

Thompson, J. E. S. 1960. *Maya Hieroglyphic Writing.* Norman: University of Oklahoma Press.

———. 1961. Notes on a Plumbate Vessel with Shell Inlay and on Chiclero's Ulcer. In *Essays in Pre-Columbian Art and Archaeology,* ed. S. K. Lothrop et al., 171–175. Cambridge, Mass.: Harvard University Press.

———. 1970. *Maya History and Religion.* Norman: University of Oklahoma Press.

———. 1972. *A Commentary on the Dresden Codex: A Maya Hieroglyphic Book.* Philadelphia: American Philosophical Society.

Thurman, M. D. 1988. On the Identity of the Chariticas [Sarh Rikka]: Dog Eating and Pre-Horse Adaptation on the High Plains. *Plains Anthropologist* 33:159–170.

Thwaites, R. G., ed. 1898. *The Jesuit Relations and Related Documents.* Cleveland: Borrows Brothers.

Tooker, E. 1964. *An Ethnography of the Huron Indians, 1615–1649.* Bureau of American Ethnology Bulletin 190, Smithsonian Institution. Washington, D.C.: Government Printing Office.

Tozzer, A. M. 1941. *Landa's Relación de las Cosas de Yucatan.* Papers of the Peabody Museum of American Archaeology and Ethnology, Harvard University.

Trigger, B. 1985. *Natives and Newcomers.* Kingston: McGill-Queen's University Press.

Tuck, J. A. 1970. An Archaic Indian Cemetery in Newfoundland. In *New World Archaeology: Theoretical and Cultural Transformations,* ed. E. Zubrow, M. Fritz, and F. Fritz, 105–114. San Francisco: W. H. Freeman.

Uhlenbeck, C. C., and R. H. Gulik. 1934. *A Blackfoot-English Vocabulary.* Amsterdam: Noord-Hollansche uitgevers-maatschappij.

Underhill, R. 1944. *Indians of the Pacific Northwest.* Vol. 5: *Indian Life and Customs.* Washington, D.C.: Education Division, U.S. Office of Indian Affairs.

———. 1965. *Red Man's Religion.* Chicago: University of Chicago Press.

Urton, G. 1985. Animal Metaphors and the Life Cycle in an Andean Community. In *Animal Myths and Metaphors in South America,* ed. G. Urton, 251–284. Salt Lake City: University of Utah Press.

Vancouver, G. 1801. *Voyage of Discovery to the North Pacific Oceans.* Vol. 2. London: Stockdale.

Van der Schalie, H., and P. W. Parmalee. 1960. Animal Remains from the Etowah Site, Mound C, Bartow County, Georgia. *Florida Anthropologist* 13:37–54.

Van Tuyl, C. 1979. *The Natchez: Annotated Translations from Antoine Simon le Page du Pratz's* Histoire de la Louisiane *and a Short English-Natchez Dictionary.* Oklahoma Historical Society Series in Anthropology, no. 4. Oklahoma City.

Varner, J. G., and J. J. Varner. 1983. *Dogs of the Conquest.* Norman: University of Oklahoma Press.

Villacorta, C., and C. A. Villacorta. 1930. *Codices Maya: Dresdensis-Peresianus-Tro-Cortesianus*. Guatamala: Tipografia Nacional.

Voegelin, E. 1936. *The Shawnee Female Deity*. Yale University Publications in Anthropology, no. 10.

von Hagen, V. W., ed. 1959. *The Incas of Pedro de Cieza de Leon*. Trans. H. de Onis. Norman: University of Oklahoma Press.

Von Winning, H. 1974. *The Shaft Tomb Figures of West Mexico*. Los Angeles: Southwest Museum.

Wafer, L. 1903. *A New Voyage and Description of the Isthmus of America,* ed. G. P. Winship. Cleveland: Borrows Brothers.

Walker, D., and Frison, G. C. 1982. Studies on Amerindian Dogs, part 3: Prehistoric Wolf/Dog Hybrids from the Northwestern Plains. *Journal of Archaeological Science* 9:125–172.

Walker, J. B. 1985. A Preliminary Report on the Lithic and Osteological Remains from the 1980, 1981, and 1982 Field Seasons at Hacienda Grande 1(2 PSJ7–5). In *Proceedings of the 10th International Congress for the Study of the Precolumbian Cultures of the Lesser Antilles, Fort-de-France,* ed. L. Allaire and F. Mayer, 181–224. Montreal: Center of Caribbean Research, University of Montreal.

Wallace, W. J. 1978. Southern Valley Yokuts. *Handbook of North American Indians,* vol. 8, ed. R. F. Heizer, 448–461. Washington, D.C.: Smithsonian Institution.

Wallis, W. D., and R. Wallis. 1955. *The Micmacs of Eastern Canada*. Minneapolis: University of Minnesota Press.

Walsh, J. H. 1879. *The Dogs of Great Britain, America, and Other Countries*. New York: Orange Judd.

Wayne, R. K. 1986. Cranial Morphology of Domestic and Wild Canids: The Influence of Development on Morphological Change. *Evolution* 40:243–261.

———. 1993. Molecular Evolution in the Dog Family. *Trends in Genetics* 9:218–224.

Webb, C. H. 1959. *The Belcher Mound: A Stratified Caddoan Site in Caddo Parish*. Memoirs of the Society for American Archaeology, 16.

Webb, W. S. 1946. Indian Knoll. *University of Kentucky Reports in Anthropology* 4:115–365.

———. 1950a. The Carlson Annis Mound, Site 5. *University of Kentucky Reports in Anthropology* 7:267–354.

———. 1950b. The Read Shell Midden. *University of Kentucky Reports in Anthropology* 7:358–367.

Webb, W. S., and R. S. Baby. 1957. *The Adena People No. 2*. Ohio Historical Society. Columbus: Ohio State University Press.

Webb, W. S., and W. DeJarnette. 1942. *An Archeological Survey of Pickwick Basin in the Adjacent Portions of the States of Alabama, Mississippi and Tennessee*. Bureau of

American Ethnology Bulletin 129, Smithsonian Institution. Washington, D.C.: Government Printing Office.

Webster, D. H., and W. Zibell. 1976. Report of Canadian Eskimo Language Survey, 1968. In *Papers on Eskimo and Aleut Linguistics,* ed. E. P. Hamp. Chicago: Chicago Linguistic Society.

Weiss, P. 1970. El Perro peruano sin pelo. *Acta Herediana Lima* 3:33–45.

Welch, P. D. 1991. *Moundville's Economy.* Tuscaloosa: University of Alabama Press.

Wellmann, K. F. 1979. *A Survey of North American Indian Rock Art.* Graz, Austria: Akademische Druck-u. Verlaganstalt.

Whallon, R. 1992. Appendix: A Statistical Analysis of Mesoamerican Writing. In *Mesoamerican Writing Systems: Propaganda, Myth, and History in Four Ancient Civilizations,* J. Marcus. Princeton, N.J.: Princeton University Press.

Wheat, J. B. 1972. *The Olsen-Chubbuck Site: A Paleo-Indian Bison Kill.* Memoirs of the Society for American Archaeology, 26.

Wheeler, R. J., and R. McGee. 1994. Report of Preliminary Zooarchaeological Analysis: Groves' Orange Midden. *Florida Anthropologist* 47:393–403.

White, C. D., and H. P. Schwarcz. 1989. Ancient Maya Diet: As Inferred from Isotopic and Elemental Analysis of Human Bone. *Journal of Archaeological Science* 16:451–474.

White, David Gorden. 1991. *Myths of the Dog-Man.* Chicago: University of Chicago Press.

Whitehead, R. H. 1991. *The Old Man Told Us: Excerpts from Micmac History, 1500–1950.* Nova Scotia: Nimbus.

Wied, Maximilian Prinz von. 1820. *Travels in Brazil in the Years 1815, 1816, 1817.* London: Henry Ciolburn.

———. 1843. *Travels in the Interior of North America.* Trans. H. E. Lloyd. London: Ackermann.

Wilbert, J., and K. Simoneau. 1984. *Folk Literature of the Tehuelche Indians.* Los Angeles: UCLA Latin American Center Publications, University of California.

Willey, G. R. 1941. *Excavations in Southeast Florida.* Yale University Publications in Anthropology, no. 41.

———. 1972. *The Artifacts of Altar de Sacrificios.* Papers of the Peabody Museum of Archaeology and Ethnology, Harvard University, vol. 64.

Willey, G. R., and J. M. Corbett. 1954. *Early Ancon and Early Supe Cultures.* New York: Columbia University Press.

Wilson, G. L. 1924. Hidatsa Horse and Dog Culture. *Anthropological Papers of the American Museum of Natural History* 15:127–311. New York: American Museum Press.

Wing, E. S. 1965. Animal Bones Associated with Two Indian Sites on Marco Island, Florida. *Florida Anthropologist* 18:21–27.

————. 1977. Vertebrates. In *Prehistoric Ecology at Patarata 52, Veracruz, Mexico: Adaptation to the Mangrove Swamp*, ed. B. Stark, 205–212. Publications in Anthropology. Nashville: Vanderbilt University.

————. 1978. Use of Dogs for Food: An Adaptation to the Coastal Environment. In *Prehistoric Coastal Adaptations: The Economy and Ecology of Maritime Middle America*, ed. B. Stark and B. Voorhies, 29–42. New York: Academic Press.

————. 1981. A Comparison of Olmec and Maya Foodways. In *The Olmec and Their Neighbors*, ed. E. Benson, 21–28. Washington, D.C.: Dunbarton Oaks Research Library and Collection.

————. 1984. Use and Abuse of Dogs. In *Contributions in Quaternary Vertebrate Paleontology*, ed. H. H. Genoways and M. R. Dawson. *Carnegie Museum Special Publication* 8:228–232.

————. 1986. Domestication of Andean Mammals. In *High Altitude Tropical Biogeography*, ed. M. Vuilleumier and M. Monasterio, 246–264. New York: Oxford University Press.

————. 1988a. Dusicyon sechurae, en contextas arqueológicos tempranos. In *La Prehistoria Temprana de la Peninsula de Santa Elena, Ecuador: Cultura las Vegas*, ed. K. E. Stothert, 179–185. Misc. Antropológica Ecuatoriana Serie Monograpica, no. 10.

————. 1988b. Animal Use by the Inca as Seen at Huanuco Pampa. In *Economic Prehistory of the Central Andes*, ed. E. S. Wing and J. C. Wheeler, 167–179. Oxford: BAR International Series.

————. 1989. Human Use of Canids in the Central Andes. *Advances in Neotropical Mammalogy* 1989:265–278.

————. 1990. Animal Remains. In *Excavations at Maria de la Cruz Cave and Hacienda Village Site, Loiza, Puerto Rico*, ed. I. Rouse and R. Alegria, 87–102. Yale University Publications in Anthropology, no. 80.

————. 1991a. Dog Remains from the Sorcé Site on Vieques Island, Puerto Rico. In *Beamers, Bobwhites, and Blue-Points: Tributes to the Career of Paul W. Parmalee*, ed. J. R. Purdue, W. E. Klippel, and B. H. Styles, 379–386. *Illinois State Museum Scientific Papers*, vol. 23.

————. 1991b. Animal Exploitation on Prehistoric Barbados. In *Proceedings of the 14th Congress of the International Association for Caribbean Archeology*, ed. A. Cummins and P. King, 360–365. Barbados.

Wing, E. S. n.d. Vertebrate Remains from the Archeological Sites in the Marismas Nacionales. Manuscript.

Winship, G. P. 1896. The Coronado Expedition, 1540–1542. *14th Annual Report of Bureau of American Ethnology*, 339–558. Washington, D.C.: Government Printing Office.

Wood, W. 1977. *New England's Prospect*, ed. A. T. Vaughan. Amherst: University of Massachusetts.

Yost, K. J., and P. M. Kelley. 1983. Shotguns, Blowguns, and Spears: The Analysis of Technological Efficiency. In *Adaptive Responses of Native Amazonians,* ed. R. B. Hames and W. T. Vickers, 189–224. New York: Academic Press.

Young, E. R. 1890. *By Canoe and Dog Train Among the Cree and Salteaux Indians.* London: Charles E. Kelley.

Young, S. P., and E. A. Goldman. 1944. *The Wolves of North America.* Washington, D.C.: American Wildlife Institute.

Zimen, E. 1975. Social Dynamics of the Wolf Pack. In *The Wild Canids: Their Systematics, Behavioral Ecology and Evolution,* ed. M. Fox, 336–362. New York: Van Nostrand.

Index

Page numbers in *italics* indicate photographs or illustrations.

Achuar: hunting dogs, 41–43, 47; word for dog, 42–43, 158; Yampani Nua spirit, 58–59

Acosta, J. de, 76

Afterworld stories and customs: Aztec, 93–94, 100–103, 190*n*28; burials of dogs in, 98–99; Cherokee, 97; Cora, 98, 121; Delaware, 96; dog deities in, 100; Fox, 98; guard dogs in, 94, 96–98; guide dogs in, 4, 93–94, 98, 102, 110, 190*n*28; Huron, 93, 96; Inca, 119–20; Inuit, 97; Maya, 95–96, *96,* 100, *100,* 121; Menominee, 97; Micmac, 98; Miskito, 98; Seminole, 96; Shawnee, 97; Shipibo, 97, 121; Sirius (Dog Star) in, 94–95, 121; sky and water journeys in, 4, 95–98, 102; Taíno, 97–98, *98,* 121; Talamanca, 98; Taulipang, 97; Tehuelche, 98, *99;* Tlingit, 98–99; Wintu, 98

Agate Basin (Wyoming), 15, 17

Ahtena: pack dogs of, 52

Alaskan malamute, x, 164

Algonquian peoples, 32; afterworld stories of, 93; eating of dogs by, 91–92; hauling dogs, 53. *See also* Arapaho; Blackfoot; Cheyenne; Cree; Delaware; Micmac; Montagnais; Ojibwa

Allen, Glover M., 30, 31, 43, 45, 107, 164

Alopex lagopus (arctic fox), 4

Altar de Sacrificios: animal remains from, 69; dog figurines from, 127–30, *128*

Alva, William, 117

Amazon peoples: hunting dogs of, 39–43, 47; prohibition against menstruating women at the hunt, 50. *See also* Achuar; Bororo; Makusi; Puri; Taruma; Taulipang; Waiwai

Ancestor spirits, dogs of, 149, 151

Andes: herding dogs in, 55–56

Anubis, 94

Aon (Arawak dog), 76, 164, 187*n*66

Apache, 86, 190*n*134; pack dogs, 52

Arabian wolf (*Canis lupus arabs*), 11

Arapaho: dog husband myth, 24; Dog Soldiers, 24; eating of dogs by, 89, 92

Arawak, 76–77; as dog spirit people, 25; word for dog, 164

Archaic period: dog burials of, 16, *16,* 103–7, *104*

Arctic fox (*Alopex lagopus*), 4

Arctic peoples: hunting dogs of, 31–32, 48. *See also* Eskimo; Iglulik; Inuit

Arikara Buffalo Pasture site (South Dakota), 91

Arroyo Hondo site (Arizona), 87

Artistic representations of dogs, 126–27, *128,* 159–60; calendar dogs, 136–37, 142–43, *143;* Chimú silver dog vessel, 127; codex dogs, 137–45, *137, 138, 140, 142, 144;* companion dogs, 153–54; composite creatures, 157–59; hunting dogs, 46, *46, 47;* on masks, 157; Nazca line dogs, *126,* 127, 151–52; on pipes, 127, *155,* 155–56, *156;* and rainmaking, 151–52, 153; and sexuality, 146, *147;* Sitio Conté pendants, 127; and transformations, 156–57; and warfare, 146–49; women and dogs in, 133–34, *135. See also* Pottery, dogs in; Symbols, dogs as

Asia: human-dog mating stories of, 23; primitive dogs of, 11

Assiniboin: pack dogs, 51; sacrifice of dogs, 89

Atahualpa (Inca ruler), 73

Atelocynus microtis (small-eared dog), 5–6

Athapaskan peoples, 32–33; aversion to eating dogs, 92; Dogribs, 23, 49, 52; Hare hunting dogs, *33,* 33–34, 182*n*9; pack dogs, 52. *See also* Ahtena; Apache; Beaver; Carrier; Chipewyan; Mountain; Navaho; Slavey; Yellowknife

Aubin Collection, 140

Austin, A. L., 194*n*47

Australian dingoes, *12,* 12–13

Aztec: afterworld story, 93–94, 100–103, *101, 102,* 190*n*28; calendar, 137; Codex Borbonicus, 138–40, *140,* 145; Codex Mendoza, 141–42, *143,* 149; coyote warrior cult, 148–49, *149;* creation myth, 25–26; dogs described, 141; eating of dogs by, 70–71; Florentine Codex, 137, 140–41; glyphs with dogs used in, 141–42; New Fire Ceremony, 139–40; origins of, 69–70; sacrifice of dogs, 103; sexuality, 139, *140,* 145–46

Barcal site (Nebraska), 90

Barkless dogs: Caribbean, 30, 76; eating of, 78–79

Basketmaker dog burials, 107, *108*

Beaver: pack dogs of, 52

Belcher Mound (Louisiana), 81

Berlandier, Joseph, 88

Biard, Father, 98

Bingham, Hiram, 56

Bison kill sites, 17–18

Blackfoot: eating of dogs, 91; hauling dogs, 53; horses, *91*

Bones of dogs: cut marks on bones of eaten dogs, 72, 76, 79, 87; fossil mandible fragments, 15–18; ornamental use of, 76, 77, 94, *113,* 114. *See also* Faunal remains; Teeth of dogs

Bororo: hunting dogs of, 41

de Bourgmont, Etienne, 51

Bourke, John, 86

Box Elder site (Wyoming), 53

Brant, Joseph, *84*

Bridges, Rev. Thomas, 45, 184*n*56

Brightman, Robert, 49–50

Brisbin, I. Lehr, 13

Buffalo-Bird-Woman, 53–55, *54*

Burials of dogs, 16, 94–95; and afterworld journeys, 98–99; in Archaic North America, 16, *16,* 103–7, *104;* Basketmaker, 107, *108;* at Cahokia, 79; Caribbean, 77–78; Fox, 98; Inca, 119–21; on the Isthmus of Panama, 113–14; in Mesoamerica, 109–13; Micmac, 98; Miskito, 98; in the Mississippian period, 107–9; in South America, 114–21, *116, 118–20;* table of sites, 122–24; Tehuelche, 98, *99;* Tlingit, 98–99; Waiwai, 41

Burr's Hill mound (Rhode Island): effigy pipe, 156, *156*

Bush dogs (*Speothos venaticus*), 5, *6,* 43

Cacaxtla site (Mexico): mural from, 136, *137*

Cahokia site (Illinois), 79, 109

Calderón, Eduardo, 155

Calendars, 136–37; Aztec, 137; Maya, 136, 137, 142–43, *143*

Canidae, 4–7

Canis dirus (dire wolf), 4

Canis familiaris (dog), 6–7

Canis familiaris dingo (dingo), 11–15

Canis ingae ("Inca" dog), 55

Canis latrans (coyote), 3, 4–5, 158; flexibility of, 7; in myths and stories, 22–23; as trickster, 85; warrior cults of, 147–49, *149, 150*

Canis lupus (gray wolf), 4–5, 6, 7, *9;* speciation of dogs from, 7–11

Canis lupus arabs (Arabian wolf), 11

Canis lupus pallipes (Indian wolf), 11

Canis rufus (red wolf), 4, 6, 7

Canyon de Chelly site (Arizona), 87

Caribbean: dogs of, 76–78; effigies, *77.* See also Arawak; Taíno

Carlson Annis Mound (Kentucky), 106

Carolina dogs, x, 13

Carrier: pack dogs of, 52

Casper site (Wyoming), 17

Castillo de Tomaval site (Peru), 116

Catlin, George, 29, 89, *90*

Cemochechobee site (Georgia), 146

Ceramic dogs, *128,* 130–34, 193*n*7; from Altar de Sacrificios, 129–30; Caribbean, *77;* Chorrera effigies, 130, *131;* of Colima, 109–10, *110,* 130, 131, 133; Maya figures, 127–30, *128,* 133; Moche, 131, 133, 151, *151,* 153–55; Nazca, 131, *151–52,* 151–53; and sexuality, 146, *147;* skeletal dogs, 131; from Teotihuacán, 130–31, *131;* Toltec dog pots, 132; women and dogs represented in, 133–34, *135;* wrinkled effigies, 129, *132,* 132–33, *148*

Cerdoyon thous (crab-eating fox), 6

Cerebus, 94

Chac (Maya rain dog), 143–44, *144*

Chahto creation story, 21–22

Chancay dog pottery, 133, *134*

Chariticas ("dog eaters"), 88–89

Cherokee afterworld story, 97

Cheyenne: dog-eating ceremonies, 89–90, 167; Dog Soldiers, 24; hauling dogs, 53; story of the origin of dogs, 19–20, *20*

Chichimec people, 69–70, 187*n*39. *See also* Aztec

Chiclero's ulcer, 142, *148*

Children and dogs, 57; and herding dogs, 56, *56*

Chilla (*Dusicyon griseus*), 5
Chimú: hairless dog effigies, *132,* 132–33, 146, *147;* silver dog vessels, 127
Chipewyan: human-dog mating story, 23–24; on menstruation and the hunt, 49; pack dogs, 52
Choctaw words for dog, 164
Chono people, 44; weaving of dog hair by, 57
Chorrera dog effigies, 130, *131*
Chrysocyon brachyurus (South American maned wolf), 4, 6
Cieza de Leon, Pedro de, 73
Classic Period (Maya): eating of dogs in, 66, 68–69; representations of dogs from, 127–30, *128;* Tomb of Hasaw-Ka'an-K'awil, 95, *96*
Clutton-Brock, Juliet, 14
Coastal Salish: Live Dog Eating Ceremony, 36; wool dogs, 56–57, *57, 58,* 185*n*101
Cobo, Bernabe, 162
Codex Borbonicus, 138–40, *140,* 145
Codex Mendoza, 141–42, *143,* 149
Codex Nuttall, *137,* 138, *138*
Codex Vaticanus A, *101,* 102
Codices, dogs in, 137–45, *137, 138, 140, 142, 144*
Coe, Sophie, 66, 71, 193*n*7, 194*n*41
Colima: ceramic dogs of, 109–10, *110,* 130, 131, 133; warrior helmet, *150*
Columbus, Christopher, 2, 76, 163, 179*n*1
Comanche: hauling dogs of, 53
Cook, James, 44
Copena Mound (Alabama): dog pipe, 127, *155,* 155–56
Cora afterworld story, 98, 121
Cortés, Hernando, 70
Coso Range petroglyphs, 46, *47*

Cotton Orange Period Site (Florida), 80
Coyote (*Canis latrans*), 3, 4–5, 158; flexibility of, 7; in myths and stories, 22–23; as trickster, 85; warrior cults of, 147–49, *149, 150*
Cozumel island: animal remains from, 69
Crab-eating fox (*Cerdoyon thous*), 6
Creation stories, 19–23
Cree: hauling dogs, 51; menstruating women and the hunt, 49–50; story of the origin of dogs, 19
Cuello site (Belize), 67–68
Culpeo (*Dusicyon culpaeus*), 5
Culture, dog participation in, 2
Cushing Site (Florida), 81

Danger Cave (Utah), 16
Darwin, Charles, 1, 13–14
Day signs, 142–45
DeBoer, Warren, 183*n*31
Deceiving Man (Penobscot mythical hero), 21
Deities, canine: Peruvian lunar deities, 116–17, *117;* Xolotl (Aztec), 26, *26,* 139, 142; in the Maya underworld, 100, *100*
Delaware: afterworld story, 96; eating of dogs, 83
Diaz del Castillo, Bernal, 70, 71
Diego de Landa, Bishop, 125, 143, 162
Dingo (*Canis familiaris dingo*), 11–15
Dinwoody site (Wyoming), 46
Dire wolf (*Canis dirus*), 4
Disease-Giver (Winnebago spirit), 85
Dog People, 187*n*39; Aztec as, 69–70; stories of, 23–25
Dogrib people, 23, 49; pack dogs, 52
Domestication: of dogs, 7–11, 15–18, 28; of horses, 39; of plants, 64

Donnan, Christopher, 118, 153–54
Dresden Codex, 143–45, *144,* 145
Drucker, Philip, 36
Duran, Diego, 60, 70, 125
Dusicyon australis (Falkland Islands wolf), 13–15, *14*
Dusicyon culpaeus (culpeo), 5
Dusicyon griseus (chilla), 5
Dusicyon gymnocercus (pampas fox), 5, *5,* 183*n*35
Dusicyon sechurae (sechura fox), 5, 114–15
Dusicyon vetulus (hoary fox), 5

Ears of dogs: sore and ripped, 142, *148. See also* Chiclero's ulcer
Eastern Woodlands: Archaic dog burials, 16, 104–6; eating of dogs in, 78–79; pipes, 127, *155,* 155–56, *156. See also* Mississippian period
Eating of dogs, 3, 91–92; and agricultural development in the Americas, 63–65; Arapaho, 89, 92; Arawak, 76; aversions to, 32–33, 44, 62–63, 73–74, 89; Aztec, 61; for ceremonies/feasts, 36, 62, 67, 69, 71, 81, 82–85, 89–90, *90,* 92; Chariticas, 88–89; Cheyenne, 89–90, 167; Delaware, 83; in Florida's Orange Plain Period, 80–81; Hidatsa, 89; Hopi, 86; Huanca, 60, 74, 92; Huron, 82–83, 92; Iroquois, 83, 92; Live Dog Eating Ceremonies, 36, 183*n*16, 183*n*18; Maya, 61, 66–69, 186*n*35; as medicinal, 82–83, 89, 90, 92; Natchez, 81; Olmec, 66; Pawnee, 90, 92; Penobscot, 60–61; prevalence of, 61–62; in Sioux feasts, 89, *90,* 92; by the Spanish, 71, 76, 78–79, 161; for subsistence, 65–69, 70–72, 75–76, 78, 90–91; and war-

fare, 155; Yokut, 37. *See also* Sacrifices of dogs
Eaton, George, 121
Effigies of dogs, 130–34; Caribbean, *77;* Chorrera, 130, *131;* at Colima, 109–10, *110,* 130, 131, 133; Maya figures, 127–30, *128,* 133; Moche, 131, 133; Nazca, 131; from Teotihuacán, 148; Toltec effigy pots, 132; wrinkled effigies, 129, *132,* 132–33, *148*
Ek Chuah (Maya merchant god), 136, *136, 137*
Eskimo, 31–32, *32;* early dog-wolf hybrid, 15; hauling dogs, 31–32, 52; and magic, 48. *See also* Iglulik; Inuit
European dogs, 162–64, 196. *See also* Spanish
Eva site (Tennessee), 103–4

Falkland Islands wolf (*Dusicyon australis*), 13–15, *14*
Faunal remains: at Cahokia, 79; of Caribbean dogs, 77–78; cranial morphology of canids, 10; of eaten dogs, 65, 67–69, 75–76, 80–81; of Florida's Orange Plain Period, 80–81; at Grasshopper Pueblo, 87; of Paleoindian dogs, 15–18; of Plains dogs, 53, 90–91; at San Lorenzo, 66. *See also* Bones of dogs
Fell's Cave (Argentina), 18
Fenton, William, 83
Fertility and dogs, 146, *147*
Fire and dogs: Aztec New Fire Ceremony, 139–40; Maya dog of fire and lightning, 143, *144;* in Maya underworld, 100; and the One Dog day sign, 137; Shasta Indian story of, 37
Fitz-Roy, Robert, 43, 44
Florentine Codex, 137, 140–41

Flushing Bay cemetery (New York), 106–7

Formative Period (Maya): eating of dogs in, 67–69

Fossil remains of dogs, 15–18, 180n40. *See also* Faunal remains

Fox, M. W., 182n90

Fox (people): burial customs, 98; White Buffalo Dance, 84–85

Foxes, 3, 4; and ancestor spirits, 149, 151; arctic fox, 4; crab-eating fox, 6; gray fox, 4; hoary fox, 5; kit fox, 4; in Nazca art, 153; pampas fox, 5, *5*, 40, 183n35; red fox, 4; sechura fox, 5; swift fox, 4

Franklin, Sir John, 51

Frison, G. C., 15

Fritz, G. J., 186n13

Frontenac Island site (New York), 104–5

Furst, Peter, 110

Gallinazo people, 116

Garcilaso de la Vega, 60, 74, 116–17

Genetics: dog-wolf relatedness, 10; of hairless dogs, 193n17

Gerry, John, 186n25

Gomez de Ahumada, Maria, 109–10

Gorden, David, 187n39

Gosiute, *38*

Grasshopper Pueblo site (Arizona), 87

Gray fox (*Urocyon cinereoargenteus*), 4

Gray wolf (*Canis lupus*), 4–5, 6, 7, *9;* speciation of dogs from, 7–11

Great Basin peoples: hunting dogs of, 38–39, 46–47. *See also* Gosiute; Northern Paiute; Shoshone

Great Medicine (Cheyenne creator), 19–20

Great Plains people: dog societies of, 24; eating of dogs by, 88–92,

189n120; hauling dogs of, 52–53; hunting dogs of, 39. *See also* Arapaho; Assinboin; Cheyenne; Hidatsa; Pawnee; Ponca; Sioux

Greater Antilles, 164

Guamán Poma de Ayala, Felipe, 55, 74, 149

Guard dogs, 3; in afterworld stories, 94, 96–98

Guide dogs in the afterworld, 4, 93–94, 98, 102, 110, 190n28

Gyles, John, 61

Hacienda Grande Village Site (Puerto Rico), 77

Haida: dog husband story, 24; hunting dogs, 35–36

Hairless dogs, 125, 133, 164, 193n15, 193n17; Mexican, x, 30, 130; and rainmaking, 153; represented as wrinkled, 129, *132*, 132–33, *148;* sexuality represented in, 146; supernatural qualities of, 155

Hare: hunting dogs of, *33*, 33–34, 182n9

Hasaw-Ka'an-K'awil tomb (Maya), 95–96, *96*

Hauling dogs, 3, *51*, 51–55, *54;* blunting of teeth of, 53; Eskimo, 31–32, 52; of the Plains, 53–55; training of, 54

Hearne, Samuel, 23, 49, 52

Helms, Mary, 193n14

Henry, Alexander, 99

Hero Twins (Maya), 129

Hidatsa: disposal of dogs, 121; eating of dogs, 89; hauling dogs, 53–55, *54*, 185n94; story of the origin of dogs, 20

Hoary fox (*Dusicyon vetulus*), 5

Hopi, 189n110; eating of dogs by, 86;

hunting dogs, 86; Snake Dance, *87;* word for dogs, 164–65

Horner site (Wyoming), 17, 18

Horses: Blackfoot, 91, *91;* domestication of, 39; and the eating of dogs, 91; impact of, on use of hauling dogs, 55

Huanca, 73; eating of dogs, 60, 74–76, 92

Huanuco Pampa site (Peru), 120

Huarochirí Manuscript, The, 25

Huascar (Inca ruler), 73

Hudson, Henry, 83

Huichol creation story, 24–25

Hunting dogs, 3; Achuar, 41–43, 47; of the Amazon, 39–43; Arawak, 76, 77; in art, 46, *46, 47;* Eskimo, 31–32; Haida, 35–36; Hare, *33,* 33–34; on the Isthmus of Panama, 114; and menstruating women, 48–50; Miwok, 37; Natchez, 82; Northern Paiute, 38; Paleoindian, 17–18; Patagonian, 43–44; Ponca, 39; in ritual and magic, 47–50; Shasta, 37; of Tierra del Fuego, 43, 44–45; Tlingit, 35

Huron: afterworld story, 93, 96; eating of dogs, 82–83, 92

Hybrids: dog-wolf, 15–18, 53; red wolf as, 7

Iglulik: hunting dogs of, 31

Illinois: sacrifice of dogs, 85

Inca, 30, 72–73, *75;* afterworld story, 119–20; burial sites, 119–21, *120;* creation myth, 25; eating dogs as abhorrent to, 61, 73–74; foxes symbolized by, 149, *150;* herding dogs, 55, *56;* Huanca conquered by, 74–75; rainmaking and dogs, 153; sacrifice of dogs, 73

Indian Knoll (Kentucky), *16,* 105–6

Interior Salish: hunting dogs, 46–47; omens about the hunt, 50

Inuit: afterworld story, 97; migration of, 179*n*1; Sedna spirit and the hunt, 48, *49. See also* Eskimo

Ipiutak site (Alaska), 103

Iroquois, *84;* Oneida Iroquois words for dog, 28; eating of dogs and warfare, 83, 92; Sacrifice of the White Dog, 83, 166–67; stories of dogs, 22. *See also* Brant, Joseph; Jemison, Peter; Seneca

Isthmus of Panama, dog burials on, 113–14

Jackals, 4, 6

Jaguar Cave (Idaho), 16

Jaguars, 3, 164; Maya jaguar-dog, 129, 158, *159,* 195*n*77

Jemison, Peter, 166–67

Jones-Miller site (Colorado), 17

Kaminaljuyu (Guatemala), 111–13, *112,* 130

Kane, Paul, 185*n*101

Kansa: hauling dogs of, 51

Kipling, Rudyard, 1, 19

Kit fox (*Vulpes macrotis*), 4

Koster site (Illinois), 16, 103, *104*

Kroeber, A. K., 38

Kulóskap (Micmac mythical hero), 21

Kutchin: pack dogs, 52

Kwakiutl: Live Dog Eating Ceremony of, 36

Lambert Farm (Rhode Island), 106

Lamoka dog burials, 104–5

Land of the Dead. *See* Afterworld stories and customs

Lathrap, Donald, 130, 193*n*14

LePage du Pratz, 81–82
Lescarbot, Father Marc, 29, 162
Lévi-Strauss, Claude, 181n73
Lighthouse Site (Peru), 115, *116*
Litter size of canids, 4
Llamas, 55–56
Lothrop, Samuel K., 45, 113

Machu Picchu (Peru), *120,* 120–21,
    192n95
Mackenzie, John, 23, 181n70
Madrid Codex, 143, *144*
Maesk (mythical dog hero), 35, *36*
Magic: and hunting dogs, 47–50
Magliabecchi Codex (Aztec), 102, *102*
Maillard, Abbé, 48
Maiong type of hunting dogs, 40
Maize, 63–64, 66–67, 80; consumed by
    dogs, 67; Maya god of, 95, *96,* 143,
    144
Makusi: hunting dogs of, 40
Mammoth kill sites, 17, 180n43
Maned wolf (*Chrysocyon brachyurus*),
    4, 6
Manito (Ottawa water spirit), 99
Marco Island (Florida), 81
Marcos, Jorge, 115
Marismas Nacionales site (Mexico),
    110–11, 133, 191n60
Martin, Paul, 180n43
Masks, dogs portrayed on, 157
Mawari (Waiwai mythical hero), 21
Maya, 66, *67, 68;* afterworld stories,
    95–96, *96,* 121; calendars, 136, 137,
    142–43, *143;* ceramic dog figures,
    127–30, *128,* 133; codices, 142,
    143–45, *144;* creation myth, 26–28,
    28; eating of dogs, 61, 66–69,
    186n35; fire-bringing dog, 100; hi-
    eroglyphic for dog, 142, 194n41;
    hunting dogs, 46; jaguar-dog, 158,

159, 195n77; maize and dogs, 143,
    144; merchants and dogs, 134–36,
    136, 137; sexuality, 145; transforma-
    tion into animals, 157, *158;* under-
    world of, 100, *100*
Medicinal use of dogs: eating dogs,
    82–83, 89, 90, 92; hairless dogs, 133
Men and dogs, 58–59; and hunting,
    49–50, 57. *See also* Hunting dogs
Menominee: afterworld story, 97
Mesoamerica: buried dogs in, 109–13;
    calendars of, 135–36, 142–43, *143;*
    codices of, 137–42; hieroglyphs of,
    142–43, *143. See also* Aztec; Maya
Miami: dog sacrifices of, 85
Micmac, 29; burial customs, 98; hunt-
    ing dogs, 47, 48; transformer hero,
    21
Midwestern peoples, eating of dogs by,
    85, *86. See also* Fox; Menominee;
    Miami; Potawatomi; Sauk; Win-
    nebago
Milky Way, 93, 95–97, 121, 190n2
Mimbres pottery, 88, *88,* 189n117
Miskito: burial customs of, 98
Mississippian period: dog burials of,
    107–9; ceramic dog effigies of, *131,*
    132, 146; eating of dogs in, 79–81
Miwok: coyote story, 22; hunting dogs,
    37; word for dog, 164
Mixtec: Codex Nuttall, *137,* 138, *138;*
    creation story, 23
Moche: buried dogs, 117–19, *118, 119;*
    ceramic dogs, 131, 133, 151, *151,*
    153–55; eating of dogs, 72; fox war-
    rior, *150;* hunting dogs, 46, *46;* "Re-
    volt of the Objects" myth, 182n87;
    Sacrifice Ceremony, 153–54, *154*
Modern dogs, 165–67
La Moderna site (Argentina), 18
Montagnais: hunting dogs of, 47–48

Moore, Clarence, 107–9
Morgan, Lewis Henry, 83
Moundville (Alabama), 109
Mountain: pack dogs of, 52
Muñoz Camargo, Diego, 153
Murrey, Charles, 90
Myths and stories: Haida hunting dog, 35, *36;* of human-dog matings, 23–25; of the origin of dogs, 19–28; social function of, 58–59. *See also* Afterworld stories and customs; Symbols, dogs as

Nagaicho (Chahto creator), 21–22
Naming of dogs, 38; Achuar, 41; Eskimo, 32. *See also* Words for dog
Narrowtail (Cree first dog), 19
Natchez: eating of dogs, 81; hunting dogs, 82
Navaho, 86, 190*n*134
Nazca: ceramic dogs, 131, *151–52, 151–53;* fox headdress, *150;* line dogs, *126,* 127, 151–52
Neoteny, 10
Nootka: dogs of, 34–35; dog husband story, 24
North America: buried dogs in, 103–9; dingo of, 13; eating of dogs in, 78–91; hauling dogs in, 51–55; hunting dogs in, 31–39; Paleoindian fossil record, 16–18, 180*n*43; pipes from, 127, *155,* 155–56, *156;* speciation of the dog in, 7–11; wild canids of, 4, 7
Northern Paiute: hunting dogs of, 38
Nouna herding dogs, 56

Oglala Sioux: dog feasts of, 89, *90,* 92
Ojibwa: hauling dogs, *51;* human-dog mating story, 24
Okanagan: hunting dogs of, 50

Olmec: eating of dogs, 66. *See also* San Lorenzo
Olsen, Stanley, 15
Olsen-Chubbock site (Colorado), 17
Omaha Big Village site (Nebraska), 90–91
Omens and portents: in codices, 137, 143–45
Ona: dogs of, 44, *44*
Oneida Iroquois words for dog, 28
Opiyél-Guaobirán (Taíno dog spirit), 97–98, *98*
Orange Plain Period (Florida), 80–81
Origin of American dogs: and dingoes, 11–15; and domestication of the wolf, 7–11; fossil record of, 15–18; myths and stories of, 19–28
Ossabaw Island Mound (Georgia), 107–9
Ottawa: dog sacrifices of, 99
Otters, 158–59
Our Grandmother (Shawnee creator), 20–21, 97
Ownership of dogs, 165–66

Pachacuti (Inca ruler), 73
Pacific Northwest people: human-dog mating stories, 24; hunter-gatherer societies, *34,* 34–37; Live Dog Eating Ceremonies, 36. *See also* Coastal Salish; Haida; Kwakiutl; Nootka; Tlingit
Pack dogs: Assiniboin, 51; Athapaskan, 52. *See also* Hauling dogs
Pacopampa site (Peru), 72
Paleoindian period, 16–18, 180*n*43
Paloma site (Peru), 115
Pampa Grande site (Peru), 72
Pampas fox (*Dusicyon gymnocercus*), 5, *5,* 40, 183*n*35
Panama, Isthmus of: dog burials, 113–14. *See also* Sitio Conté

Pané, Ramón, 97–98, 162
Paracas Peninsula sites (Peru), 115
Patagonian hunting dogs, 43–44
Pawnee: dog sacrifices in curing rituals, 90, 92; hauling dogs, 53
Penobscot story of the origin of dogs, 21
Perry site (Alabama Pickwick Basin), 106
Pickwick Basin sites (Alabama), 106
Pima: dogs of, 86–87
Pipes, dogs portrayed on, 127, *155, 155–56, 156*
Pizarro, Francisco, 73
Pohl, Mary, 186*n*23
Ponca: hunting dogs, 39; sacrifice of dogs, 89
Pope, Alexander, 3
Popol Vuh (Maya sacred book), 26–28, *28*
Port au Choix cemetery (Newfoundland), 103
Potawatomi: sacrifice of dogs, 85
Pottery, dogs in, *128,* 130–34, 193*n*7; from Altar de Sacrificios, 129–30; Caribbean effigies, *77;* Chorrera effigies, 130, *131;* Colima ceramic dogs, 109–10, *110,* 130, 131, 133; Maya figures, 127–30, *128,* 133; Mimbres bowls, 88, *88,* 189*n*117; Moche ceramic dogs, 131, 133, 151, *151,* 153–55; Nazca ceramic dogs, 131, *151–52,* 151–53; and sexuality, 146, *147;* skeletal dogs, 131; from Teotihuacán, 130–31, *131;* Toltec effigy pots, 132; women and dogs represented in, 133–34, *135;* wrinkled effigies, 129, *132, 132–33, 148*
Puna: dogs of, 29–30
Puri, *42*

Quetzalcoatl (Mexican deity), 111
Quilter, Jeffrey, 182*n*87

Rainmaking and dogs, 143, 151–52, 153
Rangel, Rodrigo, 78–79, 163
Read Shell Midden (Kentucky), 106
Real Alto (Ecuador), 115
Red fox (*Vulpes vulpes*), 4
Red Hawk: "Sioux Dog Dance," 166, 174–75, 183*n*18
Red wolf (*Canis rufus*), 4, 6, 7
Richardson, John, 53, 182*n*9
Ritchie, William, 104, 105
Rites and rituals: ceremonial eating of dogs, 36, 62, 67, 69, 71, 81, 82–85, 89–90, *90,* 92; Haida dog-eating performance, 35–36; for hunting dogs, 47–50; Live Dog Eating Ceremonies, 36. *See also* Sacrifices of dogs
Rock Cree: menstruating women and the hunt, 49–50
Roe, Peter, 159
Rogers Cave (Missouri), 103
Rosamachay Cave (Peru), 119
Russell, Frank, 86

Sacrifices of dogs, 62; for the afterworld, 98, 103, 107; Assiniboin, 89; Aztec, 103; Fox White Buffalo Dance, 84–85; heart sacrifice ceremonies, 138, *138,* 146–47, 153; Inca, 73; Iroquois Sacrifice of the White Dog, 83, 166–67; Maya, 27–28, *28,* 125; Micmac, 98; Ottawa, 99; and rainmaking, 153; Sioux, 89, 92; Winnebago, 85
Sagard-Theodat, Father, 93
Sahagún, Bernardino de, 70–71, 93–94, 125, 133, 141, 161, 162
Salinar Sites (Peru), 115–16

San Lorenzo (Olmec site), 66

Sandefur, Catherine, 75

Santa Elena Peninsula (Ecuador), 71–72

Sauk: sacrifice of dogs, 85

Savishinsky, Joel, 33

Schele, Linda, 95

Schomburgk, R. H., 41

Schwarcz, H. P., 186*n*35

Sechura fox (*Dusicyon sechurae*), 5, 114–15

Sedna (Inuit spirit), 48, *49*, 58

Seibal site (Guatemala), 68–69

Seminole: afterworld story of, 96

Seneca: dogs in stories of, 22

Serpell, James, 11

Sexuality, 3, 139, 145–46; Aztec representations of, 139, *140;* hunting dogs affected by, 48–50; Maya representations of, *144,* 144–45

Shasta: hunting dogs of, 37

Shawnee: afterworld story, 97; creation story, 20–21

Shipibo: afterworld story, 97, 121; training of dogs, 47

Shoshone: hunting dogs of, 46

Sioux: eating of dogs, 89, *90,* 92; hauling dogs, 29, 53, *54. See also* Oglala Sioux

"Sioux Dog Dance" (Red Hawk), 166, 174–75, 183*n*18

Sípan tomb sites (Peru), 117–19, *118, 119,* 154

Sirius (Dog Star), 94–95, 121

Sitio Conté site (Isthmus of Panama), 113–14; dog pendants from, 127

Slavey: pack dogs of, 52

Small-eared dog (*Atelocynus microtis*), 5–6

Sorcé site (Puerto Rico), 77–78

Soto, Hernando De, 78–79, 80

South America: Amazonian hunting dogs, 39–43; ancestor spirits of, 149, 151; buried dogs of, 114–21, *116, 118–20;* dingo of, 13–15; eating of dogs in, 71–76; fossil record of early dogs in, 18; herding dogs of, 55–57; Patagonian hunting dogs, 43–44; Tierra del Fuego hunting dogs, 43, 44–45; wild canids of, 4–6, 183*n*35

South Indian Field site (Florida), 80

Southern Paiute coyote story, 22–23

Southwest peoples: aversion to eating dogs, 92; Dogribs, 23, 49, 52; dogs of, 87; eating of dogs by, 85–88; Mimbres pottery, 88, *88,* 189*n*117; pack dogs, 52. *See also* Apache; Hopi; Navaho; Pima; Zuni

Spanish: eating of dogs by, 71, 76, 78–79, 161; esteem for dogs, 196*n*3; "hero" dogs, ix–x; warrior dogs, 161, 162–63, *163*

Speciation of the dog, 7–11; fossil record of, 15–18

Speothos venaticus (bush dog), 5, *6,* 43

Sun-Dance ceremony (Cheyenne), 19–20

Swift fox (*Vulpes velox*), 4

Symbols, dogs as: in calendars, 142–43; in codices, 137–42; in composite creatures, 157–59; coyotes in warrior cults, 147–49, *149, 150,* 158; foxes as ancestor spirits, 149, 151; and Maya merchants, 134–36, *136, 137;* in Maya vase paintings, 129–30, *136;* in Nazca line drawings, 151–52; in transformations, 156–57

Taboos: on dogs eating from the hunt, 47–48, 50; on hunting, 47–50; from menstruating women at the hunt, 48–50

Tahltan: pack dogs of, 52
Taíno: dogs of, 76; afterworld story, 97–98, *98,* 121
Talamanca afterworld story, 98
Talayesva, Don, 86
Tambiah, Stanley, 62–63
Taruma: hunting dogs of, 40, 47
Taulipang: afterworld story, 97
Teeth of dogs: blunted in hauling dogs, 53; broken teeth from Marismas Nacionales, 111; and hairlessness, 133; ornamental use of, 76, 77, *113,* 114; removal of, 78
Tehuacán Valley: dog remains in, 65
Tehuelche people, 2; burial customs, 98, *99;* hunting dogs, 43–44
Telarmachay Cave (Peru), 119
Telleriano-Remensis Codex, 139, *140*
Tello, Julius, 152
Tenochtitlan (Aztec capital), 70
Teotihuacán (Mexico): clay dogs from, 130–31, *131;* coyotes in warfare imagery from, 146–48, *149, 150;* dog remains at, 65, 111–12; effigies of dogs from, 148; murals, 127, 146–48
Thompson, Eric, 134
Thompson: hunting dogs of, 46–47
Thunder People (Oglala Sioux spirits), 89
Thurman, Melburn, 88, 190n134
Tierra del Fuego: hunting dogs, 43, 44–45. *See also* Chono; Ona; Yahgan
Tikal (Maya), 95–96
Timucua people, *80*
Tlatilco site (Mexico): clay dog figures from, 130, 193n7
Tlingit: bear-hunting dogs, 35; burial customs, 98–99; dog husband story, 24; words for dog, 164
Los Toldos site (Argentina), 18

Toltec: dog effigy pots, 132; hairless dog sculpture, 146
Training of dogs: Achuar hunting dogs, 42, 47; hauling dogs, 54; hunting dogs, 47; Shasta hunting dogs, 37
Transportation, dogs used for, 3. *See also* Hauling dogs
Travois, 51, 53, *54,* 164; training for, 54

Urocyon cinereoargenteus (gray fox), 4

Valdivians, 71–72; buried dogs of, 115
Vancouver, George, 56
Vegas people, 114–15, 149
Ventana Cave (Arizona), 87
Vérendrye, Pierre La, 51
Von Tschudi, J. J., 30, 55
Vulpes macrotis (kit fox), 4
Vulpes velox (swift fox), 4
Vulpes vulpes (red fox), 4
Vultures and dogs, 145–46, *146*

Wafer, Lionel, 114
Waiwai: hunting dogs, 41, 47, 50; story of the origin of dogs, 21
Wakoñda (Assiniboin Creator Spirit), 89
Walker, D., 15
Waorani hunting dogs, 41
Warfare and dogs, 155; artistic representations of, 146–49, *149, 150;* Iroquois war feasts, 83, 92; and Spanish dogs, 162–63
Warrior Priest, 153–55, *154*
Wayne, Robert, 10
Weaving dog hair, 56–57
Webb, William, 105, 106
Weeden Island McKeithern Site (Florida), 145, *146*
West Coast peoples, 36–37, *37. See also* Miwok; Shasta; Wintu; Yokut

Wheat, Joe Ben, 17

White, C. D., 186*n*35

White Dog Cave (Arizona), 107, *108*

Williams, Angeline, 24

Wilson, Gilbert, 53–54, 185*n*94

Wing, Elizabeth, 66, 78, 110–111, 133, 186*n*23, 191*n*60

Winnebago: dog feasts of, 85

Wintu: burial customs, 98; word for dog, 164

Wishgana cave (Peru), 119

Wolves, 3; Arabian wolf, 11; dire wolf, 4; domestication of, 7–11; fossil record of, 15–18; gray wolf, 4–5, 6, 7–11, *9;* Indian wolf, 11; red wolf, 4, 6, 7; social order of, 8–10

Women and dogs, 57, 58–59; and Achuar hunting dogs, 41, 58–59; artistic representations of, 133–34, *135;* and Coastal Salish wool dogs, 56, *58;* and the domestication of wolves, 11; mating stories of, 23–24, 48; menstruation and the hunt, 48–50; suckling of pups, 11, 12, 180*n*30; and training hauling dogs, 53–54. *See also* Sexuality

Wool dogs, 56–57, *57, 58,* 185*n*101

Words for dog, 164–65, 189*n*120; Achuar, 42–43, 158; Amazon peoples, 40; Arawak, 76, 164; Mesoamerican glyphs, 142–43, *143;* Oneida Iroquois, 28; table of, 169–73; Yahgan, 45

Wright's Mound (Kentucky), 157

Wrinkled dog effigies, 129, *132, 132–33, 148*

Xibalba (Maya underworld), 100, *100*

Xiuhtecuhtli (Aztec god of fire), 137, 140

Xochiquetzal (Aztec goddess), 139, *140,* 145

Xolotl (Mesoamerican canine deity), 26, *26,* 139

Yahgan, 184*n*56; hunting dogs, 44–45

Yampani Nua (Achuar Mistress of Dogs), 59

Yellow-Dog (Hidatsa supernatural), 20

Yellowknife: pack dogs of, 52

Yokut: eating of dogs, 37

Zorro. *See* Pampas fox

Zuni: weaving of dog hair by, 57